Thank You, Gabe

A collection of stories

PETER PURCHASE

DUNE
PUBLISHING

Perth Western Australia

First published in Australia 2024 by Dune Publishing
Copyright © Peter Purchase 2024 www.peterpurchasebooks.com

Thank You, Gabe – and other stories

Cataloguing-in-Publication data is available from
The National Library of Australia

General acknowledgement is made to the following for permission
to reprint previously published material: Use of the Australian
Aboriginal Malgana language, permission courtesy of Ben Bellottie
of Denham, Shark Bay; Photographs of the *Zuytdorp* wreck site, ©
Fremantle Shipwrecks Museum, permission granted by photographer
Pat Baker, courtesy of Fremantle Shipwrecks Museum; Photographs
of Jandamarra's Rock and the *Zuytdorp* Cliffs © Adam Monk Art
Photography, courtesy of Adam Monk.

ISBN: 978-0-9756216-4-6 (paperback)
          978-0-9756216-5-3 (epub)

CONTENTS

'Injustice anywhere is a threat to justice.
We are caught in an inescapable network of mutuality,
tied in a single garment of destiny.
Whatever affects one directly, affects all indirectly.'
Martin Luther King, letter from a Birmingham jail, 16 April 1963

'I feel confident imposing change on myself.
It's a lot more fun progressing than looking back.
That's why I need to throw curve balls.'
David Bowie

PART I

When octogenarian Australian writer,
Jon Janacek, was shortlisted for the
prestigious Dublin International Literary
Award for his latest historical novel,
The Life and Times of Michiel de Ruyter,
the greatest Dutch Lieutenant-Admiral of
them all, he refused to be interviewed.
He sent the following blog to everyone
interested in the genesis of the novel instead.

Thank You, Gabe

CALL ME NAÏVE, BUT seventy years ago, when the world was a kinder, less hostile and dangerous place, I believed that things would always work out for the best without much effort on my part.

Why? Because from as far back as I can remember I had a familiar unseen guardian angel presiding over everything I did, someone with whom I had brief personal conversations, when I, or rather we, were alone in some secluded private place, preferably behind a locked door. I'd spell out what I needed help with at the time—an upcoming hundred yard race at the school sports while I was putting on my spikes; a Maths exam I was about to sit (Maths being my weakest subject); a bully twice my size I'd decided to confront and was practising clouting on a swinging punch bag.

When I say 'spell out' and 'personal conversations', I mean *telepathically*, but no less charged with emotion and echoing loudly across the aether that separated us than they would have been if they'd been vocalised and he was real. And I say *real*, but to me he always seemed much, much more than real.

I was convinced he was an Australian pilot I'd read about, on loan to the USAF aboard the aircraft carrier *Yorktown*, shot down in the Battle of the Coral Sea on the day I was born in May, 1942. His burning Grumman Wildcat trailed plumes of black smoke before it struck the ocean with him at the controls, wounded, and struggling to save himself.

He was now assigned to protecting me—among others, but I believed I was one of his favourites—and he always came through with the goods. I'd win the race, ace the exam and demolish the bully with a surprise straight left and a right hook he never saw coming. And I never failed to thank him after the event and commend him for his effective multi-tasking.

I sensed him in his spirit form still wearing his flying gear, his helmet on with the chinstrap loose and his goggles on his forehead, his black leather flying jacket unzipped, his hands casually relaxed in his trouser pockets, occasionally taking one out to make an elegant gesture of appreciation as he listened and told me once again that it was, 'No problem, to be honest, no worries at all... any time.'

I'd recognise him anywhere. His brown, expressive eyes with their direct perceptive gaze beneath straight dark brows, his prominent cheekbones triangulating down to a slightly pointed chin with a cleft that made shaving difficult. His mouth that broke easily into a knowing grin, or a smile displaying a chipped front tooth. He was the picture of debonair cool—and when we did communicate across the spiritual airwaves I imagined his lips as motionless as those of a ventriloquist.

For no reason that I could fathom, I felt prompted to name him 'Gabe' sometime after we first met. He approved without hesitation and it stuck. I came to wonder later if the name may have applied to him and all his peers, assuming they existed, or to their Commander-in-Chief.

On occasions he'd operate without being called upon, always with such subtle and unobtrusive skill it didn't look as if he was interfering with the normal course of events.

For example, when I was twelve and was crossing Sydney's hectic Parramatta Road at Ashfield on my first visit there and looked the wrong way, I took an unexpected misstep at the last moment as if he'd held me back—and the rear mirror of the truck that would have struck and killed me if I'd taken another step whistled past my right ear.

Or when I dived from the ten metre rock wall beside Dalmanyi pool in the Kimberleys, its water brown and murky after the first drought-breaking rains, and I wrenched myself upwards at his whispered warning just in time to save myself from striking the bottom and breaking my neck. Scraping the skin off the left side of my face as I grazed the rocky bottom proved an unforgotten lesson. I still bear the scars. They show up clearly when I have a suntan.

There were other times when he'd arrange a sequence of apparent coincidences with the lightest of magical touches with immediate effect—then follow them up with long term consequences that revealed themselves years later.

The most remarkable of his on-the-spot-behind-the-scenes effects occurred in 1960, from early April to the end of August. I was turning eighteen and taking a gap year in the Netherlands to learn Dutch, before entering the University of North Wales, Bangor, to study the Dutch language, their history and culture—and then, as a consequence fifty years later, I researched the life of Michiel de Ruyter and wrote my third novel, the most successful in my *Life and Times* series.

Why the University of North Wales, Bangor? Because the family history on my Welsh mother's side went back over two centuries, with strong connections to the Methodist Revival movement.

My Australian father died when I was two, leaving my mother struggling to bring me up alone as best she could. She barely kept our noses above the breadline for years. Her strict work ethic, stoicism and unfailing persistence kept us going. I will never forget her. Short and lively, the sparkle in her dark brown eyes was accentuated by her pale and freckled skin surrounded by a mop of wiry, tightly curled black hair turning white, her moods alternately sweet and sour as she swept like a dynamo through the house in her black smocks or colourful bedgowns.

'*Never* a glass half empty, my dear,' she'd insist, the faint remnants of her Welsh lilt still evident, '*always* a glass half full, and then you make do.' And we did. 'When things *do* go south,' she'd sometimes add, 'as they often will for no good reason, you ride the wave to the beach, no matter how rough the sea.'

I took that advice throughout my years at school, and the scholarship I won for a university education in the UK proved a minor miracle. Thank you, Gabe.

And why Dutch? Well, because the four-hundred-year-old skeletal remains of marooned and mutinous sailors and passengers of the Dutch ship *Batavia*, on display under glass in Fremantle's Shipwrecks' Museum, have enthralled me since I first saw them when I was nine. The bullet holes in the shattered skulls. The shoulder blades, clavicles and ribs chipped and gouged by swinging sword blades. The mystery of the missing bones of both hands hacked off several of them. The ship was wrecked on Beacon reef in the Abrolhos Islands off the West Australian coast in 1629, and the fascination has never dimmed.

Late evening on Friday, 3 April, 1960.

A cold mist was settling over the still waters of the port of Harwich on the River Stour as I boarded the ferry for the crossing to the Hook of Holland, the glimmering lights of Felixstowe across the channel gradually disappearing as it closed in.

My cabin for the overnight trip was on the lower deck. I chose the upper bunk, stowed my haversack at my feet and prepared for an early night, the uproar I could hear in the ferry's two bars and social café not tempting me. I was feeling as uptight and excited as I had been when my adventure began—with my first flight a month ago, the surge of the UK bound Qantas Boeing 707 jet surprising me as it accelerated down the Perth runway, thrusting me back into my seat.

I woke at midnight. The sour reek of whiskey and sweat, and the regular rasp of my snoring cabin mate kept me awake for another hour. I slept fitfully after that, the sound of wharfies shouting as the ferry docked in the port of the Hook of Holland waking me at dawn.

I climbed down, and when I came back out of the ensuite bathroom, I found my cabin mate sprawled on his bunk in his well-worn jeans, his shoulders resting on his double pillows, his head against the bulkhead. I guessed he'd spent the night that way. He was shaven headed and darkly sunburned, his eyes a piercing blue, his bare, solid chest and wiry arms so heavily tattooed in blue and scarlet inks you could barely see the skin. He was smoking.

'Also, was haben wir hier? Ein Wanderer auf dem Weg zurück ins Vaterland?' he asked. His voice was deep, and what I took for his Glaswegian accent rendered the German barely comprehensible, the sharp whiff of bile and stale whiskey reaching me.

'Beg yours?'

'Beg yours! Oh, God… not another Aussie out to conquer the world. I took you for a German, son. A Fritz, for sure.' He flicked the ash from his cigarette into his calloused left palm before sprinkling it beneath his bunk.

'Me, a German? Why?'

'The buzzcut. The kraut shape of the head, if you don't mind my saying so. The tall and skinny Aryan body shape that would suit a Brown Shirts uniform. You fit the mould.' He gave me a friendly but sarcastic grin. His eyes, reflecting his humour, were spiced with a touch of cruelty. 'On second thoughts, didn't I see you in the Queensland outback at that rodeo in a clown suit? Wasn't that at the Deniliquin Muster? Or was it Mt Isa Mines?'

I laughed with him, but uneasily. 'I'm from the West, actually. Perth… but I'm often up in the Kimberleys.'

'Catching crocs?'

'Fishing, actually. Spanish mackerel and Barra mostly.'

I hefted my haversack onto my back and stepped towards the door.

'*Riiiight*, my mistake,' he said. 'So what brings you to these parts?'

I turned and looked back. 'I start Uni in September. I've come here to find work and hone up on my Dutch till then.'

He swung sideways off the bunk and stood unsteadily, stretching out to the cabin wall for balance, before following me out onto the deck. He was a foot or so shorter than my six foot three, compensated for by the breadth of his shoulders.

'*Find work?*' he said. 'What do you know that I don't?'

'What do you mean?'

'Do you have a work permit? A sponsor? Somewhere lined up to stay? Money?'

His questions stunned me and I held his stare. I slowly unloaded the haversack and placed it at my feet. 'You need a working visa?'

He gave a bark of laughter. 'My God!' He flicked his cigarette overboard and threw open his palms. 'Haven't you checked? How old are you?'

'Eighteen next month.'

'Then you should know better. Yes... you need a permit. Yes, you need a sponsor, and somewhere to stay. Jesus B Christ, do you have any money? A return ticket?'

'Enough to get by on. Just enough for a return ticket.'

'Take my advice and buy it now. Go straight back to Harwich and get yourself sorted. Unless you're a glaikit.'

'A glaikit?'

'An eejit. Someone who doesn't know his arse from his elbow... which most of the Aussies I've come across up until now generally *do* know.'

'I'm going to try finding work on a farm somewhere,' I said. 'To save some money and practice the language. I can drive a tractor... operate a forklift.'

He looked thoughtfully out over the port. The thick plume of smoke from one of the factory chimneys, flattening out as the wind caught it, trailed a long blue-grey finger pointing inland. He turned and gazed back up at me, leaning against the rail.

'Look, son,' he said, 'you may well be lucky. You may find a sympathetic farmer before his dogs rip you to pieces… or before the Immigration Officers do the same, come to that. But I very much doubt it. If I were you I'd take my advice—'

'I have to give it a go,' I cut him off. 'Things will work out. They always do… always have. I've come this far. And anyway, I've overstayed my welcome with my relatives in Berkshire.'

'Well, good luck with that if you insist. Just a word of warning though. The Dutch are still touchy about Germans, even fifteen years after the war. They copped a hit from the Nazis, as you know, and they're ready to give it back in kind. You do look German, that's for sure. You did to me. And many Dutch people won't know the difference. So make sure you advertise yourself as Aussie before they pull the trigger.'

'Thanks for that,' I said, reaching out to shake his hand before lifting the haversack. 'Jon Janacek. It's good to meet you.'

'Davie Dickson,' he grinned, 'a weegie from way back. I'm the chef aboard the *Kathleen*, a coaster in the Black Sea. She's due in Istanbul in a fortnight and I'm going to join her there. I'm stuck in Rotterdam for another week or so.'

'Goodbye, then,' I said as I headed for the gangway. 'You take care.'

'So long, and the best of British, Jon. See you around.'

'Like a rissole,' I called out as I reached the paving on the pier and took a step towards the city.

'A rissole indeed,' he raised a hand and slowly shook his head. 'Don't get yourself barbecued to a crisp, now.'

I took a bus that morning from Rotterdam travelling northwards to Leiden, to get the lay of the land. I was filled with enthusiastic optimism as the gateway to my future creaked open, after Davie threatening to slam it shut.

Unfortunately, my grasp of Dutch was still rudimentary. I hadn't progressed much beyond the chapters on greetings and introductions in my *Teach Yourself* and *Complete Idiot's Guide* books on Dutch, and that disadvantage became evident the moment I climbed aboard. The bus driver spoke no English. I unfolded my *Euromap* and indicated the green open spaces between Rotterdam, The Hague and Leiden. 'Somewhere in there,' was not good enough for him, neither was, 'Ergens darbinnen,' hoarsely translated over my shoulder by a helpful passenger with smoker's breath behind me in the queue.

To forestall the driver's growing impatience and escape the stale odour, I bought a ticket all the way to Leiden. *I can miss a meal to offset the extra cost,* I thought, and told the mystified driver, 'I'll get off when I see the sort of countryside I'm after.'

'Hij zal uitstappen als hij het sort platteland ziet warnaar hij op zoek is,' I heard the passenger explain for me as he bought his ticket.

In the end I pressed the bell at the first stop after Zoetermeer. We had just passed several goat and dairy farms, a rose nursery and a paddock stocked with alpacas.

I spent the next two days trudging along the highway and ducking down several lanes and byways to visit eight farms. Four were dairies, one a free range chicken farm with flocks of bright-eyed white Leghorns protected by two placid and gigantic white Maremma watchdogs, a specialised tulip nursery and two goat farms.

My reception at the first seven farms were all the same, with slight variations on a theme. After the dog—or dogs— had been quietened: 'What do you want? Where are you from? Where? *Australia?* Where's that?' And the eventual, 'No, we have all the workers we need.' Then the eyes lost focus and avoided mine—and the farmer or the farmer's wife retreated behind the front door, stepped rapidly away into the barn, or engaged first gear on the red or blue mud-spattered tractor and roared off into the paddock, leaving me to walk despondently back down the driveway to the road.

Except for one. The eighth. A goat farm. The last farm I visited, in fact, on the second day in the late evening, after spending the night sleeping in a leaf filled ditch in a coppice of beech trees.

The farm had an honesty market stall at the end of its driveway, with the creamiest blueberry yoghurt in its refrigerator I've ever tasted. I also bought a freshly baked hot cross bun and ate it on the spot, even though Easter was still a fortnight away.

When I reached the farmhouse, still dipping into the yoghurt with its plastic spoon, I struck the small bronze bell beside the door using a metal mallet suspended from it. The sound rang out across the acreage, and I was amused to see several bearded white goats in the lushly grassed paddock beside the house whip up their heads and trot to the whitewashed fence to investigate, their distended pink udders swinging.

The door eventually opened and a red-haired, green-eyed girl about eight or nine stepped around it. She was wearing blue stonewashed dungarees and she had a light powdering of flour on the fine blonde hairs on her forearms. She had just washed her hands and was drying them on a dishcloth.

'Kan ik u helpen?' she asked, her eyes flicking from my face to the tub of yoghurt.

'Do you speak English?'

'A little bit. I'm learning.'

I felt my hopes soar. 'Are your Mum and Dad home?'

She turned and shouted, '*Papaaaa!* We hebben een bezouker,' then disappeared.

Moments later her father peered round the door. He had a full ginger-beard and what I took for reading glasses balanced in his unkempt hair. His eyes were as luminously green as his daughter's. He stepped lightly onto the porch, nudged aside a grey cat that had followed him out with his bare foot, and closed the door behind him. In a brown check shirt and maroon corduroy trousers, he was solidly built and looked like a welterweight boxer.

'Your daughter speaks English,' I said.

'She does. I'm teaching her. How can we help you?'

'I'm looking for work—'

'I can stop you right there. I don't need anyone at present. When the blueberries need picking, yes. Early in June. You're two months too early.' He looked down at the half-finished yoghurt. 'Why don't you come in and finish that inside? More comfortable than standing out here.'

'If you don't mind, I will. Thank you. It's delicious, by the way. I was thinking the best I've ever tasted.'

'What's that accent?' he asked as I followed him in. 'New Zealand, is it?'

We spent the next hour discussing my situation and Hugo—he'd introduced himself as Hugo Bouwman— confirmed that everything Davie had told me was true.

'His advice was on the money,' he said. 'You won't find work without a permit... least of all round here. We're a suspicious lot, us farmers, at the best of times. We have a living to make, and the world out there can go jump, except for our customers as long as they're buying.' He looked at me with some sympathy, and shrugged. 'Best you beat a retreat before things get too dire.'

He fed me that night and allowed me to sleep the sleep of the dead in his barn among the bales of straw. The next morning after breakfast he drove me to the train station in Leiden and I caught the express back to Rotterdam.

So it took as little as three days for Davie's forewarnings to sink in, his predictions to come true, and for me to experience feelings of such deep despair that any thoughts of riding the wave to the beach were out of the question. For the first time in my young life I went through a range of dark emotions. I felt foolish, frustrated, desperately afraid and furious with myself in turn.

Until, that is, I stepped off the train in Rotterdam station and pushed my way through the rush hour crowd to the revolving glass door at the exit.

As I stepped into the orthogonal glass partition in the door to make my way out, someone stepped into the partition directly opposite mine, making his way in. We caught one another's eye through the glass panel as the door swept around, his a piercing blue and mine, I imagined, a depressed and defeated hazel—and a sudden surge of shock rushed through my chest.

Of all people, I recognised Davie.

I couldn't believe it, but he hammered with the knuckles of his left hand on the glass to alert me as he swept by and followed me around, wagging the forefinger of his right.

No! Not a chance, I thought, as I was catapulted out into the dazzling sunlit square outside the station and spun around as he emerged. *Not Davie. Not… a… bloody… chance.*

A hysterical burst of spontaneous laughter overtook both of us as we faced one another, before he embraced me, then held me at arm's length, his hands on my shoulders.

'Well, what do you know,' he said as he calmed down, clearly as surprised as I was, and we shook hands. 'The prodigal son returns, sooner than expected. What brings you back to these parts?'

'Just as you predicted, Davie. I've hit a brick wall.'

'So what now, son? What do you have in mind?'

'Time for me to head for the hills, I think. With my tail between my legs.'

Before I'd got the last words out he smiled and scrutinised my face, before saying laconically, 'So you're going to make a run for it? Already? You sure about that?'

'What choice do I have? Besides, isn't that what you recommended three days ago?'

'Aaaah! That was then, and I was barely sober. This is now. Come with me. I have to buy a ticket to Istanbul and I'm going to have a bite to eat in the station restaurant. The pieces they serve up in there aren't all that bad. I'll treat you.'

'Pieces?'

'Sandwiches, son. Your Aussie sangas.'

'Are you sure?'

'Of course I'm sure. No point in doing anything rash. Let's take our time and think your situation through over a steak and salad… sanga.' He gave a conspiratorial chuckle coupled with a wink. 'There's more ways than one to skin a cat. We've just got to find the right way.'

'Oh, okay, then. Thank you.'

He glanced back as he led me to the entrance. 'You only live once, Jon. And fortune favours, so they tell me. You fill in the blank.'

Three hours later we were standing in the queue in the busy Immigration and Labour Department, with which Davie was familiar. When we reached the head of the queue, Davie asked the counter clerk in basic Dutch to arrange an interview with the manager—and within ten minutes we were talking to English-speaking Guus Dekker, in his cubicle at the end of the office.

He was a friendly, middle-aged and well-groomed man,

casually dressed and greying at the temples, with a receding hairline and an alert and searching look. He checked my passport and flicked through my university enrolment documentation, his lips pursed, before turning his full attention on Davie. He listened patiently as Davie explained my situation, stressed my upcoming studies, my selection of the Dutch language and culture as a subject of study and my Australian origins.

And then, without commenting, he reached for the phone and dialled out. He spent the next few minutes conversing with someone who clearly responded positively to whatever he was suggesting. When he rang off, he smiled, placed his elbows on his desk and gazed at me over his interlocked fingers.

'This is your lucky day,' he said. 'That was my wife Coby. We have a spare bedroom at home and she will be happy to have you as a lodger. The rent will be minimal and I will sponsor you and find you work.' He paused, as if to let the good news sink in. 'On a student's wage, of course. So how does that sound?' he asked at last.

I slowly shook my head. I felt strangely powerless, as if I was a pawn swept up in the mysterious course of events with no say in how it turned out, wondering how in the world Gabe had orchestrated it.

'I can't believe it,' I struggled to reply. 'That's brilliant. Of course I accept. And thank you... and your wife.'

'A few things you need to understand,' Guus said. 'Coby does not speak English, so you are going to have to learn Dutch. And we have three children who have all now left home. They are girls, and Coby always wanted a son. So she's likely to thoroughly spoil you.'

'Half your luck,' Davie said, smiling widely.

Guus reached for a pen and a scribble pad and hastily wrote an address, sketching a mud-map below it indicating the tram that would get me there.

'Turn up any time after five and I will meet you there,' he said as he handed me the sheet. 'We will see you then.'

He stood and ushered us out of his office.

I was stunned and Davie was ecstatic. 'Well son,' he said as we exited the building. 'Never say never. We've skun the cat. Here's the beginning of the next four months of your life. Let's drink to that.'

And he was right.

Within two days I was offsider to a truck driver delivering crates of Phoenix beer around Rotterdam and The Hague, and did so for the next four months. I caught a tram to work every morning after a breakfast of white bread sprinkled with hundreds and thousands, washed down with a cup of black tea, and carrying a lunch box of sausage and rollmop sandwiches prepared by my doting second mother, plump-and-homely always-smiling grey-eyed Coby. I slept in a comfortable bed beneath a sloping roof and dormer window on the third floor of the house beside the Hillevliet canal and washed myself down in the basin at home as best I could, before bathing once a week in the nearest communal bath house. On some weekends I accompanied Guus and Coby to the art museums, the wide and sandy beaches at 's-Gravenzande and the Marantha Dutch Reformed Church on Sundays.

Until mid-August, that is, when Guus and Coby went on holiday to Belgium to meet their daughter Adrie and her children. To occupy my time while they were away, Guus enrolled me to attend a conference on the 'Seventeenth Century Indian Ocean Voyages of the Ships of the VOC', to be held in Middelburg, south of Rotterdam.

The conference lasted a week, but its indelible memories and influences lasted me a lifetime. Visits to the maritime archives; trips to the ancient warehouses, canals and docksides; examination of the saw windmills close to the port of Vlissingen; the engineering of the Haven Canal connecting the city to the sea; films and documentaries recording the famous voyages of the *Batavia*, the *Gilt Dragon*, the *Zuytdorp* and the *Ridderschap van Holland* among others.

In my later years, those seven days supercharged my determination to write my *Life and Times* series, fictional historical novels based on reality—the remarkable VOC voyages and the men and women who crewed the ships.

Once again I felt heavily indebted to Gabe.

At the conference, I met Cornelis Mertens, a dry and humorous sixty year old Professor of Marine Archaeology at Belgium's Ghent University. I discovered that he had visited Fremantle and we shared a common interest in the fate of the *Batavia*. During the week, he showed such empathy and interest in my circumstances, I opened up to him. I told him about the death of my father, my meeting with Davie and Guus, my belief in the interventions of Gabe and even let slip that I was close to broke. Most of the student's wage I'd earned delivering beer had been used to pay the rent, buy the occasional fresh bunches of tulips and other flowers for Coby and pay for my irresistible weekly treat—a pint of ChocoMilk, to which I'd become addicted.

After the conference, Cornelis came to the station to see me off.

As I was about to step up into the carriage, he handed me a book—a well-worn paperback copy of Czech writer Franz Kafka's *The Trial*.

'I want you to read this,' he said. 'Your father died when you were two, you said.'

'Yes, he did.'

'Then I'm sure he'd approve. I have to say I'm concerned that your belief in Gabe, as you call him, is excessively naïve. I'm sure your father would have advised you against it.'

'Naïve? Why?'

'In my view you've created an imaginary surrogate father for yourself. It isn't healthy, and Kafka's book will serve as a dose of reality.'

The train began to move. I thanked him, shook his hand and stepped in through the door with the book.

I found myself a seat, opened the book—and a bundle of yellow fifty guilder notes concealed within it fell to the floor. I was astonished. I gathered up the scattered notes and counted them as the train picked up speed. We were soon rocketing through the Zeeland countryside. I shook my head in disbelief. They'd pay for the ferry back to Harwich and the rail journey to North Wales, with change to spare.

I felt a rush of such excited relief that I laughed aloud, alarming and amusing some nearby fellow passengers as the train crossed the silvery marshland of an estuary, flocks of waterbirds scattering skyward.

Call me naïve? I thought. *Thank you, Gabe.*

Skating On Thin Ice

'WATCH OUT FOR CLIFFORD Farmer,' my friend Alistair thoughtfully forewarned me as we strolled around the UWA campus exhibits during orientation week.

A postgraduate student in Aboriginal Studies himself, Alistair was examining a printout of my first-year enrolment details.

'Uncle Cliff,' he went on, 'I see he's your senior tutor. Best of luck, Caleb. He's got a mind like a dingo trap and a tongue like a whiplash. If you can tolerate his sarcasm and his eccentric teaching techniques, you'll learn everything you need to know about Aboriginal history. Not to mention culture. And I mean everything. He's one hell of a taskmaster, but you'll come out the other end the better for it.' Then he sent me a knowing grin. 'If not, then you're in for a rough ride. In fact, you may as well pack up and go home now, with your tail between your legs. Avoid the torture.'

I said nothing about Alistair's warning to the other first-year students the Friday we gathered at ten o'clock outside Clifford's closed study door. *Best they find out for themselves,* I thought. *Even if it's the hard way.*

Right on time, the door swung inwards and Clifford appeared, the rich smell of percolating coffee wafting out around him.

'Brothers and sisters,' he said, giving us a formal ironic bow. 'My prospective victims. I'm pleased to meet you all. I'm Clifford, never Cliff for short, or, god forbid, *Uncle* Cliff. Not until you graduate, that is, and even then, only with my say so.'

He stepped aside and ushered us in with a vigorous circular wave of his right hand, pointing his thumb at a silver coffee percolator and several mugs standing on a sideboard to our left. 'Welcome to my lair. Tell me your Christian names on the way in. Make yourselves at home and feel free to pour yourselves a coffee at any time.'

He inspected us as we filed past, handing us each a single A3 sheet showing the dramatic illustration of a shipwreck foundering in a storm at the base of a line of towering red cliffs. *The* Zuytdorp *wreck site*, I read in capitals across the top.

'Sandy.'

'Nikki.'

'Sanjeev.'

'Kristina.'

I was the last to enter.

'Lucky last,' Clifford said, as the others took their seats, 'but hopefully not least,'

'Caleb,' I replied.

Dark brown and sharply intelligent, his eyes were deep-set beneath the protruding bony ridge behind his eyebrows. His face was lean and his cheekbones prominent, the shape of his compressed lips hinting at sardonic humour. His unruly black hair was generously streaked with silver and held in check with a woven black and white Clothing the Gap headband.

He was taller than me, and rangy, with what I took for a slight pot belly evident under a lime green short-sleeved shirt. *It may instead be a set of well-developed abdominals*, I realised, when I saw a squash racquet propped in the far corner of the study. His skin was light brown, the wiry sinews on his forearms gliding beneath it as he reached out to shut the door. His left arm was heavily tattooed in abstract patterns similar to the Maori. He wore white shorts and Asics joggers.

I took the last seat in the semicircle facing him.

Still standing, he held the picture up before us. 'Right.

Let's get down to my introduction,' he said. 'The *Zuytdorp*. She went down on the cliffs just north of Kalbarri in June 1712. The experts reckon there were up to sixty survivors. Sixty Dutch seamen brimming with semen. Imagine the consequences once they joined our local mobs. From then on, the fortunes of the next generation of my people and those who followed took a turn for the better.'

Then he sat in the chair facing us, stretched out, carefully crossed his legs, placed the picture on the floor beside him and clasped his hands behind his head. 'Or worse, depending on your point of view. Judge for yourselves. You're looking at a prime example, no less.'

He gazed at us in turn, his eyebrows raised, his eyes piercing. 'No need to pass judgement till you get to know me better, my brothers and sisters. What I'm saying, by way of introduction, is both my parents were part-Aboriginal and part-Dutch from way back. I used to wonder what that made me. I was never really sure. That is, until I came across Cyril Volkov. Any of you heard of him?'

There was an extended awkward silence. 'Anyone? Anyone at all?'

'I can't say I have, sir,' Sanjeev eventually said.

'You haven't missed much, but you're going to get to know him... and never mind the "sir", Sanjeev—unlike Price Philip I haven't been offered a knighthood yet. You'll discover Cyril was an anthropologist in the 1920s to give you nightmares. An ideological proponent of the White Australia Policy. Of course you've heard of that or you wouldn't be here.'

He looked inquiringly around us.

'Good. Anyway, I read his expert opinion on the subject of mixed bloods and he enlightened me. Quick smart.'

He rocked a long way back in his chair and reached for the inbuilt bookshelf lining the clinker-brick wall behind him. 'According to him, I'd have been classified as a quadroon. Or maybe an octoroon. But when you calculate the proportions, do you *square* the denominator? Not that my fractions are in any way vulgar. Pint for pint, I'm a pure-blood on both sides of the equation.'

He ran his finger along the spines of the books and pulled out a slim volume before resettling his chair. He flicked it open—his bookmark, I noticed, was a Qantas boarding pass—then held the book up to the sunlight pouring in through the window behind him to read from it. I saw the title in faded gold on the battered cover: *The Australian Aborigine: a Study in Assimilation.*

'You'll all appreciate this. It's a paragraph from Volkov's thesis for his doctorate regarding the definitions of caste. The first time I read it I was ready to strangle the bastard, except that he was already dead. Nowadays it's part of the ammunition us blackfellas use. It's our heavy artillery when we want to score a point about our mutual history. It's our stud book, complete with the formula for breeding out the black.'

He began to read with slow deliberation, 'Definitions of caste and the determination of aboriginality or otherwise may be derived from the inverted family tree. By counting backwards through the parentage the degree to which a person is removed from the full-blood may be calculated. For each of two parents, four grandparents, eight great-grandparents and so on, count the proportions of black or white, particularly of course where that person is already a half-blood. The fractions then become a matter of simple addition. The term half-caste or half-blood implies two parents who are full-blood, one black and the other white. Quadroon indicates one full-blood and one half-blood parent hence a quarter-blood, while octoroon results from a full-blood and a quadron, or one part in eight.'

He looked up from the page and clicked his tongue.

'Quadroon spelled with a missing "o". I like that. A slip of the tongue from an educated whitefella.' He looked at Sanjeev. 'Or educated Indian, of course.' He hesitated. 'Or Sri Lankan, perhaps?'

'Malaysian actually. From Langkawi.'

'Right. Malaysian. Langkawi. A beautiful island. Named after the brahminy kite, I understand—the sea eagle. One of our Malgana tribal totems, as a matter of interest. But back to the missing "o". I don't expect to come across similar grammatical errors in any of your essays this term. If I do, prepare for a public roasting.'

He stood, walked across to the percolator and poured himself a coffee. Then he sat back down and read on. 'Complications arise higher up the tree when new terms are required. What term does one use if five-eighths of the great-grandparents are black so that the grandparents are quadroons and the parents are octoroons? Will the person then qualify as a quadroon or an octoroon in the strict sense, being less than a half-blood; and if not, are they to be classed as Aboriginal or white? The fraction considered the determinant between Aboriginal and white is critical and for fairness, it needs to be mathematically exact. As the generations pass,' he turned the page and murmured, 'and have they what! The mathematics will become more complex. If the fraction is below the half-blood, then degrees of skin colour may be considered, and the term half-blood used as a catchall. For example, a person of five-sixteenths with light skin might be classed as a quadroon and white while one with the same proportions who is dark-skinned may qualify as half-blood and aboriginal. The mathematics may become so complicated when we deal with sixteenths that the term aboriginal may be applied to full-bloods and greater than five-eighths only, with light half-bloods or quadroons no longer classified as blacks but whites.'

Clifford snapped the book shut and waved it in the air, the bookmark with its white kangaroo trapped in a red triangle jutting from the page. He gave a dry burst of laughter. 'With light half-bloods or quadroons no longer classified as blacks but whites! What do you make of that, Caleb? Sanjeev? Nikki? Any comments? Kristina? Sandy?'

Before anyone could reply, he went on, 'The formula for a blackfella evolving into a whitefella! You need to be another Einstein! Christ! We had enough trouble coming to terms with our extermi-bloody-*nation*, let alone our exterminology.'

Unsure how to react. I wondered what was coming next. It was our first tutorial with him and he was already taking us to the heart of the Black Lives Matter debate. I'd expected bitterness and there was bitterness, but to my mind, there was also a sardonic humour that offset his rancour.

I recognised this moment as the beginning of my education. *These* were among the things I needed to fully understand.

'Times were different then, weren't they?' red-haired Sandy suggested to him, her Irish accent evident. 'People acted on different principles.'

'What principles?' Clifford shot back. 'You'll be firing blanks if you follow that line of argument. The principle of having no principles? The principle that the end justifies the means? That might is right? Or *terra nullius* justifies invasion and massacre?'

Sandy paled. 'No. They thought they were acting for the best.'

'The best? On whose behalf? Their own? Or were they doing *us* a favour?'

'They believed the changes were inevitable. They were convinced it was just a matter of time.'

'Before what? Before us blackfellas died out? So they accelerated the process and turned a blind eye to the consequences? They assumed it was only a matter of time and that gave them the foresight and the mandate to legislate the way they did and take the half-caste children away?'

He pointed at the gold-embossed name on the cover, rapping it with an emphatic forefinger. 'Only they were wrong. And Volkov here, he was one of the architects of the whitefella policy of assimilation. Assimilation my backside. Another word for annihilation. Turn the half-castes white while the full-bloods die out.' He looked enquiringly across at Sandy. 'Can you guess what I like to call him?'

'I have no idea.' Her voice quavered. She looked as though she'd swallowed a handful of ground glass.

'The mathe*mortician*. The mathemortician of Anthro-*no-apology*, with a formula for calculated genocide. We know he took his initial degree at Harvard before transferring to the ANU for his postgraduate studies. He would have learned their theory of the One Drop Rule there. It still applies in the States. One drop of black blood and if you're white you're black, not a darker shade of pale or one of the fifty shades of grey.'

He stared at her mercilessly, raising his eyebrows. 'Anything to add?'

When she didn't reply, he said, 'Looks like you've painted yourself into a corner, Sandy. Better hope you used quick-drying.'

Then he turned directly to me. I struggled to hold his gaze. 'Didn't the Nazis in Auschwitz-Birkenau render the Jewish inmates down and turn them into bars of soap before doing a Pontius Pilate and washing their hands of them? Wasn't that ethnic cleansing at its worst?' He reached for his mug and sipped his coffee. 'And didn't they make candles with whatever was left over in the vats?'

Shocked and cornered, I had no reply.

'Must have been thin candles,' he said, shaking his head. 'They didn't have much fat on them.'

Horror settled like a pool of molten lead deep in my gut. I wondered why he had directed his observations at me. *Was it my name? Did he think I was Jewish?*

'My God!' he went on, 'The things that so-called civilised human beings can own up to. White plus black equals black. The formulated logic of exclusion to preserve the imperilled white race and its culture from contamination. We all live behind the barricades and it saddens me. I find it inexcusable that it's taken so long for us to admit that we've all come through the blender and genetically every single one of us is as crazily mixed up as the next. If you go back far enough, we all have to be related.' He looked around us in mock horror. 'That means we could be having incestuous relationships if and when we get down to business, my brothers and sisters. We could be contravening the taboo.' Then he gave us a sudden, unexpectedly beatific smile, showing all his teeth. 'If you don't tell anyone, I certainly won't.'

There was another extended silence.

'Right there, on that note,' he he looked down at his watch, 'you'll be pleased to learn today's tutorial ends. Before you give a communal sigh of relief, let me explain. What I've thrown at you is the sort of argument you're going to come up against throughout this course, especially when we go out into the field and meet some of the Indigenous firebrands I've lined up for you—in their urban and country environments.

'You're going to feel at times as if you're facing a firing squad. Each embittered trigger-happy rifleman supercharged with emotion and armed with a verbal shotgun, will be sending you a scatter of pellets with what they consider rhyme and reason. You're going to have to learn to duck and weave, and avoid getting carried away... dead or alive, to complete the metaphor. You get the picture? You're going to have to sort the racist facts from the fiction. Steep yourselves in the history, in the truth. Be patient, perceptive and persistent—the three "Ps". Get organised, in other words. Do the research and apply the appropriate logic.'

He leaned back and looked thoughtfully at each of us, 'Oh, and above all, record a "yes" for the Voice when the vote comes around later this year or next, but don't let me sway you one way or the other.'

He stood, picked up a sheaf of papers from his desk, walked to the door and opened it. He handed us each a stapled document of several pages as we filed out.

'Same time next week,' he said. 'This is a short story by Kate Chopin—*Désirée's Baby*, published in *Vogue* magazine way back in 1893. It's set before the American Civil War about a baby and a racial conflict between a plantation owner and his wife. Given what we've discussed today, I want an essay giving me your analysis of the story, with no limit on the number of words. Feel free to go overboard or keep it as short and succinct as you like. Whatever you do, don't bother coming to the tutorial without it. Good day to you, brothers and sisters all. Nice meeting you all.'

He shut the door behind him, leaving us on the landing bemused and at a loss for words.

Except for Sandy.

She shook her head, her afro-styled mass of red curls bobbing and her green eyes fiery. 'What have I got myself into?' she asked, her lilting Irish accent embellishing her outrage. 'Analyse a *short story* for starters? I didn't enrol in another English Literature course. Did any of you?' When no one replied, she hissed, 'I've already *done* that, damn it!' as she stormed away.

I spent several hours on two successive nights the following week analysing the story.

Set among wealthy French Creole cotton plantations in

Louisiana before the civil war, it concerned the 'beautiful, gentle, affectionate and sincere' Désirée, a young girl abandoned on the successful Valmondé plantation. Despite her unknown origins, she was adopted by the owners. When she turned eighteen, despite her anonymity, she married Armand Aubigny, a young nobleman with a 'dark, handsome face', heir to the neighbouring L'Abri plantation.

She soon became pregnant and gave birth to a baby boy. At first, Armand was 'the proudest father in the parish'. When the baby was about four months old, however, Désirée was horrified when she noticed the pigment in the baby's skin darkening. Everyone around her confirmed her worst fears, including the slaves on the plantation, who began taking a keen interest in the child.

Armand was outraged. He vented his anger on Désirée and his retinue of slaves so that she was driven to despair. Despite her insistence that she was white and not part black, Armand exiled her from the estate. She escaped into the neighbouring bayou with the baby and was never seen again.

Sometime later, while burning all her belongings, including her love letters to him that he'd saved, Armand came across a letter from his mother to his father expressing her relief that Armand had never discovered the mixed African heritage in her line.

Seeking to preempt what Clifford was looking for, I treated the story as an essay rather than a supremely ironic short story. I did my best to unpick the themes around racial prejudice, race and cultural practice, the structure of the Louisianan social hierarchy and the devastating effect that racial profiling can have on people, both those who judge and the victims judged by them. Not to mention that Armand, who already possessed his mother's letter, may in fact have known about his African descent and he was hiding it by blaming Désirée to avoid the humiliation of his possible exposure.

I wrote just under three pages for a total of 1260 words. I spent a great deal of head-scratching time composing it and was eventually only partly satisfied with the result.

The following Friday, we filed into Clifford's office once again. This time he had a plate of lamingtons beside the coffee percolator and we helped ourselves, before handing him our essays and settling into our places.

'Right,' he said. 'It's good to see you all. So let's see how you went. Be prepared to defend your line of argument.'

He shuffled through the papers and then withdrew a single sheet with a look of surprise. There was one line typed on it, a sentence comprising three words.

I have never forgotten what happened next.

'Sandy,' he said. 'What on earth is this?'

'Read it. You did say there was no limit either way on the number of words.'

He looked down. '*Nganuralu nguba gutiya*,' he read, then gave a sudden bark of laughter. 'Brilliant! We are all of one blood, written in my Malgana language. Nicely done.'

He gazed at her, slowly nodding his approval. 'That was a smart move, sister, given the context of the story and the last tutorial. But it was a risky one. In matters so sensitive, when you think you're walking on water, you may instead be skating on thin ice and must tread very carefully to avoid falling through it and drowning.'

To Save Them From Extinction

Komodo dragons are listed as endangered. As a freelance journalist, I'm always looking for stories of interest to Australian readers—and the arrival of Cecilia, the first Komodo dragon to be transferred from Prague zoo into the Adelaide Zoo in December 2019 as part of a breeding program to save the species, gave me the opportunity for a fascinating story.

While I was researching the project, though, I came across another story so surprising it astonished me.

It began with my visit to the Prague Zoo in the Czech Republic.

Cecilia was bred there from her mother, Aranka. Housed with others in the jungles of the Indonesian Pavilion, Aranka is the prime female in the Prague zoo's world-leading breeding and scientific research program.

I interviewed the zoo's spokesperson. She directed me to Ludvik Brodsky, a middle-aged zoologist who had assisted in initiating the breeding program in 2004. With his agreement, I recorded the interview.

I began by asking him what had inspired him to join the program.

'My uncle, Jiři Springer, motivated me,' he said. 'When he was a student, he was imprisoned during World War II in the Theresienstadt SS internment camp. The Nazis set it up as a self-sufficient ghetto in the fortress outside Prague.'

'The fortress known as Terezin?'

'Exactly.'

'It's on my list of places to visit while I'm here.'

'You must. It was ideal for a Jewish internment camp with its many rows of barracks, two and three stories high. Enough room for up to forty thousand inmates, held there until being sent on to the concentration camps.'

'What happened to him?'

'He escaped in 1944, and later became Professor of Literature at the Masaryk University in Brno. He is now unfortunately deceased.' He gazed down at the tape recorder as if gathering his thoughts. 'When I was a young boy in the 1960's, he told me a mysterious fable about saving the Komodo Dragons from extinction on the Indonesian island of Flores. A teenage friend of his, Marek Löwy, who was imprisoned with him in the boys' barracks in Terezin, had written it. He published it in the boys' underground magazine, *Vedem*, secretly typed up and distributed round the boys' dormitories every Friday.'

'And the story impressed you?'

'It obsessed me. So much so that after I became a zoologist, I looked into the natural history of the dragons and joined the team setting up the breeding program.'

'I didn't realise things were that dire.'

'Oh, they are. The scrapheap of history—that's where they're headed unless we do something about it.' He looked at me for a moment, the thoughtful glint in his eyes arresting. 'You may be interested to know that Uncle Jiři told me he once heard none other than Ottla Davidová read Marek's story to a group of children in her care. She was a prison inmate assigned as their guardian when they were transported to Terezin from the Bialystok ghetto in Poland, in 1943.'

'Ottla Davidová?'

'The youngest sister of Franz Kafka.'

'Not *the* Franz Kafka?'

'The very same. Our most famous Czech literary figure. You're a journalist, you must be familiar with him? He wrote *The Trial*. And the famous short story *Metamorphosis*.'

'And *The Castle*. One of my favourites.'

'Mine also.'

'But Ottla is new to me, to be honest,' I said. 'Do you by any chance have a copy of Marek's story?'

'Not the original, no—only the one I wrote from memory. Would you like to hear it?'

'My oath… if you've got the time.'

He then told me Marek Löwy's story, surprising me by reciting it from memory. I have it on tape. I discovered later it was loosely based on *The Bucket Rider*, a short story by Franz Kafka.

I returned to Australia where I wrote the article on Cecilia. It was accepted by the *Adelaide Advertiser* and was later syndicated across other newspapers.

I then committed the next four months to researching the life of Ottla Davidová. I was privileged to discover an extraordinary woman, best described in Franz Kafka's own words as 'pure, truthful, honest, consistent, with humility and pride, sympathetic understanding and distance, devotion and independence, vision and courage in unerring balance'.

He was right.

To my mind, the extent of her self-sacrifice and dedication to those for whom she cared is beyond belief.

Ottla Davidová, an inmate in Terezin for over a year, was the first to apply for one of twenty guardian positions required to care for twelve hundred Jewish children being transferred from the Bialystok ghetto in Poland. They were due to arrive during the night on Tuesday, 24 August 1943.

She attended the interview with the Jewish Council of Elders—appointed by the SS to administer the camp—at seven in the morning on the Sunday, two days earlier.

It was cold and overcast when she crossed the lawns to the youth welfare office, half a kilometre from her Dresden barracks. The frosted grass splintered beneath her boots. Her breath was steaming and her nostrils stung in the crisp air.

After welcoming her into the warmth of room six, rabbi Leo Baeck, the senior of the three Jewish Council interviewers, said, 'The role will involve disciplining, teaching and entertaining groups of up to sixty children, aged between three and thirteen.'

'Disciplining them won't be a problem,' she replied, concerned that her voice was hoarse with the cold, 'and I'm sure I can teach, after a fashion. I'm not so sure about entertaining them, though. I don't think I have a storyteller's bone in my body. Then again, you never know till you try. My brother Franz was the writer, as you know. I'm the farmer—but with luck it might run in the family.'

She raised a forefinger to forestall the next question. 'There is one thing I could do. Young Marek Löwy from the boys' barracks—you all know him—he's been working with me in the vegetable gardens. During our breaks he's let me read some of the children's fables he's written. I'm no literary judge, but I think they aren't bad at all.' She thoughtfully rubbed her forehead. '*The Black Tulip*, for example. That one I liked. And *The Komodo Dragons*. That's special. There are several others I could recall if I put my mind to it. I'm sure he'd let me try them out on a young audience.'

Rabbi Leo asked her if she spoke Yiddish.

'Poorly,' she replied. 'No, that's not quite right. A little, yes. I can understand it. Franz and I studied Hebrew for a few months when he was living with me on the farm in Zürau and we picked up a little Yiddish at the same time. No doubt most of the children from Bialystok will speak it, as well as Polish. Communicating with them shouldn't be an issue.'

The interviewers then spent several minutes shuffling papers and conversing among themselves, before looking her up and down.

She wondered if they liked what they saw. She knew her presence was arresting, if not imperious. Fifty years old, close to six foot tall and fine-boned, she liked to think she exuded practical competence. Her chestnut hair was cut short around a delicate suntanned face and she had a slightly prominent nose, but her most striking features were her large dark brown eyes beneath straight black brows. She was aware they were calm, fearless and thoughtful, though they'd been watering in the morning chill. Despite the characteristic hint of sceptical humour in the set of her lips, which she also liked, during the interview she'd purposefully displayed a smile that she hoped warmed them to her.

She looked directly at Leo Baeck, and as their eyes met she silently challenged him to acknowledge her strongly independent mind, the depth of her courage and her loyalty to the Jewish cause. They must be beyond doubt, surely. In her application, she'd explained that she had convinced her Catholic husband, Josef 'Pepa' David, to accept a divorce exactly a year ago, to protect him and their daughters Věra and Helene from being caught up in the anti-Jewish pogroms and deportation due to their relationship with her. And then she had joined her fellow Jews about to be held in Terezin, by reporting voluntarily to the assembly area in the Trade Fair Palace, on the morning of their internment in August last year... *voluntarily*, she'd stressed, because her marriage to Catholic Pepa had previously granted her amnesty.

Rabbi Leo gazed back at her through his thick, plastic rimmed glasses, before congratulating her. 'I'm pleased to confirm your appointment,' he said. 'We have yet to interview another nineteen guardians, but we have already approved two doctors, a team of nurses, cooks and kitchen hands, laundry staff and a seamstress to care for the children. We believe the majority are orphans,' he went on. 'We're expecting them in Bohušovice station on Tuesday night. They'll remain there for two days of medical and other assessments... before the train is shunted on to the new railway siding in the fortress. You will report with the other guardians in the marketplace after elevenses on Wednesday morning, before walking to the station to relieve the incoming Polish chaperones.'

Before she departed for her barracks, he handed her a sheaf of instructions.

'You're to keep these strictly confidential,' he said. 'Commit them to memory and then burn them. They've come directly from SS Commandant Burger himself. They are top secret.'

She thanked him for his trust in her and turned for the door.

When she read the papers, she could scarcely believe her good fortune.

The Jewish children were the first consignment of an intended group of ten thousand, the SS papers read. They were to be well looked after, if not pampered with extra rations, before being exchanged for a number of high-ranking German prisoners of war and then sent to Switzerland, before resettling in Jerusalem in Palestine, their 'natural home' under the Balfour Declaration of 1917. All the pieces in the drama were in play, including Heinrich Himmler himself negotiating with Grand Mufti of Jerusalem, Mohammad Amin al-Husseini, to allow the exchange.

Ottla destroyed the papers and on a postcard to Pepa, she let him know that she was well.

Es geht mir gut, she wrote simply. 'I am fine.'

Four positive words whose message she knew the censors would allow, from which Pepa and her daughters would gather some comfort.

Deep down she was elated, both at the prospect of helping with the distressed children and with the possibility of her impending freedom in Switzerland and Palestine… provided nothing untoward occurred to change the course of the negotiations. As always, there lurked in the back of her mind a familiar shadow of distrust and doubt

On Wednesday morning she woke early. She opened the grimy window a crack to see that the pall of smoke from the overnight brown-coal fires in the kitchens and bakery had lifted, though the tarry smell of burning coal dust lingered.

She gazed at the Ohře River flowing below. Its reflections through the trailing willows changed from grey to silver as the sun rose over the Small Fortress on the opposite bank, piercing the clouds and sending shafts of light across the battlement brickwork. At the bend in the river three black moorhens scattered at a sound she couldn't hear, trailing widening arrowheads of splash behind them before settling among the reeds.

It was an image that reminded her of the farm she had managed for her brother-in-law in Zürau. She had nursed Franz there for eight months in 1917 after his first haemorrhage and the diagnosis of tuberculosis—eight peaceful months she'd never forgotten. His writing of short stories and epigrams had flourished, and he'd complimented her for carrying him on her wings through a difficult world. He'd never felt happier, he'd told her.

She had prepared the night before for the walk to Bohušovice station. She dressed and pulled on her boots, rubbing a cloth across each in turn, as was her habit, recalling Pepa's last kind gesture to her when he'd buffed them with goose fat for waterproofing.

After elevenses of half a cup of grain-based coffee and a chunk of black bread from the roll she'd saved from dinner, she made her way to the marketplace.

A red tractor was there, linked to two flat-bed trailers. They were loaded with bread and tureens of millet soup for the children, along with an assortment of simple toys the other children imprisoned in Terezin had been making for them for weeks. Gustav, the cook, and two stewards were sitting alongside each other on the first of the trailers.

She was pleased to see young Jiři Springer relaxing in the tractor seat. He smiled down at her when she arrived.

'Good to see you here, Ottla,' he said. 'Your cabbages are going to pine for you.'

'And you, Jiři. The cabbages can look after themselves for a day or two.'

A cheerful, dark-haired and good-looking post-doctoral student in literature at the Czech Charles University, he was familiar with many of Franz's writings. Now a prisoner, he was training as an earthworks machine operator, delivering meals around the barracks and collecting the corpses of those who had died overnight, delivering them to the crematoria.

She'd often supervised Jiři when he was driving the tractor on the farm beside the fortress, where she was in charge of the acres of vegetables and experimental patches of sorghum and millet.

The lively conversations she'd had with him took her back to the days when she was in her early twenties and she and Franz had argued and laughed over the merits or otherwise of his latest writings. They'd often walk along the banks of the Vltava River or lean over the parapet of the Charles Bridge, where Franz had once challenged her to see who could spit the farthest across the water. The gesture had been so unexpected she'd laughed disbelievingly before taking him on.

She scored a copper ten hellers coin from him when she won the contest, and she never forgot Franz sending her his characteristic knowing smile as he took it from his purse and handed it to her. 'Score one in the eye for life's injustices,' he said.

She later wore it as a treasured medallion suspended on a fine gold chain around her neck. She was wearing it that morning.

Dr Munk was also there, handing out a pad and sharpened pencil to each of the guardians, and Ottla collected hers.

A senior member of the Council of Elders, he was the deputy superintendent of the main hospital. When the guardians were assembled, he climbed stiffly onto the second trailer and addressed them.

'Good morning to you all,' he said. 'I will be supervising you for the next two days, while the children are held in Bohušovice station. It will no doubt take that long to sort them out and assess their situation. We don't yet know what condition they are in. Whatever the case, we will disembark them onto the platform and divide them into groups of up to sixty—a group for each guardian. Then we will identify them—hence the pads and pencils—before assessing their medical condition and feeding and clothing them. Not necessarily in that order. I suspect we may need to feed them first.' He gazed around the group. 'Are there any questions so far?'

The unmistakable high-pitched nasal voice of Lena Novotná, one of the guardians, broke the silence. 'Doctor Munk, why aren't we going straight into the siding in the fortress?'

Dr Munk peered around the group. 'Where are you, Lena? Ah, there you are. Because we don't know what sort of condition they're in yet. We can't risk them getting out of control in front of our other internees.'

He answered several other questions, completed his instructions, and forty minutes later, they reached the station, where they met the incoming Polish chaperones and a contingent of SS guards and Czech gendarmes, who'd been patrolling the platforms since the train's arrival.

In the station waiting room, two emaciated, shivering teenage boys dressed in filthy rags were roped to a bench. One of them was barefoot, the other in battered sandals. They'd clearly been thrashed and were under guard.

'Escapees,' one of the gendarmes told Ottla when she

enquired. 'We caught them red-handed, running for it during the night.'

'Have they been beaten?'

'No more than they deserved.'

Then Ottla's heart was wrenched when she glimpsed three small corpses in the far corner of the room, face down and head to toe beneath a hessian blanket that barely covered them. Suppressing her outrage and the tears that came with it, she drew closer. Three discarded skeletal dolls she estimated were no more than five years old, a girl and two boys who had not survived the last night of the journey.

She tore herself away and boarded the first carriage.

She walked down the central corridors between the mostly silent, staring children crammed onto the wood-slatted seats, gradually overcome with the immensity of the task that lay before her.

She'd entered an appalling scene from Dante's inferno, one that would have horrified even Franz, she thought, despite his ability to conjure inhuman scenes as frightful and outlandish as the one unfolding around her. Dressed in soiled and threadbare clothes and many barefoot, they too were bony and sunken-eyed, their faces grimy, their hair matted. The stench of unwashed bodies and urine was acrid. She found at first glance that their expressions were uniformly glazed and traumatised, as if they'd been exposed to such unspeakable terror it had ripped away their childhoods.

A mix of emotions swept through her. Empathy and pity for the children so deep she found herself about to weep, just as other guardians were. Outrage that life could be so unjust, cruel and inhumane to children so young. And then a pressing anxiety as to how she could best approach the problem of connecting with them to understand their pain and help them through it.

When they reached the third carriage, she could bear no more. She forced her way through those ahead of her until she reached Dr Munk.

She put her left hand on his shoulder. 'I can't believe this,' she said. 'It's far worse than we imagined.'

He turned to gaze at her, his face grey. 'It is. And we have another seven hundred in the carriages ahead of us. We will give them a quick inspection and then decide on our next course of action. All right?'

'Yes, but it's unspeakable. My first reaction is to strongly suggest we can't remain here for another two days identifying and inspecting them. We will have more deaths on our hands if we do.'

He peered at her gimlet-eyed through his rimless glasses. 'You are Mrs Davidová, are you not?'

'Ottla.'

'I agree, Ottla,' he said, turning away to resume the walk along the carriage. 'I take your point.' He looked back over his shoulder. 'I have already considered that.'

With some of the terrified children unwilling and others stubbornly refusing to cooperate, it took them until mid-afternoon to disembark them, settle them down on the platform, organise them into twenty supervised groups and feed and identify them, before distributing the toys to those who wanted them.

Dr Munk then selected one or two of the older children in each group to assist the guardian.

Fortunately, thirteen-year-old Abram Novinski, allocated to Ottla, spoke fluent Czech. He proved a godsend. He was a respectful, shy adolescent with lank blond hair and eyes a sky blue so pale they took Ottla by surprise the first time she looked into them, his suffering evident. Short and thin and mature beyond his years, he had a certain charm and gentle humour to which the younger children, most of whom seemed to know him well, quickly responded.

He translated for Ottla as she calmed them down. He located four sets of siblings among them and placed them together, before helping Gustav and the stewards serve them the millet soup and slices of rye bread.

Late that afternoon, after a brief but heated discussion, Anton Burger, the newly appointed SS Commandant Obersturmführer, accepted Dr Munk's decision to shunt the train into the siding within the fortress.

They boarded the train again, and arrived at the siding in the late evening.

On Sunday afternoon a fortnight later, Ottla took her sixty charges into the coppice of birch trees within the Western compound. She arranged them three deep in a semicircle in front of her, and sat facing them on a small wooden stool she'd brought with her.

She gazed at them in silence for several moments, deeply pleased at the progress they'd made since the violent riot that had erupted on their first night within the fortress. When she'd led them to the bathhouse showers that night, several frantic older boys had screamed hysterically that they were about to be gassed, igniting panic across the group. It took her and three SS guards many minutes to restrain them, convince them that the showers were safe, and get them to submit to the delousing and washing processes. Hours later, fed and with their hair trimmed, in laundered clothes and repaired shoes, they'd settled into the barracks.

Abram sat cross-legged on the fallen leaves beside her, leaning back against a beech tree, his eyes closed, sunlight filtering through the leaves playing across his face. Ottla nudged him awake. 'Time to translate,' she whispered, before gazing acround the group. 'My beautiful children,' she began, pausing between phrases for Abram to translate, 'today I'm going to read you a story about Komodo dragons. It was written by one of the boys in the camp here, our own Marek Löwy. He's fourteen years old.'

She withdrew a sheaf of papers from her apron pocket and unfolded them. Before beginning to read, she looked thoughtfully down at Marek's carefully pencilled handwriting.

He had handed the story to her a month ago. 'I liked your brother's story *The Bucket Rider* you told me yesterday so much I've written this one for you,' he'd said breathlessly. 'I especially liked the way Franz describes the man flying in his magical empty bucket through the streets looking for coal. The thoughtless coal merchant's wife refuses to give him any, just because he can't pay her at the time. She even pretends to her husband, who would have given him some, that he isn't there when she answers the door, before she slams it shut in his face. So he disappears into the icy mountains and is never seen again, his bucket empty.'

Ottla had been taken aback. 'You wrote this last night, Marek? All seven pages?'

'It's about Komodo dragons. It didn't take long. The coal bucket was like a flying carpet. That gave me the idea. I love Komodo dragons, you see. They're in danger of dying out, like the dodo bird of Mauritius, so I didn't really have to think about it. The story almost wrote itself.'

Ottla had smiled and stroked his hair. 'You sound so much like Franz,' she said. 'He would have liked you. He wrote *The Bucket Rider* when he was living with me on the farm in Zürau. I remember the day he read it to me as if it was yesterday. It shows you how cruelty and injustice can result from ordinary actions and beliefs. We can all inflict pain on one another—every single one of us—you don't have to be a monster to be cruel. Sometimes even doing nothing can have the same effect.'

'That's why I write my stories,' Marek said. 'I can't stand doing nothing.'

'I know. Neither could Franz.'

She looked up at the ring of faces in front of her, then back at the writing and began to read. 'Komodo dragons. I'm going to tell you all about them. And about a young Czech boy called Jakob Ježek. His surname means "hedgehog". It suited him very well because he was very shy and could get quite prickly and curl up in a ball when other people teased him.'

At that moment Jiři Springer appeared on the tractor, bouncing along the cobbles, towing a trailer loaded with clanking empty soup tureens. He slowed and then stopped when he drew alongside them under the trees.

He switched off the tractor. 'What's this, Ottla?' he asked. 'Nature study?'

'Story time,' she replied. 'I think they're ready for one of Marek Löwy's fables.'

'Aha! Young Marek and his famous stories.' He made himself comfortable in the seat. 'Do you have room for one more? I have ten minutes to spare.'

'Be our guest,' she said. She nodded at Abram and looked back down at the manuscript. 'Well, children, are you ready? Here we go.'

She began by describing Jakob's interest in the nearby Prague zoo's reptile park, especially the Komodo dragons. The giant poster in his bedroom showing several females guarding their eggs on a beach on Flores Island. His quiet conversations with them every night before he went to sleep—and his regular vivid dreams, when he fought with local poachers digging up the eggs. The strangest night, when everyone else was asleep, and he slung his empty school satchel over his shoulder and stepped into his mother's magical sewing box. The tornado that swept him up—standing in the box and clutching its handle—then out through the window and across the roofs of Prague, before crossing the volcanic mountains of Flores Island and gliding down onto the beach.

The seven eggs he found in a nest, all about to hatch. How he carefully placed six in his satchel, and then fought off three local poachers armed with bamboo sticks, who beat him mercilessly as he rescued the seventh, before the sewing box soared skyward again and carried him back to Prague.

Then Ottla deliberately paused and gazed around the group. 'Are you all comfortable?' she asked. 'Would you like me to go on?'

There was a loud chorus of assent.

'Very well,' she said, looking down and reading on. 'The next morning Jakob said nothing to his parents about his overnight flight. There were five hatchlings already free of their shells and wriggling around in the satchel. The other two were still emerging. He put them carefully into an empty cardboard shoebox and packed a towel round it to soundproof their hissing squeaks, before hiding it beneath the books in his satchel.

'Then he made sure he was wearing a long-sleeved school shirt to conceal his bruises, ate his breakfast in a rush, kissed his mother goodbye and sprinted all the way to the zoo. The gates were open and when he got to the reptile park one of the keepers he knew was hosing down the walkways.

'"These are for you, Karel," he said, as he took the shoebox from his satchel and unwrapped it. "You may not believe it, but there are seven Komodo dragons inside!"

'He removed the lid. The attendant could not believe what he was seeing, as they carefully helped the last two dragons emerge from their shells.

'"Where on earth did you get these?" he asked. "This is truly a miracle."

'"You don't need to know," Jakob said. "It's a long, long story anyway, and you'd never believe it if I told you. Let's just say I did what I could to save them. I rescued them just in time from poachers."

'So that's how Jakob succeeded in preserving the Komodo dragons. They survived and will live on for as long as we all look after them.'

Ottla looked up and smiled at the children. 'The end,' she said.

There was a long silence, broken by the groans of some children who wanted more, and then by Jiři, who applauded loudly, the children following his lead.

'Jakob discovered there's far more to the natural world than we realise,' Jiři said, raising his voice as he started up the tractor, 'Someone very wise, much wiser than me, once said we should reach out to life in all its fullness. Everybody lives it, but few know much about it, and wherever you touch it you'll find it interesting and even magical. Nice one, Ottla! I will see you all at dinner time, children.'

Ottla nodded and raised her hand in farewell before looking round the faces in front of her. 'Jiři's right, children,' she said. 'Jakob did what he could to make the world a better place. We must learn to do the same before it's too late, mustn't we?'

Three of the older boys leapt up and sprinted along beside the tractor, grinning up at Jiři until he exited the gate.

Four weeks later, on Tuesday, 5 October, the complement of 1196 surviving children and 53 carers, including Ottla, were ordered to evacuate the Western Barracks and board a transport train leaving the fortress at midday.

They were instructed to remove the Star of David they'd been forced to wear in the fortress, and had to sign pledges agreeing not to reveal Nazi atrocities once they were freed.

I can imagine Ottla's heart-crushing despair an hour later, when the train turned east instead of south to Switzerland.

She didn't know it, but Himmler's negotiations with

Mohammad Amin al-Husseini had broken down. The Mufti refused to allow the exchange. He balked at sanctioning the migration of yet more Jews into Palestine.

I'm certain she would have been determined not to communicate her horror to the children. She would have kept their spirits up throughout the journey, perhaps entertaining them by reading *The Komodo Dragons* to them for the second time, despite the deep irony in its theme, considering their predicament.

The train arrived at the second disembarkation ramp in the Oswiecim freight station, half way between the Auschwitz and Birkenau concentration camps, late on Thursday evening.

I can find no records of it in the archives, but I suspect that the SS Commandant there had been instructed to immediately exterminate them all, without going through the usual selection procedures.

I picture Ottla bravely and calmly conducting her children from the train, before assisting them up onto the trucks lined up to deliver them to the gas chambers and the crematoria. And I imagine her at the end, shaven, dignified and defiant, kneeling to bring her face closer to theirs as she spreads her arms like wings and gathers the children around her, her heart charged with deep regret that she hasn't been able to make amends for the horrendous misfortunes they've suffered, as the gas chamber doors slam shut.

She was an extraordinary, deep-spirited, courageous and generous hearted woman it has been a privilege to come to know. She did all she could to console the children she was caring for, never abandoning them once she'd chosen her course of action, knowing as she did so that her efforts to save them from extinction may come to nothing.

The Closest I Came
To Believing In Ghosts

ONE UNFORGETTABLE NIGHT IN August 2022, our mother Jolanda showed us three kids her latest pastel sketch for the first time. It showed an exquisitely carved and polished wooden box.

We were sitting round the table after dinner and she held it up to each of us in turn.

'This is my treasure chest,' she said, sending us her familiar cat's-got-the-cream smile. 'It's made of the finest West Australian jarrah, with a polished brass latch and key, designed to hold jewellery and look the part on any discerning woman's dressing table.'

She placed the sketch on the table—upside down from my point of view.

'It's going to hold a dozen millionaire's shortbread chocolate biscuits to die for, my darlings,' she went on, with the emphasis on 'die'. Her voice was intimate, rich and mellow and her Belgian accent as strong as it always was when she was talking about chocolate. 'They'll be wrapped in gold and silver paper. I'm not convinced of their design yet. I'm thinking maybe the Florentine scudo right now, but either way, they'll sell like hot cakes. They'll put Tim Tams out of business. I'm sure of it.'

'Like the rest of your inspirational ideas?' our father asked, sliding his rimless reading glasses down the prominent bridge of his nose as he peered at her over his newspaper from the other end of the table. 'You promised us that last time. What's your point?'

'As I said, the taste will be to die for. I can guarantee that, as you all well know. And the boxes will not only keep the chocolate biscuits intact, they'll be collectibles. Women will be proud to keep their jewellery and knickknacks in them once they've eaten the biscuits. We'll have wooden and cardboard versions of them. Just think of Mother's Day and Christmas.'

'Sounds feasible,' my father said, giving her a sceptical glance before pushing his glasses back up and retreating behind the paper. 'Just don't break the bank this time.'

Our mother laughed. 'Ah, come on Marcus, it takes money to make money. You know that. Look where we are now. We've opened a second shop and paid off our mortgage on the house thanks to my chocolate quokkas, the little dears.'

'Fair point,' he conceded, with a shake of the paper as he turned the page, 'but my advice to fill their pouches with chocolate buttons went a long way towards their popularity. Not to mention Roger Federer's photo on the advertising poster.' He peeked round the page at us as he asked slyly, 'And whose idea was that?'

Then he added with what our mother always called his smart-Alecky grin, 'And he's *Swiss*.'

'Wash your mouth out!'

We had no idea where she'd got the idea of the treasure chest from until we pressed her. Her answer completely bamboozled us.

'From my DNA test,' she said. 'You know the one I took six months ago because I'm researching our family ancestry on my side and the test is part of the process.'

'What's a DNA test?' my younger sister Hanna asked. 'And what's a scudo?'

'A scudo is an Italian gold and silver coin used round the world a few centuries ago and a DNA test helps you find out where you and your ancestors are from, by examining your genes.' She put her hand up, palm outwards, before Hanna could ask her next question. 'If you're going to ask me what genes are, they're the mysterious building blocks of life and they're turtles all the way down.'

We heard our father give a suppressed snort behind his paper, but it may well have been our plump old golden cocker spaniel Delilah, stretched out asleep at Hanna's feet, expressing wind from either end.

We looked at each other, eyebrows raised. Turtles all the way down? If that was meant to be funny we saw no point in asking what she meant just then and possibly making fools of ourselves. We'd catch her off guard and ask her later, our glances agreed, when she'd forgotten she'd said it.

'I've found out I'm mostly Dutch and Belgian,' our mother continued, 'as I expected, but also partly Viking Scandinavian, which I approve of, and I have some Spanish too, but no Italian at all. That was unexpected. With my great-great-grandfather Isaak's surname Carletti and coming from a family in the international port of Antwerp, I was anticipating a percent or two.'

She paused for a moment, sending us each her familiar raised eyebrows look, with its half-smile hinting at a confidence she was about to share. 'It's the *Asian* proportion that really surprises me. Roughly three percent of me is possibly, if not probably, Korean. *Korean*, of all things! That threw me. I had no idea at all. I mean look at me. I have no hint of their eye structure or skin tone, do I? I'm a fair-skinned natural blonde with blue eyes. The only thing I will admit to is the kimono I like to wear around the house and some of the pottery designs and ornaments I prefer. And the food, of course, but they're all more Japanese than Korean aren't they?'

'Does that mean we are too?' my middle sister Martine asked. 'Partly Korean?'

'Clearly, but with a slightly smaller proportion than me, I expect.'

'Wow!' Hanna said. 'Wait till I tell Myeong tomorrow. Now there'll be two of us in the class.'

'Don't rush things, Hanna. You're blonde and blue-eyed too, so she's going to find it hard to believe.'

Hanna gave her a brilliant gap-toothed smile. 'It's all right, Mum. I'll tell her what you said—I'm Korean turtles all the way down.'

Our mother left the table, propped the drawing face out and upright on the sideboard against her favourite iron red and turquoise Japanese Satsuma vase with its delicately gilded floral patterns, and turned to face us.

'I didn't believe the results for one minute,' she said, 'so I had a second test and that confirmed it. Not only that, it adjusted the percentage *upwards*, increasing it to five percent. *Five!* I know it doesn't seem much, but when you analyse it, it means one of my great-great-grandparents was one hundred percent Korean. So I hired a professional researcher a while ago to look into it for me, starting with Mama and Papa in Antwerp. Her name is Bronwyn. She has sent me her report. I received it yesterday. What a surprise!'

'So?' I asked, on behalf of all of us.

She shook her forefinger at us—a sure sign she was going to keep us in suspense.

'No, not tonight. Tomorrow, perhaps. Right now you three can clear the table and settle down to your homework, if you have any.' She turned to me and pointed at the piano. 'I want to hear you practice that Debussy piece again before you head for bed, Lucas. The competition is only three weeks away, remember. Before your fingers get too rusty.'

'And your brain,' Martine murmured, 'Clair de Lune-*atic*.' She squealed when I dug a bony knuckle into her ribs.

'Korean. Who'd have guessed?' our mother murmured as she turned and left the room.

Martine looked at me and grinned. 'Koreans are brilliant musicians, aren't they? Maybe that's where you get your piano-playing skills from. Now you've got no excuse if you don't win.'

'So who'd you inherit your tin ear from? The milkman?'

After dinner the following evening, our mother asked us to gather around the table. She sat at the head, the three of us on either side of her and Delilah squatting on the floor, peering up attentively as if she didn't want to miss out on whatever was coming next. Our father was working late.

She had an envelope in her right hand, and with the long fingers of her left, she opened the flap and withdrew several loose-leaf pages, which she slowly unfolded, as though she really was about to reveal a mystery to us.

'I mentioned yesterday I hired Bronwyn to look into our so-called Korean ancestry,' she said. 'Well, I'm here to tell you, my darlings, that she's given me undeniable proof that we are, indeed, partly Korean. Isn't that interesting?

'She has discovered that we are related to one Antonio Carletti. That's not his real name but his adopted one, and she believes—but isn't certain—that he once lived in the fortress city of Namwon in the southwest of what is now South Korea. I've worked out that he was our great-grandfather fourteen generations ago. Bronwyn has explored his history and she has a fascinating story to tell us, taking us back over four hundred years to 1597. And you want to know the most surprising thing about him?'

'What?' Hanna asked.

'He was one of the first chocolatiers in Antwerp that no one knew about until she dug through the archives and uncovered him. She believes he and his Korean wife opened their shop roundabout the year 1616. A chocolatier, just like us. Isn't that amazing? Would you like to hear her report?'

'Of course,' Martine said.

'Very well. Listen carefully.' She opened up the letter, but before she began, she looked up from the page. 'The words Bronwyn uses in this report are quite complicated in places, my darlings. They might sail straight over your heads. What I'll do is read it through to you once, then we can talk about it bit by bit, in words we understand. How does that sound? All right?'

'All right,' Martine and I said in unison.

'How boring is it?' Hanna asked.

Our mother smiled. 'You tell me when I get to the end. I think the bit about the stray dogs will interest you, as long as it doesn't give you nightmares.'

'Ooooh! Stray dogs and nightmares! It must be scary!' Hanna said, looking down at Delilah, who wagged her tail when Hanna nudged her with a toe.

'I won't spoil it for you.'

She looked down again and began to read.

'Dear Mrs Vermeulen, with regard to your request that I look into the estimated five percent Korean genetic component of your ancestry, I am pleased to advise that I have some pertinent facts to report. They concern a certain gentleman by the name of Antonio Carletti, a resident of Antwerp in the early seventeenth century. I am sure you will find his details deeply interesting and relevant to your investigation.

'To begin with, Antonio Carletti was a Korean boy, aged about sixteen, captured during the siege of the fortress city of Namwon in the south-west of the Korean peninsula. This occurred during the Japanese invasion of Korea in the early days of the Chongyu war of 1597.

'He adopted the surname Carletti in 1598 when he was baptised into the Roman Catholic faith in the city of Nagasaki, in Japan. That ceremony occurred after he was purchased in the public square on Nishizaka Hill during the auction of Korean prisoners of war, who were being sold as slaves. A Florentine merchant named Francesco Carletti, then on a trading mission with his father Antonio around the world, paid the princely sum of twelve Florentine scudos, roughly equivalent in buying power to fifteen US dollars today, for him, along with two other Korean boys and two girls.

'The other unfortunate Koreans who were not purchased were used as targets for Japanese samurai warriors testing the effectiveness of their swordsmanship and the quality and sharpness of their blades. In the memor he later wrote, Francesco reports that the executions were indescribably gory and he confirms that their discarded body parts were fed to the city's stray dogs.

'Thankfully, Antonio avoided the butchering by the sheer coincidence of Francesco's presence that day and his having enough small change available in his purse. You won't mind my commenting at this point, considering what follows, that had that not been the case you would not exist and I would not have had the privilege of undertaking this research for you.

'Francesco Carletti then took his five Korean charges with him on his voyage to Macau, where his father Antonio unfortunately died, and then on to Portuguese Goa, in India. There he released four Koreans, retaining Antonio as his personal manservant for the remainder of the voyage to Europe.

'He boarded the fully loaded Portuguese carrack, the *Santiago*—in Portuguese the *São Jago*—on Christmas Day in 1601 and arrived at the mid-Atlantic Island of St Helena on 14 March 1602. Again, by sheer coincidence, three Dutch ships were anchored there. The *Santiago* captain prudently sailed past them and anchored in a northern bay, where he had been instructed to wait for Portuguese naval men of war sent to escort his ship home.

'Unfortunately, the Dutch ships, also returning home, attacked and captured the *Santiago* after a lengthy sea battle the next day. They then sailed in convoy to Middelburg in Zeeland, the southernmost of the states of the Netherlands. There Francesco's valuable cargo was confiscated and he and

Antonio spent the next three fruitless years suing to recover it. They eventually returned to Florence virtually empty-handed.

'Interestingly, I discovered that Francesco had a large consignment of Mexican cacao beans in his cargo. These were released to him, the Dutch considering them valueless at the time. In his fifth chronicle, Francesco notes the popularity of the chocolate drink made from them, sweetened with cane sugar and spiced with nutmeg, to which he and Antonio introduced the Dutch during their stay.

'There is evidence that when they left Middelburg for Florence in December 1605, they visited the Louvre in Paris and met with King Henry IV of France and his councillor Villeroi. I report this because in 1602, the king offered protection in the southern port city of Bayonne to large numbers of Sephardic Jews previously expelled from Spain. These Jews were experts in the making of chocolate.

'On his voyage back to Italy, Francesco's vessel called into Bayonne. It is beyond doubt that he and Antonio would have investigated those chocolate-making techniques, given the number of chocolate shops newly established on the Rue Port Neuf at the time his vessel was berthed there. Francesco refers to these in his sixth and final chronicle.

'In my view, this led young Antonio to the next stage in his adventurous life—opening the earliest recorded chocolate drink shop in Antwerp sometime before 1626.

'I discovered evidence of a chocolate drink shop in Antwerp named Chocolaterie Carletti, marked on the corner of Kasteel Straat and Lambermont Plaats, on two street maps dated 1626 and 1632. The reference maps are in cartographic collection Z2 in the Antwerp Archives. Antonio must have opened the shop earlier than 1626, given its proximity to the town centre.

'In 1617, world-renowned artist Peter Paul Rubens created in his Antwerp studio a series of sketches and a large-scale chalk drawing of a Korean man dressed in silk robes and wearing a transparent headdress. Now considered one of his masterworks, I strongly suggest that Antonio Carletti was his model. For one thing, Antonio and his family were in Antwerp at the time. For another, given the accuracy of the national dress, it is highly likely that Rubens used a live model for inspiration, rather than draw on his imagination or memory.

'I also found seven references to the Carletti family in the period after 1615 in the Antwerp censuses and marriage, births and deaths records. The Carletti, Jeong and Park families are closely interconnected in those records. Jeong and Park are common Korean surnames. This leads me to conclude that after returning to Italy in 1606, Antonio may have travelled back to Korea sometime during the period from 1608 to 1615, to reconnect with his family in Namwon.

'Subsequent to that, he has clearly returned to Antwerp, most probably with a small group of his countrymen and women, to take advantage of the thriving commercial opportunities there, including the opening of the Chocolaterie Carletti, mentioned above.

'In conclusion, I believe there is sufficient evidence to confirm that you and your family are related to Antonio Carletti. In view of the estimated five percent Korean genetic component in your DNA, it would appear that the full-blood Korean line was maintained until three generations ago. In other words, your great-great-grandparents. As you pointed out to me, the remains of your great-great-grandfather, Isaak Carletti, are buried in the Putte Drihoek Communal Cemetery. He appears to be the last in the male line carrying that surname.

'It remains for me to congratulate you on discovering your family roots and to wish you well with any further investigations into more recent segments of your family tree. Thank you once again for entrusting this assignment to me. It has been a fascinating undertaking. My services are always available should you need them in future.

'For your interest, I have listed my archival sources below.

'Yours sincerely, Bronwyn Johnstone.'

Our mother then placed the report face-up on the table. I reached across and spread the pages out beside each other so that we could examine them. I silently read the reference notes at the bottom, though they made little sense to me:

Source 1: Antonio Carletti: Ragionamente (Chronicles) of Francesco Carletti in Biblioteca_Angelica Rome—Codice 1331.

Source 2: Capture of the *Santiago:* Zeeuws Archives, Middelburg—Admiralty Records 1602–5.

Source 3: Antwerp maps: *Rijksarchief te Antwerpen in the Verzameling kaarten en plattegronden.*

Source 4: Korean Portrait: Man in Korean Costume (1617), Peter Paul Rubens, J Paul Getty Museum (1983).

Source 5: Civil records and Burial sites: Belgique, Anvers, *registres d'état civil,* 1588–1913.

Our mother then went carefully through the major points for the second time, responding patiently to Hanna's annoying questions. Where exactly was Namwon? How long ago was 1597? What did the word coincidence mean? What was a Samurai sword? Did they *really* feed the butchered bits and pieces of the executed Korean prisoners to the stray dogs, and if they did, 'How *horrible.* I'm glad I wasn't born then!' And so on.

When Mother had gone through the report again and Hanna had run out of questions and comments, our mother leaned her elbows on the table, interlaced her fingers, propped her chin on her joined hands and looked at each of us in turn.

'So,' she said. 'Now we know for certain we're part Korean.

What do we fill my treasure chests with? Millionaire's biscuits or pralines with all our special flavours?'

Pralines won by four votes to one, with Delilah preferring biscuits when Hanna posed the question to her and she wagged her tail. Circular flattened pralines, in fact, shaped and embossed as Florentine scudo coins with *peppermint* centres, because, our mother told us excitedly, 'There's a Mint Chocolate Chip craze going on in Korea *right now*.'

She opened up her laptop, logged in and googled the Korean Minchodan website. She turned the screen so that we could all take in the gaudy, mouth-watering pictures of peppermint and chocolate products revealed as she scrolled down the screen.

'Can you believe that? It's another remarkable coincidence that will work to our advantage. The boxes will fly off the shelves that fast we'll have trouble keeping up with demand, my darlings. We'll use the authentic Korean mint plant called *Agastache rugose* for the fillings, just like they do. They've been eating it and using it as a medicine for centuries. They call it baechohyang, or bang for short. It's delicious, and it has the slight tang of licorice. Imagine that? It grows well in Tasmania and I've already contacted Uncle Yannick in Meander to grow some for us.'

Our mother. She isn't one to sit around!

'With Antonio Carletti on our case,' she went on, 'I've already had our new poster designed. Would you like to see it?'

She disappeared into the study and emerged moments later with a cardboard tube from which she withdrew a rolled-up poster. With Hanna reaching out to hold down the far corners, she straightened out an exquisite copy of Peter Paul Rubens's meticulous depiction of the man in a Korean costume, the silk shimmering in a play of light and touches of red chalk highlighting the man's observant face, his knowing expression displaying a gentle humour. *Jolanda's Treasure Chest*, the title read, *The finest after-dinner chocolate mints. Inspired by the legendary Korean Chocolatier, Antonio Carletti.*

'We can play with the words,' our mother went on, 'but I can feel his presence sitting here right now with us, approving of everything we're doing as if it's all his idea. Can't you, my darlings?'

'Perhaps he's whispering to you through your DNA,' Martine suggested.

'Or maybe it's one of the turtles,' Hanna said, as she stood, retrieved the appropriate silver cutlery and a fresh plate and wine glass from the sideboard and laid a place of honour for Antonio beside her.

That evening was the closest I ever came to believing in ghosts.

I saw Antonio materialising in the chair beside Hanna, as real and magical a presence as he must have seemed to her. The illusory rustling of his silk robes was magnified in the echo chamber of my DNA as he reached out to the plate of Florentine scudo chocolates with their peppermint centres, unwrapped the gold foil and took an experimental bite, before he turned to our mother and politely nodded his approval, complimenting her on its perfection… or I imagined it, as he faded from my thoughts.

The Eulogy

THERE WE WERE, ANITA and I, UWA postgrad students in English Literature, head down bum up, previewing the entries to the 2023 Kimberley Literary Review Short Story competition. It was early February, a month since the contest opened, and the entries were piling up. Already over three hundred deep.

The competition was closing in April and we were culling them for the three official judges—we had to present them with a long list of twenty by the end of March for the final judging.

'In the "definite" or the "maybe" pile?' I asked, when we'd both stopped laughing at *The Eulogy*, the latest we'd read. 'Or through the shredder and another one bites the dust?'

'The story of a twelve-year-old boy losing his virginity in a Kalgoorlie brothel during World War I? Not a chance,' Anita said, pointing at the shredder, her lips pursed now that she'd controlled her giggling and recovered her breath. 'When pigs fly, if I have my say.'

'I wouldn't be so quick to judge. It's the "definite" pile for mine. We both got a good laugh out of it after all.'

'That may be, but let's face it—there's no way any of the judges will think it meets our standards of appropriateness. Let alone the obscenity. They'll wonder why we approved it. You know that. Why waste time discussing it?' She tapped the growing pile of entries between us. 'We've still got these to plough through, for heaven's sake.'

'Oh, come on now, Anita. They aren't that prudish.' I looked down and skimmed through the paragraphs. 'Where's the obscenity in "she lowered his shorts and complimented him for eating his spinach" or "he got his money's worth in a transaction that lasted three seconds flat"?'

'It's not so much the phrasing as the concept,' she said. 'The idea of an underage boy on his way to primary school accosting a cherry-popping madam in Kalgoorlie? I ask you. Where's the theme? The story arc? The twist?' She gazed at me, her pencilled eyebrows raised as she always did when she thought she had me on the spit and was roasting me over the coals. 'Besides the flippant tone. We have the magazine's reputation to maintain. I rest my case.'

'I take your point,' I said to pacify her, 'but I'll have another read, while you make the coffees, if that's okay with you. I'll judge it purely for its qualities as a short story, based on our criteria.'

'It's hardly a short story. It's a blokey outback yarn at best,' she said, before delivering her parting shot with a withering look as she left the room. 'A vignette. A *shag*-gy dog story, pun intended.'

I picked up the manuscript once again and began to read it.

The Eulogy

The second time I said goodbye to Karel 'Rip' Van Winkel, he was dead.

He was lying in his pinewood coffin at his funeral service in the Fremantle cemetery chapel. He'd sent me a signed invitation written on a neat white card with embossed edges resembling a medical appointment reminder. It read: *You are cordially invited...* etc, with the time and place written in his neat blue cursive, and ended: *RSVP Alan 'Awesome' Wells, 08 354 1666.*

I rang Awesome and said I'd be there.

'You right for the eulogy?' Awesome ambushed me when I called. 'Rip said you'd do him proud. You're the scribbler, after all. Any problem?'

I didn't hesitate. 'None. I'll have another gander at James Joyce's short story *The Dead*. That should set me up.'

'Whatever you think is best.'

'I wouldn't miss it for the world.'

Apart from the uncharacteristic smudges of rouge on his cheeks and touch of lipstick to liven him up, Rip hadn't changed much, even with his eyes closed. I looked down and saw a wizened but wise old man, his broad forehead deeply indented, as if he had an empty socket for a missing third eye. Several lines ridged from the corners of his almond-shaped eyes to his temples, as though grooved in leather. His white hair was dragged back in a sparse ponytail that strayed across the shoulder of a freshly laundered t-shirt, faded yellow, with the *Life Be In It* logo imprinted across his chest. He was wearing jeans stained red with dust and his iconic yellow Blundstone working boots that still appeared to be several sizes too large for him.

His battered face confirmed a life lived to the full. He still looked inscrutable and shrewd, and I had no doubt that had he unexpectedly opened his amber-coloured eyes as I looked down at him, they'd have shown that spark of sly humour in which I always detected a touch of malicious joy at putting one over on you.

His right hand was holding the neck of his prized Alhambra acoustic guitar across his abdomen, his left about to strike the strings. His stiffened fingers with their surprisingly well manicured fingernails were artfully arranged as if he was about to fingerpick the opening E major chord for his favourite flamenco piece, '*La Malagueña*'. It was one thing he'd arranged to have cremated with him in the coffin, the other was his decorated didgeridoo lying beside him.

I thought he was looking as laid back as he always had—so

relaxed it seemed he'd just stretched out for a twenty-year sleep in the Catskill Mountains. He refused to wear a watch, he told me once, withdrawing a large glass marble with a bright green spiral down its centre from his pocket, because winding up a watch reminded him his life was winding down. He held the marble up to the sun. 'Two fifteen *pee em*,' he'd said, checking the sun's reflection in its sphere. 'Circular time. The only way to tell it. When you've got one foot in the grave? Amputate. Or one foot in life's out-tray and the other on a blancmange? Give death the slip.'

He hadn't, though.

Awesome told me over the phone that he'd died trying to stop a brawl in the canteen at Camp 232 between the surveyors and a group of TI railway tracklayers.

'Thursday Islanders,' he said. 'The rail laying crew. You know what they're like. Built like Arnold Schwarzenegger, each and every one. Brick shithouses. Once they get going there's no stopping them. Rip fell back on a broken beer jug that sliced through an artery and that was that. He bled to death. Four of us gave blood for him that night in Tom Price Hospital, but it was hopeless. He just had time to write the invites.'

'He wrote them himself? While he was bleeding to death? Pull the other one.'

'He did, believe it or not. You know what he was like. Stubborn. I don't know how he managed it, but he did.'

'I thought I recognised his handwriting. Where did you find the cards?'

'Snuck them from the matron's office.'

'Are any of the boys coming?'

'No. Just me. I came down with his body. They're too busy with the final grade at the Paraburdoo end. The tracklayers are catching us up. It's a race against time.'

'A race against time. That's ironic. It's exactly the sort of thing Rip would have said about life. So who's going to be there to see him off?'

'Close family, mostly. Some old school friends from Kalgoorlie, maybe.'

Awesome met me at the door to the chapel. Six foot six and two axe handles across the shoulders, eyes an electric blue beyond description, blond hair sprouting through a shaven skull on a bull neck, you couldn't mistake him. He was our gun grader operator, our Colossus of Main Roads, our Ninth Wonder of the World.

'How'd you be?' he asked when I arrived, peering down his long Grecian nose at me, his voice its usual double bass. 'How are your studies going?'

'Good as can be expected under the circumstances. You?'

'Same. You got your spiel worked out?'

I tapped my back pocket. 'Got it all down pat. Are you the maître d'?'

'I am. Appointed before the old bloke passed away.' He tapped the side of his nose with his forefinger. 'I'll give you the heads up when you're on.'

It wasn't long in coming.

I strode to the coffin, looked in and promptly did a double take. I could have sworn I saw Rip wink. A quick twitch of his right eyelid. A flicker of his brow.

I looked across the rows of gathered mourners. There were no faces I recognised. Most of them were very old, but I'm certain I saw among them here and there a knowing smile, a clenched jaw suppressing a laugh rather than tears.

Knowing smiles? Clenched jaws? Is this whole setup a hoax? Is my leg being pulled? Is Rip about to sit up and strum his guitar, singing 'Gotcha!' as he used to? I wouldn't put it past him, but there's no piking out now.

I left the eulogy I'd prepared in my back pocket and decided to ad-lib. I had to get in first, attack from left field.

'Among practical jokers,' I began, 'Rip Van Wrinkles was the practical joker extraordinaire. The rib-tickling best of the best. Whenever he got round to telling us his yarns, they were rippers. I thought it'd be most appropriate today to tell you one of his liveliest—about the time he lost his virginity when he was twelve years old, during World War I, to a sturdily built madam in Kalgoorlie, where he was brought up. The way he told it, he used to pass her Roe Street brothel on his way to primary school each day and give her a wave, until he was game enough one cold July midwinter morning to call in and ask the price. "Five quid," he was told, "but for a little fella like you we'll make it one."'

No response.

The guitar in the coffin was as silent as the grave.

For the first time in my life, I understood exactly what the cliché *you could hear a pin drop* meant, no matter the number of angels dancing on its head.

'So he saved up his school lunch money for the next six months at tuppence a day,' I went on, 'and then dropped in before the last day of the December term a lot thinner, but with all the coins he'd saved in a sock. He followed the madam into one of the bedrooms. She counted out the coins, lowered his shorts and complimented him for eating his spinach.'

Not a sound.

Again, for the first time in my life, I understood exactly what another cliché *you're putting your foot in it* meant.

Where do I go from here? I'm only digging the hole deeper.

'He told us he got his money's worth,' I stammered on, 'in a transaction that lasted three seconds flat. "But you never forget your first, do you?" he told us. "That's the one when time stands still. I wore my green and gold school cap throughout the performance, and the cap was at a much more rakish angle and my voice two octaves deeper when I got to school and had to work up a excuse as to why I was late."'

Total silence.

A collective intake of breath, the shuffling of feet, creaking pews and shaking heads, even though I thought I'd made a decent fist of imitating his accent and his voice.

No roars of laughter drowning out the triumphant twanging of his guitar like those I'd heard the first time he'd told us the full story during smoko, sitting round a blazing night-shift fire beside the Fortescue River, crackling sparks spiralling upwards into the night sky swarming with stars.

I couldn't leave it there. Too much loss of face.

I stepped across to the coffin, took out the original eulogy I'd written from my back pocket, unfolded it, and leaned in to arrange it face up on his chest. The back of my right hand ran across his throat and jaw. His skin was cold, its waxy feel carrying the hint of bristle since his latest shave. I knew at that moment with a sense of shock that had I touched his cheek as a mark of respect before I'd begun, I'd have saved myself a truckload of embarrassment.

'There you go, Rip,' I said. 'That's the eulogy I should have given and you deserved. You were a great man. One of the best I've been privileged to know.' I faced the mourners. 'Vale Rip,' I said, as forcefully as I could. 'R.I.P.'

I raised a hand in salute as I left the dais and joined Awesome at the back of the chapel.

'That went down well,' I said.

'Lead balloon,' he murmured. 'Seems you told them something they never knew or dug up a family secret they'd rather forget.'

'Tell me about it,' I said, as the eulogy I had prepared for him ran through my mind:

The first time I said goodbye to Karel 'Rip' Van Winkel he was very much alive. He was sitting on a barstool, leaning back against the jarrah bar in the 232-mile camp canteen, pool stick in hand, waiting his turn to play his characteristically uncanny skill shots and clear the table.

I was returning to Perth the following morning at the end of the summer vacation in 1972, to rejoin the UWA for my fifth and final year. I'd spent the last four months driving the Acco man-haul for the earthworks final grade crew and their dingo-kelpie cross mascot Bazza, taking them to and from their scrapers and graders at the latest workstation on the Tom Price to Paraburdoo railway line, then under construction.

Given his age at seventy, Rip, our geriatric Peter Pan, was appointed Billy Boy for the crew and he travelled with me. That's Billy Boy with capitals, because he was the best Billy Boy on the line, bar none—voted five star and multiple chef's hat awards.

He'd sling a blue tarpaulin between ghost gums for shade and protection from raucous flocks of white and sulphur-crested cockatoos gathering overhead, before setting up a trestle table and benches filched from the camp dining hall, along with every condiment under the sun. Polished cutlery and white plates followed, and then he'd magically conjure two dozen eggs fried in olive oil and as many T-bone steaks and strips of bacon as he could fit on a four-legged two metre by half metre barbecue plate, with bowls of garden salad and buttered toast on the side.

And last but far from least, piping hot tea, made from water boiled in a billy till it had rocks in it, swirling with fistfuls of tea leaves and swung around his head in the traditional manner, poured into steaming half-litre green enamel mugs.

He'd always save a bowl of scraps for Bazza and lettuce leaves for any stray goanna scavenging round the table, violet forked tongue sliding rapidly in and out to taste the air. All this in a breathtaking landscape of red sand spiked with tussocks of spinifex and clusters of purple Mulla Mulla flowers stretching from horizon to horizon across the hills and lower slopes of mountainsides under a big blue sky.

When the crew arrived and they were tucking in, he'd always have a practical joke or a yarn for them: "Did you hear the one about the line of crucifixions celebrating Nero's birthday?" or "Did I tell you about the time I fell arse over tit off the jetty in Mauritius when I hooked that giant Trevally?" or "There are cold beers in the esky over there, boys", pointing at an esky into which he'd secreted a six-foot black-headed banded python that had wandered into the campsite during the night shift. Even if they'd heard them before or suspected he was having them on and let him know in no uncertain terms, he'd sail ahead anyway, invariably drawing the laughter and applause he intended.

I'll never forget him. I have his smiling image tattooed on my memory, standing beside a fully laden table in his campsite, wearing his favourite t-shirt, faded green, with a hole at the armpit and "Sex Appeal—Give Generously" imprinted across his chest. He'd be wearing jeans so caked in sweat and red dust he swore he used to stand them up in the corner of his donga when he took them off, his latest yellow Blundstone working boots a size or two too large for him protruding conspicuously from the cuffs.

The crew loved him and so did I.

Especially so did Bazza, his tail wagging so fast you couldn't see it when Rip filled out a daily timesheet for him with his canine goings-on, before handing it in with all of ours.

He was big-hearted, generous, thoughtful, empathetic, shrewd and dry as dust. He was the Billy Connolly of the bush, and I was privileged to have known him.

He told me once the only thing worth dying for is living longer. Can I suggest that for his epitaph? It says it all. Vale, Rip. R.I.P.'

At the end of March, Anita and I handed over our twenty potential finalists selected from over a thousand entries to the judges, copies of *The Eulogy* by coincidence on top.

Alan was the first judge to finish the manuscript. He looked up at the others sitting opposite him, tossed it on the table and stretched back in his chair.

'*The Eulogy*,' he said. 'Now that tickles my fancy,' before giving a customary bark of laughter. 'It's in the "definite" pile for mine.'

Moments later Sarah followed suit with a series of hiccupping breathy chuckles.

Katerina wasn't far behind. 'Sex appeal—give generously,' she said, smiling broadly, 'and a *Life be in it* t-shirt on the corpse. They were unexpected.'

'So, is it in the "definite" pile?' Sarah asked. 'Or relegated to the bin?'

'My vote right now is in the bin,' Katerina replied. 'I think it's crossed the line and is a little shallow, for what it's worth.'

Anita tightened her lips, arched her eyebrows and sent me a smug *what did I tell you?* look.

'I'm not so sure,' Alan said. 'We all enjoyed it. Let's have a second read before canning it. I can see it right up there, winning the People's Choice award.'

As they skimmed the story once again, their widening smiles developed into a communal burst of catchy laughter that ended with Alan's characteristic coughing fit, his right fist gently banging the table as he caught his breath, his thumb extended upwards.

I grinned across at Anita and mouthed her a '*Gotcha!*' on Rip's behalf, imagining him sitting bolt upright in the coffin after all, his triumphant eyes alight as he strummed an opening E chord.

For The Love Of Evie

Be good, sweet maid, and let who will be clever;
Do noble things, not dream them, all day long:
And so make life, death, and that vast forever
One grand, sweet song.
— Charles Kingsley, *A Farewell*

* * *

Evelyn 'Evie' Sinclair was born unlucky. The odds were stacked against her from the start. In the genetic lottery, her numbers scored the family curse—a faulty pituitary gland perched on the Turkish saddle bone at the base of her skull—from which vantage point it played havoc with her metabolism, secreting unseasonal growth hormones like nobody's business.

In short, she was tall, she was big and bulky, and she had no say in the matter.

On the other hand, her face was her saving grace. She had a natural, eye-catching large-boned beauty that turned heads even at a young age, her features so marvellously proportioned they took your breath away. Imagine Michelle Pfeiffer at twelve years of age. Evie had that captivatingly symmetrical face with its full lips, high cheek bones and sparkling dark brown eyes that had the girls around her eating their hearts out, let alone the boys. Her hair flowed long, black and shining across her broad shoulders.

She carried her singular beauty unselfconsciously as she matured, without ostentation or pretence. She seemed genuinely uninterested in the advantages and powers of attraction it gave her. She developed early and was simply a bigger kid than the others her age.

None of this was an issue until her early teens.

'Why'm I so much taller than the other girls at school right now?' she once asked her mother when she was thirteen and helping out in the kitchen. 'I hate being so different.'

'It's just an early growth spurt, dear. You're maturing earlier than your friends,' her mother replied, dusting the pastry she'd rolled for the Anzac biscuits they were making with a light shower of flour and grated coconut.

'Friends? I wouldn't call them friends. Not any more. Josephine even told me today she was sick of looking up my nostrils.'

'Listen Evie, look on the bright side. Enjoy the advantages your size and weight give you while you're ahead. Before the others catch up. Your speed and strength in little athletics shotput and discus, for one thing. You've got excellent hand-eye coordination on the netball courts… and goal-keeping on the hockey pitches, for another. Your cabinet's filled with sporting medals and ribbons galore after all.'

'I know, I know. It still hurts though.'

'And what about the dancing? You're musically pitch-perfect and rhythmically in sync, as far as I can see. You match anyone on the dance floor. Bar none.'

'I almost punched her. I will next time.'

'Now then, sweetheart, you know that won't help anyone.'

'It will me.'

During her adolescence, she developed a self-confidence that served her well, along with an acute awareness of the world and an accompanying sense of humour and intelligence beyond her years. She held her own with anyone who crossed her, putting those game enough to tease her back in their place with such consummate and cutting skill they rarely tried it twice. And she reassured the adults in her extended family, who were alarmed at the rapid acceleration of her growth and searching for non-existent remedies for her increasing weight, that she'd accepted the hand she'd been dealt and would strive to make the best of it.

She continued to do so into her late teens, when her size

eventually overtook her. It was then that she became aware that her world was crumbling around her and the advantages she'd enjoyed as a younger girl were now illusory. She privately acknowledged that had she been able to continue to live and perform with the unconscious freedom and intensity she'd enjoyed as a young girl she'd have led a successful and fulfilled life as an adult.

But that was not to be.

She discovered instead, without admitting it to anyone but herself as she grew larger, that what she really wanted was to be as slim, petite, attractive and seemingly lovable as her younger sister Larissa ('Lara'). She attracted boys like moths to her flame and more often than not, sent them packing with their wings scorched.

Yes, she wanted to be as lovable and she wanted to be as frequently loved, too. Eventually, even just the once would do. As time wore on, however, even that seemed more and more unlikely. Until she turned twenty-one, that is, and cut the birthday cake on Saturday, 21 January 1939.

Standing six feet three and eighteen stone, her floral dress ballooning round her to her ankles like a giant blue tent and her IQ up around the Mensa standard on either test, *Just the once*, she whispered to herself, as she blew the candles out and the knife slid through the icing and the sponge and never touched the plate. *Someone to love me just the once. Please, God, grant me this favour. Remember, even if I am beginning to wonder about you these days, up till now I've always thought of you with wonder.*

Her wish was almost granted the next day, a day she marked in her diary without words at first—just three heavy black asterisks she stabbed into the page, their meaning known only to herself. Months later, when she was calmer and feeling confident about the changes in her life's direction, she went back to the page and copied out the second stanza of her favourite poem, Charles Kingsley's 'A Farewell', above the asterisks.

The aircraft carrier HMS *Ark Royal*, pride of the British fleet and commissioned the month before, called in to Kilindini Harbour in Mombasa for a week's stay on its maiden voyage round Africa. She'd arrived three days before Evie's birthday, after undergoing sea trials in the Indian Ocean and Red Sea, with the clouds of the World War II gathering across the world.

Evie was standing with Lara on the cliffs at the seafront beneath the stately line of baobab trees, along with most of the island's population, carrying balloons and streamers to welcome her as she steamed in through the channel to the harbor.

Across the water, Evie saw a long line of sailors standing stiffly to attention on the starboard runway deck, their starched white uniforms a blinding white in the stark sunlight, the Marines' brass band going for it, the strains of Louis Armstrong's hit 'When the Saints Go Marching In' carrying across the water.

The *Ark Royal* and the Likoni Ferry, which was crossing the channel at the same time, were on a collision course. Loaded with trucks and cars and a cohort of passengers, the ferry churned violently away to starboard at the last moment even though it had the right of way, the passengers and onlookers gasping a communal groan of relief as it escaped a sinking.

Might is right, as always, Evie silently observed with a disapproving shake of her head.

On Sunday night things got interesting.

A dinner dance was arranged on board, in the open on the runway deck under multi-coloured lights and crepe paper decorations, with cocktails and bowls of punch appropriately laced and an open invitation to all the eligible young ladies across the island and on the mainland as far south as Diani Beach, north to Mtwapa Creek and up in the Changamwe hills to the west.

And they all came flocking.

Evie was among them, looking forward with nervous optimism to an exciting evening, but feeling vulnerable and exposed in her red silk dress and white sash before the hordes of woman-hungry sailors.

Seemingly aeons later that evening, sitting alone, a steadily shrinking violet well away from the floodlights, she sipped her third Kenya-style gin martini with a lemon twist after sitting out several waltzes, three foxtrots and a number of sambas with no one asking her onto the floor. With a touch of envy, she watched Lara, breathless and elated, dancing her way through a line of partners, the belle of the ball, as always.

Evie was torn between ordering a fourth martini, retreating homeward down the gangway, or—she smiled to herself—*jumping overboard to cause a scene and get myself rescued* when she spotted one of the sailors opposite her detach himself from the group and make a beeline for her.

Omigod! At last! There's no doubt about it!

Their eyes locked across the crowded flight deck, hers an apprehensive brown and his a hypnotic lime green beneath his crewcut red hair with its parting down the middle. He held out his right hand, his crooked forefinger signalling her to join him. Dressed in his crisp blue sailor suit, he was grinning, she thought, like an attractive shot fox with freckles.

Flooded with relief and fearful anticipation, her heartbeat racing, she downed her glass.

'We can't have this,' he said, his Geordie accent difficult at first for her to follow, 'it's time we got you on the floor, my bonny lass. Roddy Randall at your service. You can call me Randy.'

'Evie Sinclair,' she replied in her refined contralto as she stood, thankful she was still in shadow as she loomed over him. 'Are you sure about this, Randy?'

By name and nature? The question flashed across her mind. *Probably not, by the skinny look and feel of him. On the other hand*—she smiled to herself—*why on earth not?*

'Never surer.' He laughed. 'Come on, pet. Let's show them what we're made of.'

He reached up to gather her in his arms, the left one held out stiffly, already gripping her right hand for steerage.

At which point she looked down at the crown of his head a foot or so below her, and while the magic didn't quite end, it seemed to pause until the music struck up a rumba and they readjusted their positions. He turned into Fred Astaire and she his Ginger Rogers, matching him shimmy for shimmy, pirouette for pirouette, and sliding sideways step for step, the pair of them gliding in unison and apart across the floor, weaving between the other dancers as though they were made for one another, both skating on thin ice and never missing a beat.

From that moment on, dancing the night away was truly magical for Evie, who hoped it would never end. Of course it did and all too soon, but not before she'd invited Randy home the next day and he'd accepted.

'I'm looking forward to sharing what's left of your birthday cake for starters.' He smiled as he led her to the exit gate at the end of the night. 'And any other treats you can dream up to serve for afters.'

A strange thing happened when they reached the gangway, where Lara was waiting patiently with three expectantly admiring partners. Another sailor Randy introduced as Mikey Taylor handed him an upturned sailor's hat filled with crisp white Bank of England five-pound notes.

'A hundred and twenty quid. I've done the rounds. They've

all paid up,' Mikey said, as Randy scooped them up, licked his forefinger and quickly counted. 'You've earned every penny.'

'Here,' he said, counting out a dozen notes and handing them to Evie. 'Sixty pounds. It's your half. You deserve it.'

'What for?'

His answer came the moment she posed the question. 'We won the dancing contest, you and me. We were judged the best-performing couple on the floor.'

Mikey suppressed a burst of laughter with a snort, his eyebrows shooting up as Randy spoke. Evie, her normally perceptive scepticism blunted by the euphoria of the moment and the gin martinis she wasn't used to, took his apparent surprise for congratulations on their success.

'Oh. Thanks so much. I had no idea. And thank you for tonight. I loved it so. You will be coming round tomorrow?'

He took her hand in both of his. 'I'll be there, Evie, trust me. I wouldn't miss it.' He looked down at the hat still full of notes. 'Not for quids.'

'I'll see you then.' She smiled as he released her hand. 'Sweet dreams.'

'After tonight? With you in them? Way aye, they're bound to be, pet.'

'You smooth talker, you.' She pocketed the roll of notes before stepping gingerly sideways down the bouncing gangway.

'He seems nice, even if he does come across a bit full on,' Lara commented as they walked away towards the car park, before adding, with her nose a little out of joint, 'It's strange that no one mentioned a dancing competition to the rest of us. I wish I'd known.'

Things came to a surprising head the next evening.

After meeting Evie's parents and with an hour to kill

before dinner, she and Randy set out on a walk around the seafront to take in the atmosphere and colours of the twilight on the open ocean as the sun set inland behind them.

Hand in hand, they mingled with the crowds heading down Salim Road towards the Likoni Ferry, lined with Evie's favourite African Tulip trees bursting with upright brilliant orange blooms. They joined the groups of muscular and cheerful Africans in flowing kanzu gowns or multi-coloured kikoi waistcloths walking home from work to the rhythmic twanging of their thumb piano tines among the smoke-and-spicy smells of curried samosa stands and roasting corncob braziers.

They stopped at one peanut vendor's barrow to buy a serve of Evie's favourite flavour, watching him miraculously cascade a shower of salted and chilli nuts from an aluminium scoop held high above his right shoulder into two newspaper cones he'd twisted into shape with his other hand, without a single nut falling astray. To wash them down, they shared a green *madafu*, an unripe coconut with its top lopped off, sucking its cool sweet milk through a single bamboo straw they shared, turn and turnabout.

The crowds thinned on Azania Avenue, leading further around the seafront. Indians and Sikhs in their silken saris and tight-wrapped turbans sat in rainbow coloured family circles on the lawns beneath the baobabs, loping dogs and children chasing one another round the enormous trunks, the salt air on the breeze refreshing as the dark descended.

When they turned to cross the seafront golf course for a shortcut home, Randy let go of Evie's hand and slipped his arm around her waist.

He pulled her into him. 'You don't mind, pet? I can't resist it.'

'No, that's all right,' she replied. 'You don't have to ask.'

A few strides later, though, when his hand slipped up

her cotton blouse and his fingers felt beneath her breast, she reached wordlessly across and calmly placed it back above her hip where it had rested before.

They crossed the sixth tee and sat on the iron bench there, facing the ocean, and when the upper quadrant of the gibbous moon crested the horizon, speckling the sea with flecks of light, Randy leaned across and tentatively and gently reached up, turned Evie's face filled with expectant wonder to his, and became the first man ever to kiss her.

'Ah, now *that*, that was nice, my bonny lass,' he said. 'That was a belter.'

'It was,' she replied, adding with a smile, 'even if we shared the taste of chilli peanuts over again.'

'It's just the start, lassie, just the start. Let's see where it takes us,' he said. 'Now close your eyes.'

He kissed her again, with the promise of many more to follow, which at first, she didn't mind at all. Her body pleasurably glowed as she adjusted to the novelty of each kiss and she tried to match the unfamiliar moves of his lips and tongue—but it was the sudden fondling that followed that caught her off guard. She felt she was getting in over her head, the uninvited pressure of his stroking fingers at her breast, his lips moving to the flesh beneath her ear and throat. The fumbling invasion of her personal space and privacy unexpectedly dismayed her, until she pleaded all too gently, 'Stop, please, Randy. Stop.'

Then she suddenly felt sick and stiffened as Randy began to grope her inner thigh, an unanticipated rush of primal dread forcing her to her feet screaming, 'Stop! Stop! I'm not that sort of girl!'

He jumped up without a word, and with his arms around her they fell violently forward, Randy's forehead striking the metallic Par Aide golf ball cleaner beside the bench with a ringing thud so loud she'd never forget the sound. Whether she'd caught her heel in a divot on the grass and tripped or he'd attempted to force her backwards to the ground she would never know. Either way, desperately winded after breaking his fall, she thrust him aside and struggled up from beneath him.

He was unconscious for several minutes.

She used her sash to bind the four-inch gash and stem the bleeding as best she could. When he came to, dazed and concussed, she held him up and walked him back to Azania Drive, where an Indian couple picked them up and drove them to the emergency department at the Mombasa English Hospital three kilometres away. There the doctor signed him in for an overnight examination and an x-ray because his pupils were alarmingly dilated and he hadn't spoken since the fall, as though he knew that words could never serve to mend the rift.

Evie, exhausted, shocked, concerned and confused, rang Lara to pick her up and drive her home.

She slept fitfully that night, unwelcome thoughts and emotions raging through her mind and body. Why had she reacted so immaturely to a situation for which she'd been preparing herself during the past several years? It wasn't as if what had taken place had happened too soon or caught her unawares, so why had that realisation heightened her feelings of shame? Why did she feel so defiled and taken for granted? So disrespected and reduced to a lump of flesh? She wasn't that naïve and prudish, was she? Surely not. She'd been enjoying the interaction up until a certain point. If she'd so narrowly escaped being raped, why should she feel so guilty about leading Randy on and inviting his attentions?

And is that what it was? She wondered. *Attempted rape?*

That thought stilled her mind and brought some focus to her confusion. In a calmer moment, she re-examined everything that had occurred since he'd beckoned her onto the dance floor two nights before. The group of watching sailors—yes, Mikey Taylor was among them, as far as she could recall. Were they judging the dancing? Hardly. The alleged competition hadn't been officially announced. If that was a lie, then why the hundred- and twenty-pound prize?

She froze. Mikey Taylor's suppressed laugh was one of scornful surprise at Randy's quick thinking, not congratulations.

Omigod! They'd paid him to dance with me and he gave me half his fee to conceal the fact.

If they'd been so cruel and calculating then, what more had they done after that?

His visit to her home. What was his motive? What goal did he have in mind? Her thoughts raced. *My virginity! How much did they judge that was worth? Double or nothing?*

She lay on her back staring in dumb shock at the ceiling. Her imagination ran away with her. She imagined him confirming on his return to the ship that yes, he definitely had scored and legitimately deserved his three hundred pounds sterling winnings. The wound on his forehead? It was her signet ring. Put it down to the passion of the moment when she lashed out in her ecstasy; she was a big girl, after all. And, no, she was not a virgin, she needed little urging. As for the panties he was supposed to provide as a trophy to prove he'd done the deed, well, she hadn't been wearing any.

When that imaginary conversation ran through her mind, she tore off the sheets and rushed to the top drawer of her dresser. She took out the bank of England notes tightly wrapped in a green rubber band. She tipped her brooches and necklace from the bowl they were in, put the notes in the bowl and with a match from the box she kept to light her scented candles, set the notes alight. She watched them burn down to a fine ash. That done, she poured the ash into a blue Croxley envelope, wrote three words on a page of the writing pad—*Shame on you*—tore it off and folded it, before placing it in the envelope and sealing it. She addressed it to Leading Seaman Roddy Randall and propped it against the dresser mirror.

The next morning her father's enquiries at the hospital confirmed that Randy had signed himself out at four o'clock that Tuesday morning and he'd returned by taxi to the *Ark Royal*. She sailed at midday. Evie did not go round to the seafront with Lara and her friends to farewell her.

Randy's letter to her arrived the following day. His apology was polite and to the point.

Dear Evie,

Many thanks for the invitation to spend time with you and your family. It was a privilege and I appreciate the efforts you all took to entertain me.

Especially you. All I can do is let you know how sorry I am we were so clumsy and things turned out the way they did. I can assure you I never meant to harm or hurt you, even if you might believe I got what I deserved.

Thanks again for seeing to it that I was taken to the hospital and stitched up. Apart from a splitting migraine, I am healing well.

Your friend,

Randy

P.S. I will write you from Aden if I get the chance, pet.

We were so clumsy? We? And to crown it all—pet?

Evie vented her fury in her bedroom, tearing his letter to shreds before throwing it into the bin along with the screwed-up envelope of ashes on the dresser. She reached for her diary and marked Monday's entry page with three solid black asterisks, jabbing them in place with her indelible black felt marker pen.

She never heard from him again.

It was then, as she looked down at the asterisks in the pale light of the breaking dawn, that she took what she called her 'vows of chastity', and her life changed course.

She resigned that morning from her position as the receptionist in Elsie's Beauty Salon, the only women's hairdresser on Kilindini Road in the centre of the town.

With her father's permission, she opened a children's crèche in the family's spare games room, with a comprehensive playground of sandpits, swings, seesaws and climbing frames in the shade of the mini forest of gnarled old Frangipani trees in the back yard. Within six months she'd built a clientele of thirty lively children, a boisterous family group she and two cheery African ayahs cared for throughout the day.

By the end of the year, she'd published four children's early readers along the lines of Beatrix Potter, using African antelopes, meerkats and anteaters as her protagonists, with more stories in the pipeline.

When her father died two years later and she inherited the house, she gathered up all his clothes and shoes, as well as other useful belongings, and passed them on to the Kenya Red Cross for distribution to anyone they saw fit.

Within four years she was also caring for Lara's two children, Jacqueline (Jackie) and Alexandra (Lexie), before they transferred up country to Nairobi. She proved so effective and caring a surrogate mother they became attached to her for life, loving her as deeply and depending on her as much as they did Lara.

She opened up her heart to the world, as though that was what her heart required, and the world around her responded.

Take little Feisal Ali, for example.

A skinny, ten-year-old Omani Arab boy, he turned up at the house one afternoon with a battered brown leather suitcase balanced on his shaven head, his left hand holding it in place. She invited him in, and they conversed in Swahili.

'*Jambo sana, memsahib...* my name is Feisal and I have come all this way especially to sell you some bargains you will not be able to resist.'

'*Jambo*, Feisal. You think you're going to convince me so easily?'

'Of course, *memsahib*. I have everything in here you need at bargain prices. I will save you the long drive into town to buy them.'

'How can you be so sure?'

'How can I not? You are a white *memsahib*, after all, like all the others. And they cannot resist me when I show my wares. Now let me show you.'

He placed the suitcase on the table between them, undid the strap and opened the lid. It was filled with a wide variety of trinkets, small toys and haberdashery items. He carefully took each one out and lined them up, looking Evie in the eye with a cheeky grin as he did so.

He waved a hand across them. 'There you are,' he said. 'Now take your pick and we will agree a price.'

Deliberately pursing her lips and frowning, Evie cast her eye across them.

'Now let me see,' she said as she settled on a two-piece stainless steel manicure set, comprising nail scissors and clippers. 'How much is this?'

'Ah, that, memsahib. You have very good taste.' He paused, sucked in his cheeks. 'It is very rare. For you, because it is your first... *shilingi kumi*, ten shillings.'

'*Shilingi kumi!*' Evie gave a burst of laughter. 'I'm not paying ten shillings, you little rogue! I'll give you *tano*, five.'

Feisal frowned deeply, paused, and then slowly nodded. 'Only for you, *memsahib*, *saba*, seven.'

'*Tano*, I said. That's my last offer. Take it or leave it.'

'*Sita*, six. I can go no lower. I will lose money.'

'Alright, six it is.'

He smiled, reached out and shook her hand, before she retrieved her purse and counted out the coins.

He explained that his parents had provided him with the suitcase and the items within it, to teach him the mercantile art of striking a hard bargain early in life; and he continued visiting Evie at odd times after that, his head regularly shaved against lice.

She invited him into the house whenever he arrived, never missing the opportunity to offer him a steaming cup of black sugarless tea and his favourite, a slice or two of toast and honey, before choosing between hairclips, buttons, pinking scissors, reels of cotton or packets of sewing needles for which she had no need, testing his developing salesman's skills at bargaining and then paying for her selection at an inflated price that always favoured him.

Or the team of six African garbage collectors, whose rubbish truck arrived every Friday to empty her two galvanised steel waste bins. Without fail every week, she'd have a jug of iced water, freshly squeezed lemon and the latest batch of pancakes or buttered scones laid out for them on a table beneath the Mango tree beside the garden tap. As regular as the calendar of passing weeks, the truck would pull up and they'd gratefully take a ten-minute break there, hosing down her bins and themselves in the heat, and thanking her before they drove away.

Her reputation spread, and for the rest of her short life, she wore with pride the respectful Swahili name by which she became known—*Memsahib Mkubwa*—Mrs Big. Far from demeaning, it acknowledged her generosity and signified the love and respect with which everyone regarded her, including those who'd only heard of her in passing.

It was sixteen-year-old Jackie, staying with Evie at the coast during a vacation break from her Nairobi Secondary School, who found her at nine-thirty am that fateful Sunday morning in April 1962.

Jackie knocked on her bedroom door, tiptoed in and drew the curtains. She was lying in bed, as though she'd peacefully overslept. When Jackie gently shook her, she was cold and unresponsive. Jackie's heart lurched and she jumped backwards, a hand to her mouth. Then she crept forwards, leant over with her ear to Evie's mouth and heard no breathing. She felt for a pulse, gingerly pressing into her inert and wax-like flesh, but felt none. She dropped Evie's forearm and stood paralysed before she screamed, and one of the children's crèche ayahs came running to her aid from her outhouse living quarters.

Evie was forty years old.

When the ambulance arrived and the two African paramedics confirmed that she was dead, they called for reinforcements to lift Evie from the bed onto the gurney, and a second ambulance arrived. Jackie watched on, sobbing in the ayah's arms at the sight of Evie overflowing the narrow stretcher of the gurney and threatening to slide off as five grunting paramedics manoeuvred her with clumsy control down the polished red veranda steps, before heaving her into the back of the closest ambulance.

Lara and Lexie flew in the following day.

Lara worked frantically over the next fortnight to finalise Evie's personal affairs, put the children's crèche up for tender and the house on the market, auction her personal effects and finalise the complicated funeral arrangements at the new Nyali Cemetery on the mainland.

These included the construction of a made-to-measure mahogany casket, the hire of an appropriately sturdy green utility truck to carry it and, given the regrettable experience of the paramedics and the gurney at the house, the use of a forklift with an appropriate counterweight supplied by the Mombasa Municipality to cart the casket from the cemetery gateway to the grave along the gravel walkway.

Lara was astonished at the size of the silent crowd congregated at the cemetery gates on the Sunday morning of Evie's burial. Close to three hundred Africans were there, she guessed, when she drove up behind the truck, along with a surprising number of Mombasa's European, Goanese, Indian and Arab communities.

Only a handful appeared to be the gawking lookers-on, who were all she had initially expected to turn out.

An extraordinary thing happened when the truck backed up to the pillars of the cemetery gates and the forklift operator started up his machine. Six powerful garbage collectors, tall and broad-shouldered in their smartly laundered khaki municipal uniforms and wearing tight-fitting intricately embroidered white skull caps, stepped forward from the crowd. One of them ordered the operator to shut down the forklift and park up, while another walked across to Lara and asked her in Swahili to allow them to act as Evie's pallbearers.

'Using a forklift would be disrespectful to Memsahib Mkubwa,' he explained. 'She deserves better.'

'Of course,' she replied, taken aback, glancing at the name sewn over his shirt pocket. 'If you're sure you can manage it, Juma.'

He sent her a wide smile and placed a large reassuring hand on her forearm. 'We can,' he said, before adding as if reading her mind, 'and we will not require payment, *memsahib*. Your sister was very good to us. We are doing it for her.'

The garbage collectors took over, moving aside the funeral director's assistants who'd clambered onto the back of the utility to slide the casket onto the forks of the machine. With three on each side of the casket, they grasped the handles, and with a grunted '*Harambee!*' heaved it onto their straining shoulders. They stood for a moment, braced themselves and evenly adjusted the weight, before setting off down the path at a steady, unfaltering pace towards the grave, jaws set, the taut cable-like tendons in their necks standing out, the crowd trailing behind them.

When the ceremony was over, Lara noticed that the six pallbearers were among the last to leave. She stepped across to thank them and shook each by the hand. They removed their caps and bowed to her in turn.

'She was a saint,' Juma, the last of them confirmed simply, with beads of sweat—or were they drying tears?—still glistening among the tribal scars along his cheeks.

'Well, yes, perhaps she was. She did bring out the best in people.'

Jackie was especially quiet in the car on the way home. While they were crossing the Nyali pontoon bridge to Mombasa Island, she said, 'I feel so sad for Aunty Evie.'

'Of course you do,' Lara said. 'We all do. We're going to miss her.'

'No, I mean really, really sad.'

'Why?'

'She didn't have someone special in the crowd today. A husband or a boyfriend, someone who really loved her.'

Lara gathered her thoughts before gazing sideways at her. 'Ah, that all depends,' she said.

'On what?'

'On what you mean by love.'

The car rattled across the planks on the bridge as though providing a drumroll as it broadcast a message in Morse code loud and clear, and she thought, *It's such a shame she wasn't alive to appreciate it.*

First Cab Off The Rank

Ryan worked on his short story without a break throughout the day. His eleventh. He completed it as night fell. He had one more to write.

His conversation with his publisher earlier that day was ringing in his ears. 'A deadline is a deadline is a deadline,' Gunnar had insisted in his clipped Nordic manner. 'No more extensions. Twelve short stories for a total of at least sixty thousand words on my desk by 3 January, as we agreed. Or you will have missed the bus for next year's publication.'

'Two more weeks, Gunnar. That's all I'm asking. I've written eleven. Short stories don't grow on trees.'

'Not this time, Ryan. No.'

'Or fall out of the sky.'

'Then you had better find one that writes itself. You've got five days.'

The next morning the wind had swung onshore. Cooled by the Pacific, it cleared the smoke from bushfires that had raged across Watagan State Forest and the slopes of Mt Warrawalong kilometres away the day before, spurred by swirling westerlies. Showers now swept in across the coast at Lake Macquarie, assisting the firefighters and turning the ash that had fallen like black snow around the converted boathouse into slush.

Ryan had rented the boathouse for the past month. Gunnar had recommended it to him. The idyllic scene and the silence would be conducive to writing, he'd explained. While there was still sufficient light, he stripped down to his bathers, walked out into the rain, checked the damage and began the clean-up. He hosed down the boathouse veranda and did what he could to sweep the lawn, which he'd spent an hour mowing earlier that week.

The tide was out. He swept the muck over the embankment and onto the narrow beach where it was easier to shovel it into the wheelbarrow. He deposited it on the flowerbeds.

He did the same to the jetty, spraying the pier and the two yellow kayaks there before scrubbing the matting on the farthest pontoon afloat in deeper water. He took a breather when the light faded and the showers eased, squatting at the end of the jetty.

The lake stretched like undulating silk into the blue twilight. He watched patches of sludge drifting shoreward buffeted by the breeze, and a paragraph from the scene he'd spent hours revising the day before in his eleventh story came to mind. He blurted the words into the dusk, 'Much of the spoiled sea-soaked pepper was carted from the holds and thrown overboard, its dark stain curving away behind the carrack like a fan of coral spawn. Floating ribbons of discarded silk unfolded in a rainbow blaze in the pepper-smear, and scavenging sailors from the *White Eagle* launched two skiffs to retrieve them, hauling them in like fishnet…'

He was unable to recall word for word what followed.

While writing, he'd made it a habit to read selected passages aloud to himself. He focused on the sound and sequence of the words and rhythms of the phrasing, tinkering with their placement and resonance. Now, reciting to himself, he grinned at the thought that anyone overhearing him would consider him a prime candidate for a straitjacket and a padded cell.

Then he heard an unexpected voice gleefully call 'Encore!' from the cliff above, and someone applauded.

He turned to see a young couple leaning on the railing at the cliff top, where coloured lights strung beneath protective sails danced on the breeze.

He returned their wave and clambered to his feet. Beside the boathouse, a flight of steps climbed the cliff face to the boarding house. He made his way up and when he reached the top, he met the couple he'd seen signing in the day before.

'You caught me red-handed,' he said.

'Seems we did,' the woman answered. 'Hello, I'm Caitlin—Catie for short. And this is Iain.'

'O'Dwyer,' her companion said.

'Hi, I'm Ryan.'

She appeared to be in her mid-twenties. Her cropped black hair was sculpted round an elfin face of appealing fragility. He saw a mix of laughter and reserve in her eyes. *Are they green?* he wondered, their colour confused by the lights swinging overhead. He thought she was blushing, but the lights were deceiving, and if she was, he wondered if the fact that he was half-naked in his bathers had triggered it. The delicacy of her features and the quiet huskiness in her voice added to her apparent shyness.

'So is a carrack what I think it is?' she asked.

He recognised her singsong Irish accent and wondered if her raven hair hinted at Spanish forebears, survivors of the Armada limping home down Galway's rugged west coast.

'If you think it's a Portuguese cargo vessel built in the sixteenth century from oak mostly, then you're right.'

'I *knew* it,' she said, a pair of astonishing dimples marking her cheeks when she smiled. She turned to Iain. 'I was right, mister.'

'So you were.'

She held out her left hand, palm up. 'So pay up. Now!'

'I'll deduct it from your tab.'

'Skinflint!'

'I've just finished a short story about one,' Ryan said.

'You're a writer?'

'Wearing P-plates. I'm putting the finishing touches to my first collection.'

'Have you had many published?'

'A couple. One in *Westerly* and the other in *Meanjin*. The rest are waiting for the pigs to fly.'

'Do you think they'll ever take off?'

Ryan laughed. 'The kosher ones might. At least I hope so. I'm hanging my hat on this collection. I need one more to round it off. Just the one. If they don't sell I'm skint and it's back to shovelling iron ore in the Pilbara.'

Iain reached out and shook his hand. His brown eyes coolly assessed Ryan through gold-rimmed John Lennon glasses. His dark hair was tied back in a ponytail, the shadow of a week's stubble accentuating his jaw line. Ryan noticed his Pink Floyd t-shirt—*The Dark Side of the Moon*.

'We didn't expect this rain,' he said, his accent echoing hers.

'It shouldn't last,' Ryan said.

'Let's hope you're right. This is our third anniversary and we forked out a bundle for our stay.'

Catie stepped back and gazed at them both, her eyes sparkling. 'Well, look at you two, would you now? Spitting images! Never mind your glasses and hair, Iain. Ryan could be your older brother.' She broke into a laugh. 'Both of you from Clonmel, Tipperary, and me from Wicklow having trouble telling you apart.'

'Then I'm glad you married the right one.' Iain smiled.

For the briefest moment, Ryan noticed a speculative look passing between them, as though a private question had been asked and answered, before they both glanced back at him. Unwilling to appear curious, he turned away and watched a curtain of rain smothering the peak of Coal Point opposite, before turning back to them and pointing as it churned across Kilabin Bay. As he met their gaze he sensed a subtle change in mood, a heightened tension in the moment, before Catie gave him an enigmatic but engaging grin.

Is she laughing at me? What have I said?

About to ask, he changed his mind. He suggested instead they make a move before the shower swamped the shore. 'It should clear up overnight. The fireys will have the bushfires completely under control by then. It should be a good day tomorrow.'

'Let's hope so,' Iain replied, as he stretched up to switch out the lights.

After a momentary pause, Ryan added, 'Listen, tomorrow's New Year's Eve. Why don't you join me down below to see in 2008? I've got some coral trout in the fridge; best fish in the world. I'll dig out a recipe to knock your socks off. And a red Ned, or white, if you prefer, to wash it down.'

The approaching shower lashed the shoreline, rattling on the sails.

'That's an offer we can't refuse,' Catie said. 'What do we bring?'

'How about yourselves, and maybe salad for three?'

'Sure, then. It's a deal. And I'll bring my violin along to sing the New Year in.'

'Sounds good. I've got a flute and a guitar to give you some backing.'

'The violin you might regret,' Iain shouted over his shoulder as they ran hand in hand up to the house in the pelting rain. 'There's no stopping this one when she gets going!'

Catie shrieked with laughter as Iain swung her slender body childlike into the shelter of the veranda.

Ryan stepped out from under the sails and stood, arms outstretched and face to the sky. The cold sting of rain beat at his skin. By the time he reached the boathouse, the gutters were overflowing, sluicing the remains of the black snow across the lawn and over the embankment.

The next evening as darkness fell, Ryan lit the veranda lamp and mosquito coils and stepped out to check the effect.

All it needed was music. He took his circular stone flute from the shelf and placed it on the table. *I'll teach Catie the fingering for 'Waltzing Matilda' if things go quiet.*

He picked up his acoustic guitar, tuned it by ear and then sorted through the CDs stacked on the coffee table. The young couple was Irish so he selected Horslips *The Book of Invasions: A Celtic Symphony*. It was a favourite of his from the late seventies. He slipped it into the CD player and turned up the volume.

The couple appeared just as the catchy third track was playing.

Catie bounced barefoot off the last step. She wore a lime green mandarin dress with enticing slits in the sides, its open collar elaborately embroidered in gold. She caught Ryan's eye as she whirled into a jig, a bowl of garden salad held over her head in one hand and a violin and bow in the other, as she sang along to the chorus in a hoarse soprano:

'Trouble, trouble.
I try to chase trouble but it's chasing me.
Trouble. Trouble with a capital T.'

She gave a regal bow and a cheerful 'Taraaa!' as she placed the salad in the middle of the table. 'I do love that song,' she said, turning to Iain descending the steps behind her carrying a bottle of wine, which he passed to Ryan. 'It sounds like we've found ourselves an Aussie who's not a barbarian. He's heard of Horslips!' She gave a burst of laughter. 'See, I *told* you he was your long-lost brother. He's one of us, a Paddy through and through.'

She took up the violin and began to play, circling the table as she sang joyously:

'High on the mountain stands a boat,
But are they gods or real folk?
We can't see the fire but we smell the smoke.'

'The Four Poxmen of the Horslypse!' Iain said 'Magic!

We've got the CD of their Belfast gigs recorded live in the Whitla Hall up in the room.'

'So that's where the name came from,' Ryan said.

'It sure is.'

'We're in for a good night,' Ryan shouted over the lively violin. 'We can jam later and wake the neighbourhood.'

'Later?' Catie laughed. 'What's wrong with right this minute?'

'Not while we're still sober.'

'What else do you have?' asked Iain.

'I've got a new CD I'm sure you'll enjoy. It's an Aboriginal group called *Ingga Thaaka*, unplugged, recorded in Munich. It's their latest. They've called it *Rocktoberfest*. With a didge to die for going for it all the way through."

'That's a new one on me. I'll look forward to it.'

'It seems we share the same tastes,' said Catie.

'We do, by the sounds.' Ryan pointed at the hissing gas barbecue. 'What about your taste in fish?'

'You said it was the best in the world.' She placed her violin on one of the chairs. 'It's our socks you're going to knock off, if I remember rightly, only I'm not wearing any.'

'Then I've already succeeded. You be the judge.'

He poured the wine and unfolded the fish, steaming white flakes falling from the bone. Pungent flavours of lemon and thyme pervaded the veranda.

They enjoyed the meal, and as the twilight deepened, fireflies beyond the boathouse began to light up, signalling to each other in a flashing display. Delighted, Catie captured one. She placed it carefully on one of the wax-white vermillion-freckled blooms of the Stanhopea orchids flowering in hanging baskets attached to the veranda eaves, but it took off towards the lake. The pulsating tracer of its tail zigzagged away into the dark.

'Special effects, courtesy of the house,' Ryan said. 'They must have hitched a ride on the wind coming down from the Blue Mountains during the fires. I've never seen them this close to the coast. I doubt they'll survive this far from their habitat.'

Later that evening the quarter moon rose over Lake Entrance. Its reflection uncoiled in blue and white ripples towards them and Catie, who'd been experimenting with the stone flute and was now a little tipsy, insisted on walking down its stairway in the shallows. Seemingly weightless, she lifted her skirt to her knees, her unsteady footsteps scattering tiny whiting fry. When she returned to her chair she stretched out, her head tilted as she contemplated the dark sky swarming with stars.

'Guess what this reminds me of, Iain. The wallpaper in my bedroom back home on the farm.' She turned to Ryan. 'When I was a kid, I plastered the walls and ceiling with stars and moons. Luminous ones. Whenever I woke, it was like the room had disappeared and I was out in space astral travelling. There were times I woke up screaming until I realised I was safe in Ballinvalley.' She paused. 'Ah! How I miss my Vale of Avoca.'

'Astral travelling in the Vale of Avoca—it sounds very Celtic,' Ryan said. 'Your bedroom must be the perfect place to ask yourself what on earth you're doing in a universe where for no reason at all there appears to be something rather than nothing.'

Catie glanced at her watch, leaned forward and vigorously shook an extended index finger under his nose. 'Enough of that,' she said. 'We have half an hour. No time for a metaphysical debate, but a fine time for a story. So never mind the fact that reality is not what it seems, *nothing* must be *something* to exist. We want to hear about your carrack and the scavenging sailors from the *White Eagle*. You can resume where you left off last night.'

Iain was finger-picking Ryan's guitar, a broken thumbnail occasionally catching on the strings. He looked up. 'It's the perfect night for it,' he said, 'and it's still young enough. What better than a story about the sea after such a tasty meal that hit the mark?'

'And we want it unabridged,' Catie added. 'We don't want you censoring those sex scenes. We want lots of those, Mr Joyce… the ones you're famous for.'

Ryan shook his head good-naturedly. 'James Joyce? I wish!' He looked at Ian. 'Insistent, isn't she?'

'Oh yes, trust me, it's her strong suit. And she's always right. Better comply or wear the consequences. It never pays to argue with someone with a PhD in Philosophy from Trinity College, Dublin. Especially if she happens to be a woman,' Iain replied, recoiling as Catie reached out and dug a finger into his ribs.

Ryan gave a burst of laughter. 'Oh, okay then. Let me think. I could read you the short story I've just finished. The one you heard me quoting from last night—*The Sea Battle*, about the capture of the Portuguese carrack the *Santiago* by the Dutch, near St Helena Island, in 1602.'

When he'd finished, Ryan looked up from the file. 'That's it,' he said. 'That's the capture of the *Santiago* right there, and I need a drink.' He drained his glass and reached for the bottle to recharge the glasses. 'So how did that go down?'

'Interesting. Unexpected.' Catie looked at her watch. 'And you're right on time, two minutes to midnight… but you did let us down I have to say.'

'Let you down? How?'

'Where were those sex scenes we expected?' She clicked her tongue. 'It's a yes for the fish, that was sexy, and the wine had a great body to it. But I expected *so much more!*'

Iain laughed. 'Give the man his due, Catie. The sea battle qualifies. That was sexy.'

'Not sexy enough. I wanted a *real* sex scene. A sex scene that makes me frisky. Some seductive hussy doing a Molly Bloom… a red rose in her hair and her arms wrapped around someone about to have a cardiac arrest, intoxicated by her breasts, all perfume. Yes, and his heart going like mad and yes, she says, yes she will, yes. How does that sound?' She gave Ryan a long shrewd look, her eyes alight. 'What d'you think, Ryan? A sequel to *Ulysses* starting right where Molly left off?'

Ryan smiled and pointed out across the lake. It was black and flat as vinyl oilcloth. 'I've heard they're setting off rockets on Birriban Reserve any minute now, across the water over there. They'll be sexy. They'll have to do for now.'

As he spoke, the ridge of Coal Point erupted in a blaze of multi-coloured lights as rockets burst above the tree line and faded into the lake beyond the headland. Catie danced round the table to kiss them both, fusillades of midnight rainbows behind her lighting up the distant sky for several minutes.

When the show was over, Ryan was astonished to see Catie unbutton her collar, reach down to the hem of her dress and lift it overhead. She threw it across the back of her chair. Beneath it, she was small-breasted and narrow-waisted naked, an ankh on a silver chain about her throat, a gold ring through her navel and the faint shadow of pubic hair at the junction of her slender legs.

She turned to look at the lake. In profile, Ryan found her breathtaking.

Then she looked down at him. 'Don't disappoint me now, Mr Joyce. I'm sure you of all people don't shock easily! And

I'm certain you've seen many a map of Tasmania before now. Come on Iain, it's time for us to skinny-dip and make like we're back in Finland. Let's baptise 2008 like we did last year!'

Iain hauled off his shirt and jeans. 'We were in Helsinki this time last year, mate. It was bloody freezing and I needed tweezers to find my tackle when I got back in the sauna. This'll be a piece of cake. Why don't you join us?'

They ran down the jetty and leapt into the watery darkness, Catie's shrieks echoing.

Ryan shook his head in amazement at her bubbling vitality, amused that he'd thought her shy and fragile when they first met. Then he slipped out of his clothes, picked up three towels and trotted out to them.

They were clinging to the end of the pontoon, watching him approach.

'Bravo, Ryan!' Catie said, beating at the pontoon with her left hand. 'Come on in and join us.'

The water was warm and welcoming, and he circled them as they spun in an embrace, before Catie detached herself and swam back to the pontoon. She trotted to the boathouse, towelling herself off. She picked up her violin and walked out to them. Standing at the pontoon's edge, she tested a string and then began to play as she sang. Her husky voice and the rhythm of the music carried over them.

'We've a dragon nearby who arrives twice a year
And he strikes all our virgins with terror and fear.
Oh! No! Not again! They all scream as they flee.
You leave me alone now, don't you pick me!
For beautiful girls you've developed a taste.
They always are lovely, they always are chaste.
For the purest colleen is your favourite fare,
And you serve them up barbecued medium-rare.
Now the answer we've got, well it's magic for sure:

We won't cross our legs like we used to before.

If you're looking for virgins to roast and then eat,

You won't find a virgin at all for your meat!'

Bathed in moonlight, her body swayed to the music. Ryan was mesmerised. He swam to the nearest yacht and climbed aboard. Sitting cross-legged on the deck and listening, the thought struck him. *I'll make a note of all this the minute they're gone. Catie on the pontoon dancing to the Celtic rhythms. The veranda lantern a spotlight for her lithe, pale body gliding with the violin from move to move.* A rush of joy consumed him. *I'm certain there's a story in there somewhere to complete the collection. It will come to me.*

Catie then threw herself into 'The Wild Colonial Boy' before breaking into a sequence of traditional tunes for several minutes, some at a spirited pace, others melancholy. When she tired and she and Iain called out their farewells, Ryan waved from the yacht. He watched Catie climb unsteadily back up the steps, the towel wrapped around her, Iain's arm supporting her at the waist, her voice fading:

'When Irish eyes are smiling,

Sure, 'tis like the morn in spring.

In the lilt of Irish laughter

You can hear the angels sing…'

The next morning, he was surprised to find he was not hung over.

He put on his bathers and walked to the end of the jetty, where he dive-bombed his undulating reflection to freshen up. He trod water and looked up at the boarding house. There were no signs of life. He imagined Iain and Catie wrapped in each other's arms, snoring off the effects of the wine.

Back in the boathouse he prepared toast and a pan of tomatoes and sausages. While they were frying, he flicked through his draft prints and picked out the completed eleventh short story for a final edit.

He ate out on the pontoon. And then, before he could begin reading, he was interrupted by approaching footsteps, the pontoon bouncing. Catie was walking towards him, wearing dark glasses. Her face was shaded by a wide-brimmed straw hat with a freshly picked scarlet hibiscus threaded through its band. She was barefoot, wearing plum-coloured shorts and an orange t-shirt.

'Morning.' She looked down at the papers he was holding. 'Hope I'm not intruding. I've come down for the salad bowl and to give you a hand cleaning up.'

'All done last night. I thought you two must be out to it.'

'Half out to be sure, but don't remind me. It serves me right. Iain's been called back to Newcastle to cover an emergency. On New Year's Day, would you credit that?'

'Is that the luck of the Irish?'

'Must be. That's what you get for administering a hospital. There's been an accident out on the New England Highway. He has to get things sorted.'

'I see you're dressed for a hangover.'

She took off the sunglasses, grinned as he acknowledged the faint shadows beneath her eyes, and then replaced them. 'You can rest easy, Ryan. I'm respectable this time. It was a great night, though. We enjoyed it.'

'Me too. Iain said you had two more days. When are you leaving?'

'First thing tomorrow. Back to Newcastle.' She hesitated, gazing thoughtfully down at him. 'If you don't mind me asking, why are you here alone? You're wearing a ring, after all.'

He lifted his left hand and glanced at the gold band. 'A trial separation. I should have removed it. Maybe I'm hopeful,' he smiled thinly, 'but it seems she has other fish to fry.'

'Oh, do you have kids?' she asked, then frowned as though she'd spoken out of turn. 'I'm sorry, I don't mean to pry.'

'We do. Just the one. Hanna. She's about to start year twelve. Like you, she plays a mean violin. I'm going to enjoy describing you and Iain to her.'

She gave him a quick smile. 'Good for you. For the child I mean, Hanna. Not the separation. I'd love one myself, and so would Iain. So far no such luck. I've been getting *really* clucky lately...' She broke off and pointed at the papers. 'So where are we at this morning?'

'Staring at a blank screen, I'm afraid. Working up ideas for my next story—the twelfth and last for the collection. And it's a struggle, so far.'

'Would it be rude of me to ask if I could read some of your work? I won't get in your way. I could read up in the boarding house if you like. I've got nothing else to do today except moon about.'

'Of course you can, but you must promise to be critical,' he told her. 'I need the feedback, even if I appear to take no bloody notice.'

'Hang on, then. Let me get a drink. I'm parched.'

When Catie returned from the boathouse with a bottle of cold water and two glasses, Ryan announced that he'd changed his mind.

'You've made up your mind to change your mind? You sound like Iain. And you men talk about us women being fickle.'

'No, no. Let's get back to the veranda and out of the sun. You can read there and tell me what you think.'

'Ah, so you haven't given me the shove. Good. You had me worried for the minute, boyo.' She gave him a quick curtsey. 'I still feel wanted. That's nice. And you trust my critical faculties? Me, a virtual stranger? I'm truly honoured.'

'Don't go soft on me now. I need you to be picky.'

'Oh, I can be picky, Ryan. Miss Picky to the bone, Iain sometimes calls me. But like he warned you, I'm always right.' She gave a throaty chuckle. 'As you're about to discover.'

They walked back to the boathouse veranda and sat at the table, facing the lake.

Catie removed her hat and placed it on the chair beside her. 'You'll be wanting to know if I'd go out of my way to buy your book after a preview?' she asked, as Ryan handed her a thick folder. 'I can tell you that already.'

'Well?'

'The answer's no.'

'No? That was straight to the point.'

'No, I'll expect a complimentary copy, personally signed, sealed and hand-delivered.'

'Then I'd better get stuck in and get it out there.'

'You better had, indeed. There's nothing to be gained from wasting time.'

She made herself comfortable, pulled her left knee up and wrapped her arm around it, balancing her heel on the seat of the chair. 'Right then. Which one should I start with?'

'Why not *Shark Fin Soup*? It's light. It should amuse you.'

'Who's it about?'

'An old joker called Karl Voight. A cray-fisherman from Geraldton, in the west. He has a free-for-all with a white pointer and doesn't come out second-best. I think you'll like him.'

She rifled through the stapled pages and selected it. 'Let's get a good look at you, Karl,' she murmured. 'Don't be shy. I'm Catie, and it's good to meet you.'

She began to read.

A moment later Ryan sensed her gazing across at him engrossed in firing up his laptop. Before he began to type, he looked up. As their eyes met he caught her quiet, knowing smile. An unexpected, irrepressible rush of warmth coursed through him before she turned back to the page.

Catie left late in the afternoon. She hugged him before leaving, going up on her toes and whispering, 'It's so nice to have a part of you inside me, Ryan. It's a miracle.' She turned at the bottom step. 'I'll be over the moon in a few weeks' time, thanks to you. I will never forget you.'

'Nor I you.'

He sat back at the table gazing out over the lake, its surface shimmering with wavelets leapfrogging each other shoreward. Thoughts of their earlier encounter flooded his mind. He lifted his left hand, extended his fourth finger and removed the gold ring. He placed it on the table and sat looking at the band of white skin in the tan. It wouldn't be visible for long.

Then he recalled Gunnar's advice and smiled at the irony. The story *had* written itself. All it needed now was a subtle twist to the ending. Then he could amend the names and personalities of the characters and write the surprising narrative.

He had to complete it by tonight.

Better get on with it.

Start with the ending.

After concentrating for some time, he fired up the laptop and began rapidly typing, using the first person point of view for the intimacy:

It wasn't until 2018 that I came across Catie and Iain again, and then it was purely by chance. I was in my rooms at the University of North Wales in Bangor, where I was lecturing in creative writing.

I was updating my Author's Facebook page. On an impulse, I typed the name 'Catie O'Dwyer' into the search engine. Seven names were listed, and I discovered to my surprise she was among them.

I opened up her page and there they were, photographed in the banner. Catie just as I remembered her, smiling, little changed but clearly more mature. Iain with a beard, his temples turning to silver, and four, yes, four children standing in descending order between them.

I jerked forward and peered at the oldest boy. Dark-haired, attractively featured and smiling, he struck me as confident and competent-looking for a ten-year-old—the splitting image of myself at the same age, in fact. No doubt about it. The broad forehead. The long fingers. Those big knees and spindly legs. But the others! The two girls and the youngest boy, born more than likely two years apart. While their features carried subtle hints of Catie in the eyes, in the shapes of the ears and the chins, they could not have been more different from one another. A blond, a brunette and the youngest boy red-haired, his ranga's pale skin heavily orange-freckled. He looked to be about four years old.

But it was the backdrop that brought a gasp of surprise.

They were standing on the veranda of the converted boathouse, the steps up to the boarding house visible to the right, the two yellow kayaks moored to the jetty, the white and vermillion orchids strung like brilliant butterflies on long green stems in the hanging baskets, just as they had been ten years ago.

The flowering orchids confirmed that the photo had been taken at exactly the same period in December that I had been there and met them.

Then the thought struck me—Who took the photograph?

My suspicions aroused, and with the time I had spent with her that day unreeling in my mind, I pressed the 'friend request' button.

When the 'request denied' message appeared on my page almost simultaneously, my suspicions were confirmed.

I shut down the laptop, closed the lid and gazed out across the university quadrangle.

Despite the knockback, I will relive my interaction with

her for the rest of my life, I thought. If things do turn out the way I suspect they will, and they have a fifth child, at least I was the first cab off the rank.

It took him until well after midnight to complete the early sections of the narrative, refine the dialogue and setting, hint at the theme, change the names of the protagonists and settle on the title—*First Cab Off the Rank*.

He undertook a rapid edit and then, with a disbelieving shake of his head, he emailed the finished story to Gunnar.

He went to bed soon after, wondering before he fell asleep if Iain had actually been called out to an accident on the New England Highway.

Only A Matter Of Time

'**M**ARCEL PROUST MAY HAVE had the taste of a madeleine biscuit dipped in his Aunt Léonie's lime blossom tea to jog his memory of Combray, Monty,' my father Louis said out of the blue, as he cut into the orange, 'but that's small change compared to the taste of oranges. It always reminds me of Lidice.'

I was twelve years old when he surprised me with that statement.

For one thing, I had never heard of Marcel Proust, let alone a madeleine biscuit or Combray. For another, my father hardly ever shared confidences with me during the long and awkward silences that extended between us. I'd grown used to it and had long forgiven him. Just being in his company was enough.

That morning, his voice was so emotionally charged I was concerned for him. He had mentioned his experience in Lidice in passing to me a year ago, and I knew better than to ask him to elaborate on it now.

It was a Saturday, 17 February, 1968. I recall the date precisely because I was looking forward to taking part in the inter-school soccer competition grand final that afternoon. I was hoping he'd attend but was achingly aware it was unlikely.

We were slicing a dozen ripe Seville oranges I'd harvested from the two citrus trees we could see through the kitchen window in our house in Geelong. They were intended for my soccer team during the half-time break. I watched him lift a slice to his lips and tear the juicy flesh from the peel between his teeth. He chewed the orange before he swallowed, basket-balling the skin neatly into the kitchen tidy.

'Not quite as bitter as the slices I recall,' he said, wrinkling up his eyes and wiping a forefinger across his lips, adding with a quick nod, 'but sour enough, I'd say.'

Louis Novak was my Czech father and I loved him deeply, in spite of his introversion and the faults that I suspected others found in him: his intolerance for what he considered examples of their naïve stupidity when he came across it, his sarcastic tongue that cut them to the quick when he chose to use it, his short-tempered sensitivity when he judged that racist insults were being directed at him for his Jewish religion, his guttural mid-European accent or the way he looked.

At sixty years old, he was stocky, sharp-eyed, wiry, suntanned and quick on his feet. At first glance, the determined set of his nose, mouth and chin suggested someone quick-tempered and not to be messed with. That may have been true, but he was always gentle with me. He was regrettably distant most of the time though, and I came to appreciate him as a man who valued his privacy and preferred his own company.

The occasional unfocussed expression in his dark brown eyes was apparent only now and then; suggesting that he'd survived some trauma, some kind of hell he'd rather forget.

'You need to remember what your father's been through, and do your best to understand him and forgive him. Be patient, in other words,' my mother Miriam often advised me when I was younger. 'It's not that he doesn't love you when he gets moody and goes into his silences. He does. He always will. It's just that in those times he needs be alone to quieten his memories.'

Originally named Louis Novalecki, he was a highly-qualified academic, a professor in literary studies at the Czech University of Life Sciences in Prague. He'd been rounded up and interned with other Jews in Terezin Castle prison outside Prague in 1941, before being railed to Auschwitz III-Monowitz in 1944. In January 1945 he survived the first horrific death march to Loslau, before being railed to Buchenwald, where the American forces liberated him in April, along with a handful of other survivors who had taken over the camp.

He disembarked from the SS Orcades in Melbourne in 1949 as a Czech Jewish refugee.

He started working that year as an earthworks grader operator on the Snowy Mountains Hydro-Electric Scheme for the contractor Thiess Brothers. During his internment in Terezin he'd worked on the roads and railway yards as a grader operator and Thiess had assisted with his migration.

'That's my song, Monty!' I remember him shouting at me one evening when I was six years old. He gave an uncharacteristic burst of laughter, gazing bright eyed at me across the dinner table with his loaded fork half way to his mouth. Astonished, I wondered what had come over him. 'You will never guess what they called me years ago, on my first day on the job up in the Snowy—when I passed my grader operating test and was meeting the crew.'

The TV was on and I distinctly recall hearing the Mortein jingle for the very first time.

'Called you? Called you what, papa?'

'Listen...' he said, chewing on his steak and shaking his now empty fork at the TV in time with the song.

I heard the name, and when the song ended I read the advert. 'Louie *the Fly?*' I asked, incredulous.

'Exactly so. I remember when my foreman Syd Hill was introducing me to the crew. "This is Louis Novalecki," he said, stumbling over my surname. "That's Novalecki spelled n, o, v, a... Ah, bugger it! Too much of a mouthful. From now for us lot you're Louis the Fly. Nice and simple, like us blokes. Got that?" And it stuck. Good and proper, because in those days the bush flies really took a liking to me... in their hundreds.' He sent me a quiet smile as he reloaded his fork. 'I've been Louis the Fly ever since... and soon as I could after that, I changed from Czech to Aussie and Novalecki to Novak.'

'But this is the first time we've heard the song,' I said.

'So? Syd Hill must have had second sight thirteen years ago.'

From then on he constantly used the nickname whenever he introduced himself. I flinched when I first heard it that night, even though I was only six. I thought there was something derogatory about it, something demeaning and verging on insult, until I later realised that was why it appealed to him. He wore it like a camouflage, a mask that turned him into one of the boys. It obliterated a history he'd rather forget.

He sliced the final orange and saved another piece, tore off the flesh as he had before, and began to slowly chew, while I used plastic wrap to cover the two plates loaded with the remaining slices. I placed them in the fridge. He missed the kitchen tidy with the next piece of peel, so I stooped to bin it as he washed his hands, before he opened the door to the garden and settled on the top step.

The pervasive tangy citrus scent of oranges followed him out.

He moved aside a terracotta pot of my mother's overflowing Maidenhair ferns so that I could sit beside him. It was so unusual and rare an invitation I couldn't believe my luck and gave him an uncertain smile as I sat.

He was on one of his infrequent visits home during a period of two weeks' leave from the Snowy at the time. Each time he'd returned lately, he seemed to have become more taciturn, reticent and reclusive, making me less and less sure how to approach him—but on this day things were different.

I wasn't sure why and I was wary.

Leaning slightly forward, his arms stiff and his hands beside him on the step, shoulders hunched, he peered around at me. His calm brown eyes were thoughtful and, I thought, a touch bemused.

'What do you know about Reinhard Heydrich?' he asked. 'Nothing?'

'Yes, nothing. Why? Who is he?'

'I'm not surprised. No reason why you should. He was a nasty piece of work. He was the SS Nazi chief of the Gestapo, among other things. He was Hitler's right-hand man, his "man with the iron heart" that matched his Iron Cross, First and Second Class. He was appointed as the Deputy Reich Protector of Moravia and Bohemia in 1941. I was already in Terezin prison at the time.'

There was a long pause, during which I watched him apparently gathering his thoughts, his lips pursed. As the silence lengthened, I thought he wasn't going to continue.

'Terezin?' I asked at last, concerned he wouldn't go on. 'Where's that?'

He raised his left arm and placed it across my shoulders. His unaccustomed gesture both pleased me and left me feeling uncomfortably awkward.

'I think you're old enough.' He exhaled a sigh, his voice terse. 'It's short for Theresienstadt Castle, half an hour from Prague. Many of us were in there. Jewish writers, intellectuals, musicians, philosophers, scientists, the cream of the cream from all over the provinces.

'We had been arrested the year before and sent there after the place had been converted into an internment camp. In fact, the Nazis had dressed it up as a cultural holiday destination, a comfortable five-star health spa designed specifically for Jews. To hoodwink the Western Allies and the Red Cross.' He gave an unexpected laugh with an ironic edge to it. 'I did gain one advantage while I was in there that's served me well, though. I became a hot shot on the grader, even if I say so myself. A gun operator. The best of the best. Still am.'

When he and his fellow prisoners heard that Heydrich had assumed control, he went on, they knew he'd unleash a program of terror, arrests, executions and deportations, not just of fellow Jews, but any form of resistance to the Nazi regime.

'It turned out to be worse than we predicted,' he said. 'It was so bad our government in exile in London organised a hit squad to assassinate him.

'I remember the day they messed up the ambush. It was in late May 1942. I forget the exact date. A couple of Czech agents who had parachuted in tossed a hand grenade into his Mercedes and tried to fire a jammed Tommy gun at him to finish him off. It happened north of the river in Holesovice on the corner of Salvation Army Avenue and Haji Street. They destroyed the back of his car and punctured a tyre, but they missed him.'

'He didn't die, then?'

'Thankfully he did, a week later. Sepsis got him. From shrapnel, we were told. Bits and pieces of the car seat's leather and horsehair stuffing got stuck in the wound.'

He removed his arm from around my shoulder and stared across the garden, his hands on his knees, his gaze fixed on the road beyond the picket fence, following a passing car.

I knew better than to ask what had happened next.

Then, with a slow shake of his head, he looked back at me at last. 'Heydrich. He got his revenge in the end. Well and truly, even though he was dead. Adolf Hitler went berserk at first. He ordered the execution of thousands of Czechs, but the Police Chief Hermann Frank calmed him down, and he agreed to the destruction of the village of Lidice and the murder of its five hundred inhabitants instead.'

'Lidice?' I asked, to keep him talking. 'Where's that exactly?'

'It's a village twenty-five kilometres from Prague. On a hillside, in sheep farming country.'

'Why did they pick on Lidice?'

'They suspected someone there had looked after the agents.'

'Had they?'

'Who knows for sure? Either way, the people of Lidice picked the short straw.'

A shudder ran through him as he stretched and crossed his arms. 'Thirty of us were trucked in from Terezin to bury the dead,' he said, 'with picks and shovels and barrels of lime.'

It was 11 June, 1942, he explained, the day after the massacre. Every man and boy over sixteen from the village had been murdered. One hundred and seventy-three bodies lay strewn next to the wall of the barn beside which they'd been clinically shot by a firing squad, blood-spattered mattresses propped against it.

The grave was the size of half a tennis court and three metres deep.

'We marked it out with lime from the barrels we later used on the bodies after we dumped them in the pit,' he went on. 'We worked three shifts. Right through the night and half the next day. Ten of us in the grave at one time. It had to be deep enough for all the bodies. It was hard going, very rocky further down. On the second day, we shared some oranges from a crate one of our Czech gendarmes found in one of the barns. They were dry and sour, nothing like the ones we've just sliced.'

He did not elaborate, except to mention that the German officer in charge of the firing squad salvaged a vintage portable HMV gramophone. He used wooden needles from one of the houses their engineers were blasting and bulldozing as they razed the village. He'd also rescued a pair of 78 vinyl records. One was a Jelly Roll Morton recording of *Wolverine Blues*.

'I can still hear it like it was yesterday,' he said. 'The officer got one of the older prisoners to rewind the gramophone and play it again and again,' he took a deep breath, 'while he and his SS soldiers picked over the corpses for valuables that hadn't been handed in before they were shot.'

Then he gave another dry laugh. 'Every now and then he appeared at the edge of the pit, screaming at us to dig faster, in time with the piano's rhythm.'

I pictured him in the working party, armed with a shovel, sharing the slices of oranges in the pit before climbing out on the shoulders of a fellow prisoner to drag the stiffening corpses to the grave's edge, where they were ordered to remove their shoes and identification papers. They lowered them hand and foot to prisoners below, who stacked them, sardine-like, head to toe, in rows across the bottom and poured lime across them. All the while the German engineers set fire to the dynamited village.

'That experience is a stone in my shoe,' he said at last, 'one I haven't been able to wipe from my memory. It's been a constant reminder of my history—a reminder that you carry your past with you, stored in your memory like you're some miracle of a time machine.' He peered bleakly at me. 'And you learn to live with it, Monty. Some of us better than others. Maybe that's what time really is, each of us imposing our personal flow of time on the timeless mystery of the world around us as we recall the past and anticipate the future.' He sent me an unexpected smile. 'Does that make any sense? It does to me. Life is only a matter of time, after all.'

He died a month after he'd come to watch us win the inter-school soccer grand final trophy that memorable afternoon.

He amazed me and my team by handing round the orange slices at half-time, urging us to play as we'd never played before. And we did, encouraged by his surprising confidence in us.

He was working on the final grade of a rain-soaked embankment for the Jounama Dam, my mother was told, when his off-side grader wheels bit into the verge and the earthworks gave way. An avalanche of mud and rock buried him and his young survey hand, the grader on its side, one slowly spinning wheel protruding. The rescue crews reached them too late.

The fortnight before his cremation, I helped my mother unpack his belongings returned to her from Tumut. I watched her withdraw from among his things the yellow star he had saved, one he'd been forced to sew onto his jacket before his imprisonment. He'd mounted it in cellophane, along with the red triangle marked with the black 'T' he'd worn, indicating his Czech nationality.

It was the last thing she expected. She squatted, grief-stricken, on the edge of the bed, her body doubled over and shaking as she'd ducked her head to sob. She held the packet at arm's length on her upturned palm, staring at the star and the letter 'T', her fingers rigid, before she turned her hand over to drop it back into the battered leather suitcase as if her skin was scorched.

She pinned the badges to his suit at the cremation. They may have been intended to symbolise the fact that he had been among the less-than-human when imprisoned, but to my young mind, he wore them in his coffin with defiant and dignified pride on that last day, as though the victory was his.

My father's will had been specific and my mother observed his wishes—he insisted on cremation despite the Halachic prohibition, followed by the scattering of his ashes in Port Philip Bay at Barwon Heads.

A gusting wind snatched at the smoke from the crematorium chimney after the funeral, driving ash across the handful of mourners outside the chapel as my mother thanked them for attending. She handed out roses and lilies to them, detached from the wreaths and floral sprays she unravelled. Faint traces settled across her shoulders and I can still remember the grainy feel of it as I brushed it away.

I looked down at the residue of white dust on my twelve-year-old hands and was aghast at the sudden thought—*so he ended up in the ovens after all.* The world fell away beneath my feet. Drained and emotionless, I could not drive away the emptiness that overtook me at that thought, and I felt guiltier for thinking it. I buried the moment deep within.

'Ashes to ashes, Monty,' my mother murmured, before adding remorsefully, 'As Louis used to say, life is indeed only a matter of time.'

Here I am, thirty years later, a published writer, visiting the Lidice Garden of Remembrance outside Prague after exploring Theresienstadt Castle. I am walking in my father's footsteps, long after his death.

Over the past two years, I've compiled my latest collection of short stories. To my mind, the story my father told me that day in the back garden in Geelong would make an apt inclusion and provide me with an appropriate title for the book.

When I arrived, I sat for a long time in the multi-coloured, subtly scented rose garden at the top of the hill. The sprinklers among the rose bushes were spinning spirals of silver spray across them. I gazed down the hillside at the ruins, deeply moved, before following the concrete pathways to inspect the monuments and what was left of the village more closely.

When I had completed the circuit, I doubled back to revisit what I considered the most remarkable of the memorial sculptures—two rows of teenage girls and children cast in bronze, some with infants carried in their arms, standing clustered on a concrete plinth. They peered in distress down the clover-covered hillside at the gravesite of the murdered men and older boys, marked by a tall crucifix carrying a woven barbed-wire crown of thorns.

When I sat cross-legged on the grass at their feet, my mind reeled as I imagined my father labouring in the grave beside the burning buildings. I was appalled by the injustice recollected in that moment—an assassination attempt on a street corner in Prague, which had been followed, as night follows day, by the massacre of all the men and teenage boys and the gassing and imprisonment of the women and the girls.

I held my head in my hands, fighting back tears. *Acts of revenge! Will there never be an end to the carnage? Where are the dependable landmarks to navigate through confusion? Where the keystones that will hold? Where the shared processes that can be relied upon to reach reconciliation?*

Then, as though I'd heard my father's voice, his words came back to me: *That memory is a stone in my shoe.* In that excruciating moment, I pictured him limping on the march from Auschwitz III-Monowitz to Loslau train station in transit to Buchenwald, a worn yellow star stitched on his threadbare blue coat, a fragment of gravel lodged in one of the battered brown shoes he'd inherited from a dead friend, unable to stop and remove it for fear of being shot and abandoned on the side of the road.

I remember once again a reserved and private man who had told me on that one and only memorable occasion about his imprisonment in Terezin and Auschwitz. Before that, his only concession had been to hint vaguely at a circumstance before retreating into silence as though scalded. I know the wounds ran deep and he didn't want them exposed or to impose them on me or any others. I understand his pain and forgive him for the distance he maintained between us as a result.

Only a matter of time. I recall my father's last words to me when he described his experience at Lidice, and I know I will always associate the taste of oranges with that surprising conversation and with the soccer trophy presentation that afternoon, with him proudly in attendance.

My father, Louis—I'd introduced him to the other members of the team as Louie the Fly and seen him nod as he shook each of them by the hand. 'That is definitely me,' he'd said. 'I have a reputation to keep up, you see, when I'm working on my grader.'

It has taken me years to forgive myself for the conflicting emotions I experienced at his cremation when I found myself standing paralysed and seemingly unfeeling on the edge of an abyss.

To help me through that process, I've taken out my notebook and a biro from my backpack, opened it to a blank page, and made myself comfortable on the lawn beside the sculpture.

I'm about to record everything I can remember of our conversation, imposing my own personal flow of time on the timeless mystery of the world around me.

After a couple of false starts scratched out, I believe I've nailed it. This is what I've come up with so far for the opening paragraph:

'Marcel Proust may have had a madeleine biscuit dipped in his Aunt Léonie's lime blossom tea to jog his memory of Combray, Monty,' my father Louis said out of the blue, as he cut into the orange, 'but I've got the bitter taste of oranges, shared with my fellow prisoners, to remind me of Lidice.'

The Possibility of Happiness

SUNDAY, 20 DECEMBER 1998. Lennard and Stefan arrived at the glassworks on Bathers Beach in Fremantle just after sunrise. Standing on the front step facing the ocean, they were surprised to see a yacht ghost across the entrance to the bay, only a hundred metres out, the mainsail sliding down the mast. The anchor rattled out and then a lone figure emerged from the cockpit and observed them, eyes shaded against the rising sun. The sea was flat, the wash at the water's edge advancing and receding with the lightest hiss.

'This looks interesting,' Lennard said, 'Drug runner, you reckon? With a consignment of pot for the pottery next door?'

Stefan noted the silver bikini bottom, then the top, as the figure picked it up from the cabin roof and clipped it over her breasts. He gave a broad smile. 'Got your binoculars handy, Ace? It's a woman. I don't see anyone else aboard.'

'A *woman*? That's a lookup for the books, bro! You've gone without for how long now since Tania did a runner and you still remember the difference? I told you we'd find you a bushfire blonde to put the sting back in your tail if you came across to Fremantle! Even if you said you wouldn't be interested.'

They watched the figure wave and then dive, striking out strongly for the beach; a trained and stylish swimmer. When she reached the shallows, she stood and walked towards them, her blond hair darkly streaked with water and falling to her shoulders, her sunburned body sleek as a seal, her tan accentuated by the silver bikini. Her face seemed disproportionately small and oval, and her eyes, even at that distance, ice blue as the sun struck them.

'Jesus, bro. It's Ursula what's-her-name from Doctor No— the petite version.'

'Ursula Andress?'

'*Un*dress more like. Your luck is in, by crikey!'

'Howzit boys?' She gave a wide engaging smile as she walked up the beach towards them, speaking with a South African accent. The lines of windburn at the corners of her eyes stood out. She appeared to be in her early forties, but the wiry strength in her trim physique suggested she was a little younger. She had the face of a weathered Madonna, her eyes candid and engaging. 'How are things?'

'Good,' said Lennard. 'Welcome ashore. That's quite a body you've got there. I was going to say yacht, but why beat about the bush?'

She gave a peal of laughter. 'Thanks for the compliment, but I promise you it'll get you nowhere. Are you guys from the Pottery? I heard there were hand-made ceramics for sale here.'

'What did I tell you, bro?' Lennard chuckled.

'You doing some late Christmas shopping?' Stefan asked. He indicated the far end of the building to his right with his thumb. 'They're next door, but they don't open today.'

'Ceramics? What do you want with second-rate ceramics, sister? Now the brother here, he's got *exactly* what you're after, and more. First-class bracelets made of glass and semi-precious stones, rose quartz necklaces, citrine pendants, tiger eye anklets. Lucky charms to keep you safe when you're all at sea! You name it and he'll even knock you up something personal made to order and you can watch him make it. Check him over, his samples are inside. Show the lady your wares, bro.' He winked at Stefan. 'All of them.'

Stefan reached out a hand. 'I'm Stefan,' he said, 'Stefan Novak.'

'Mischa Kruger,' she took his hand, 'all the way from Durban and the Seychelles, but not in that order. And that's my faithful *Dromedary* out there.'

'Just call me Ace,' Lennard said, giving her a broad smile, 'all the way from up north around Kalbarri, a proud blackfella Australian Aboriginal, in that order.' Then he pointed at the yacht. 'The *Dromedary*? Strange choice of name. She doesn't look that ugly to me. You must have your reasons.'

'The ship of the desert?' suggested Stefan. 'Twin masts?'

'Yes, she's a ketch... and I named her after Jan van Riebeeck, actually. He sailed aboard the *Dromedaris* when he was first sent out from Holland to settle the Cape in 1652. That was the only name that rang true for me when I had her built.'

'So what are you? A solo yachtswoman sailin' round the world?' Lennard asked.

'More or less. This trip I sailed from New Zealand, Taranaki actually, and through the Torres Strait.' Her voice had a lilting quality to it, her liveliness arresting. 'I was heading home to Durban and called in to Mahé in the Seychelles to cruise the islands, waiting for the Trades to change. Just beautiful that was, so beautiful I overstayed and ran out of time. Now I'm on my way back to a teaching job in Auckland. My dog's in quarantine at the moment, up in Byford. Two more months to go.'

'What? They found him seasick and thought it was catching?' Stefan asked.

'Her, actually. Corryn. She came ashore with me on some of the islands so she has to do her time.'

Lennard nodded. 'That's Australia for you. They must suspect those tortoises over there are carrying some sort of rabies virus they don't want imported, the ones you saw frothin' at the mouth.' He placed a hand on Stefan's shoulder. 'Let's not stand around gettin' cold feet, bro. Let's show the lady here a good time, startin' with the best Arabica coffee she's ever tasted.'

Over coffee in the glassworks, Mischa asked if either of them knew of anyone with a room to let. She had a berth for the yacht at the Fremantle Yacht Club for the duration of the quarantine, she explained, but was yearning to spend some time ashore on solid ground. Stefan offered her the spare bedroom at his unit.

'I'll be no bother. It'll only be for two months and I can help with the rent. I'll keep out of your hair. I'll be working on the yacht most of the time anyway, and visiting Corryn whenever I can.'

'*You* no bother? It's not you I'd be concerned about.' Lennard grinned. 'It's the brother here. You've only just met him and he's been through a dry spell for the past year. You sure you can trust him?'

'Oh, I can trust *me*, Ace,' she said, flexing a bicep. 'First sign of any funny business and I'll have him flat on his back.'

'Way to go, sister. That he *will* enjoy!'

They both broke into laughter and Stefan, with a quiet smile, wondered what he'd let himself in for.

She moved in the same day. Stefan picked her up at the yacht club on the scooter. She was carrying a mountaineer's red backpack bulging at the seams. She was talkative and animated when she settled onto the pillion.

'It's chock full of photo albums I have to sort through,' she shouted in the slipstream as Stefan fought to keep the scooter upright on the turns. 'I want to submit some seascapes for a competition in Finland. It's closing in a month and I've got some classic underwater shots and others of a storm at sea. They'll give me something to bore you with in the evenings if we run out of conversation.'

That won't happen. Stefan smiled to himself. *She's talkative, this one. Probably comes from having only the dog to converse with.*

He grinned when she echoed his thoughts. 'It'll be nice having someone real to talk to, Stefan. I'm fed up with carrying on one-way chats with Corynn for days on end. I can never get any sense out of her.'

'You'll have to learn to bark. What breed is she?'

'Jack Russell. She's only a brick and a tickey high, but she's a real character and she is good company. I nearly lost her, though. She fell overboard twice in mid-ocean on the way here. The second time there was a real blow on. It was quite a strain getting back to her. I was *so* tempted to leave her to sink or swim.'

'How'd you get her back aboard?'

'Like a hooked trout, with a landing net. Just as well she's a strong swimmer with stamina to burn. She makes it look easy. She heads straight for the net. I sometimes wonder if she's just trying me on. Practicing canine lifeboat drills.'

That evening, they joined Lennard and his partner Alicia in their nearby house on Bellevue Terrace for dinner. Mischa and Alicia, both teachers in different fields and global travellers, shared an enthusiastic common bond, swapping stories about their academic interests and places both had visited.

Mischa brought them up to date with her cruise. She described a massive group of whale sharks she sailed among south of the Maldives. 'I counted more than a dozen. I dropped the sails and hung off a line at the stern as we drifted among them. Unreal, it was. Ah man, it was most *bakgat*, I tell you! They're usually so solitary.'

She described a disastrous stranding on a sandbank off West Island in the Aldabra Atoll when she thought she'd lose the boat. Her hour-long struggle neck-deep in water to free the ketch proved so strenuous and traumatic, her panic so all-engulfing, she found herself lactating a day later. 'All over myself, my boobs aching like you wouldn't believe.' She gently stroked her right breast. 'They leaked on and off for a couple of months after that but seem to have stopped for now. There's no sign of an abscess or cancer, thank God. They've given me a clean bill of health... and here I am.'

'Yes, here you are, indeed,' Stefan said. 'It seems you've dropped in and joined us at just the right time.'

'Isn't that interesting though, the timing?' She sent him a knowing look, her blue eyes sparkling. 'Most of my crockery gets smashed in a storm off Reunion Island on the way here and I need replacements, and when I swim ashore for them there you two are. My saviours, to be honest.'

Three days later, it was Mischa who proposed sleeping with him. Stefan had been concerned, wondering if she'd get round to it and hoping she wouldn't. His feelings for his absent partner Tania were still too raw. He recalled the warning she'd delivered about her combative reaction to the first sign of any funny business and took her at her word—she wasn't interested.

When she first moved in and they were getting used to one another, she was quiet and unobtrusive. She made a conscious effort to avoid being invasive. As the days passed, though, there were moments when he sensed a certain electric tension between them, a meaningful glance or a shared smile quickly cut short, and he suspected they were both behaving out of character. When she did eventually suggest it, he was aware it would never have occurred to him to put it so brazenly.

It was late evening. She was in the bathroom after a shower, a towel wrapped around her tucked at the shoulder. She appeared at the door.

'Stefan, I want to move in with you.'

'Move in? You have.'

'Don't play hard to get. Into your bedroom, into your bed.' He felt himself freeze and saw her smile. 'I think I should. It will do us both the world of good. No more pussy-footing around. It's been a long time for me and twice as long for you, you tell me.' She gave a gentle laugh. 'We're missing out. The world of sex is passing us by. Look, it's not as if it's going to be a permanent arrangement, just two months... and we've already wasted three days.'

He didn't reply, saw her frown and sensed her reading his silence. 'We should share something to remember each other by. I want to remember you and I hope you're not going to insult me by suggesting you want to forget me. Not yet, anyway.'

'It's not that,' he murmured.

'Then what?' Smiling uncertainly now, she walked across to him. 'I'm no spring chicken? All the more experience. I'll get pregnant? Not a chance. I'm carrying an STD? I'll sign a guarantee to the contrary.' She looked down at him thoughtfully. 'Or are you saving yourself for someone else? For the rest of your *life*? And you think making love to me will be some sort of transgression?'

With thoughts of Tania racing through his mind, he found the situation confronting. He had denied himself for so long since she walked out—and he'd declined the few temptations that came his way, his love for Tania overriding any impulse to take them up.

He wondered if this moment was another as the rising tension gripped him.

'You don't think I do this with every man I meet and you're just another, surely? Far, far from it. I'm choosy and you tick all the boxes.' She gave an infectious laugh as she leaned over and touched his shoulder. 'So far, that is. There's just one more tick to go.' He didn't react, a confused mix of emotions stifling him. Denial. Uncertainty. Rising desire.

'Are you attracted to me or not? You don't have to say. You can just nod or shake your head. Your look will tell me.'

He glanced up at her, feeling cornered for a moment, then gave her a sheepish smile.

'That wasn't the answer I wanted.' She turned back towards the bathroom. 'That was a yes *and* a no.'

Then, unable to control the impulse, he stood, turned her gently around and took her in his arms.

'You are lovely,' he whispered, 'just lovely.'

'That settles it then.' She tentatively kissed him, both hands on his shoulders, before settling into his lap when he sat down. Then she gave him a second kiss, joyful and uninhibited, and the physical intoxication of it carried them both away.

The next morning, relaxing naked at the window in the first rays of the sun, her skin aglow, she asked, 'So who's Tania? You were talking in your sleep.'

Leaning on an elbow, watching her, he responded, 'My ex. I hope I didn't keep you awake.'

'I was out like a light, but I woke early like I always do. I tend to sleep in shifts, one ear out for any change in the behaviour of the wind or the sea. But you sounded troubled, so I woke you. Do you remember the glass of water I brought in for you?'

'Vaguely.' He glanced at the empty glass on the bedside table. 'Yes. That was good of you.'

He silently recalled being pierced by unbearable regret the moment Mischa received him, an unexpected emotion so powerful and raw he felt riven, until moments later, a burst of joyous relief overwhelmed him.

She walked across to the bed and sat beside him, one leg tucked beneath the other. She stroked his hair. 'When you're ready, you can tell me about her. It sounded to me like you are damaged goods.'

'It hasn't been easy. It's like I'll never get over it.'

'I stirred up memories? That's bound to happen when the wounds run deep.' Her eyes filled with concern. 'It sounds as if it's going to take you quite a while.' She wrapped her arms around him and squeezed the breath out of him. 'I had no such worries. Trust me, you ticked that final box—and *twice*! That I did not expect. So let's get a good look at you.' She stood and, gripping the sheet, she pulled it slowly from the bed, leaving him naked, hands behind his head on the pillow.

'Gorgeous!' She said, kneeling beside him. She ran her hands down his flanks to his feet and began to drag him from the bed. 'Time we were up. It's a beautiful day outside. Let's not waste it.'

It took Stefan weeks before he opened up to her about Tania. Then one evening, with Mischa lying beside him after making love, her head resting on his shoulder and his right arm about her, the words welled up.

'I met her in Kyoto,' he began, 'in the foyer of the Granvia Hotel. I was stocking a glass cabinet there with samples of my jewellery and miniatures. Sales in Japan had got off to a flying start and I had contracts in different cities, including Nagasaki and Hiroshima, interestingly. I didn't know it, but the Aboriginal Bangarra dancers were in Tokyo presenting *Ochres* at the time. When I turned round after locking the cabinet, there she was, standing behind me with another dancer, admiring the collection of miniature crystal marsupials I'd made—koalas, bandicoots, numbats, bilbies.

'She told me they'd snuck a trip to Kyoto between performances and she'd admired the miniatures when she'd arrived two days before, surprised to find Aussie fauna there to welcome her. They were on their way to the station that morning and saw me arranging the display.

'She told me she was particularly taken with the little swamp wallaby. It had particular significance for her. I wasn't sure what she meant and was about to ask when she picked up her bags to leave. So on an impulse, I selected a wallaby from the two I had on display and gave it to her.

'It was the wrong move. She didn't have the money on her to pay for it and she refused to accept a gift from a complete stranger, fellow-Aussie or not. But she took my card and said she'd get in touch back in Melbourne. I didn't believe her, so I did the next best thing. I posted it to her via the Tokyo theatre with the message that payment wasn't necessary and returning it to me would be a disappointment.

'To cut a long story short, she turned up at my glass studio in Brunswick one morning to return it... and one thing led to another.'

He slowly shook his head. 'We were together for just over two years. I look back on them as the best of my life, even though the backside was falling out of my business. I was hopelessly undercapitalised. Customer interest was there, especially in the jewellery, but I couldn't produce enough to meet demand. I was a one-man-band trying to sound like a symphony orchestra. The biggest mistake I could make. What a disaster!

'Then it was compounded by Tania walking out on me a year ago. Without warning. She went,' he snapped a finger, 'like *that*, and my world fell apart.' An excruciating rush of bitterness and regret tore through him. 'The day she left she looked as if I'd driven a dagger through her. I had no idea what the problem was. I've been wondering ever since.'

Mischa turned and balancing with her elbows on each side of his chest, she looked into his eyes, and then leaned to kiss him on the forehead and the cheeks and at last on the lips. Then she clicked her tongue. 'My poor Stefan, let down by the woman who stole your heart. And you still don't know why she left?'

'Not for sure.'

'What were the signs? Were you getting along? Did you argue?' She dug him in the ribs with a forefinger. 'It couldn't have been the sex. I have no complaints.'

'She may have met someone else.'

'If she did, it would have been written all over her. You would have picked up on subtle changes in her behaviour she couldn't hide, those tell-tale hints and changes that surface once the lying begins. You'd have sensed it the first day she met him.'

'Or her.'

'Or her. But I doubt that if you were keeping her as satisfied as you are me.'

'And you me.'

She frowned thoughtfully. 'Was it the money, perhaps? She must have been concerned about your prospects.'

'Of course she was, but she was helping me deal with it.'

'Perhaps she made herself scarce to give you one less thing to worry about?'

'No, I can't believe that. She'd been very concerned and loyal up till then. If we were going down, she insisted we were going down together.'

'So what else was there?'

'I figured it may have been her brothers, Rex and Richie. The Aboriginal thing. The resentment and the misunderstanding. The first time I met them early in the piece it was a disaster. We spoke at cross-purposes and I was completely unprepared for the outburst they delivered at my expense—at my ignorance of their circumstances and apparent lack of concern for their history. Fortunately, Tania came to my rescue that afternoon, but the damage was done. Maybe she thought the bridges were beyond repair.'

'I doubt that, my dear,' Mischa said, 'but I completely understand. I was back home in Cape Town in 1990 when Nelson Mandela was released. I remember wiping off the spit when I was waiting for a bus. I still am, in a sense, waiting for that bus and wiping off the spit. It takes time to achieve reconciliation and make positive changes.'

'So it seems.' He looked thoughtfully up at her, wondering for a brief moment whether he should go on discussing issues he'd found so confronting, issues for which he had no answer.

Then he shook his head and plunged on, searching for the words. 'Tania had me reading up on her people's history before she left. She believed it would give me some insights and patch things up with her brothers, but I found it confusing and so far in the past it seemed pointless. My heart wasn't in it. And I know she was offended.'

He looked away as another surge of deep regret tore through his chest so that he could no longer speak. He fought to suppress it for several tense minutes, before he regained control. 'That was before I met Lennard,' he said at last.

Mischa nodded and stroked his hair. 'The white man built this country, made this nation what it is, so why don't you blacks snap out of it? The future beckons. Take responsibility. Assimilate. Don't waste our time or yours.'

'That's one way the argument runs,' Stefan replied, 'but now, here in Fremantle, in the glassworks with Lennard, I'm learning to see things in a very different light.' He paused, regathered his thoughts. 'I really don't know what else could have upset her. She wanted us to have a child, but that was out of the question with our bank balance in the red and she agreed to wait.'

'That must have concerned her. How old was she?'

'In her mid-twenties.'

'And you were what, in your late thirties? A twelve-year difference is not insurmountable.' She broke into a peal of laughter. 'Until you hit the slide in the sixties and she's in her sexy mid-forties and more demanding!'

Mischa sat up in the bed and looked down at him. 'Maybe she just wanted her freedom, Stefan. She's a dancer. She's used to expressing herself through her body, moving freely as she follows the choreography she's learned. She's disciplined but carried away in the flow of the moment. That must be as intoxicating as the ocean is for me. There are times when I simply have to up anchor and tear myself away, no matter how agonising the departure may be. Perhaps that's how she was feeling. She needed space. Time out to reassess things. And she couldn't talk to you about it because she didn't want to hurt you. In the end, she couldn't help it.'

She reached out and stroked his cheek. 'If that is the case, my friend, I think your luck is in. I think she'll come back to you as freely as she left once she regains her balance. I really do.'

Two weeks later, they joined Mischa as she motored out into the channel and set sail southwards for Albany and the eastern states. Lennard had arranged for a friend to follow them out in his centre console Quintrex to give them a lift back to the yacht club.

Out in Gage Roads, Corryn strutted up and down the deck re-establishing ownership over her territory, yapping excitedly at the choppy sea, putting it in its place. She was zipped up in a West Coast Eagles neoprene jumper designed for dogs her size, donated by Alicia.

'They didn't have one for the Western Bulldogs "Doggies"', she said to Corryn when they fitted it, 'so you'll have to make do with second best.'

'Oh, she's not fussy,' Mischa said, 'but I'm not sure she'll wear the beanie. I can see that going over the side first chance she gets.'

The wind was gusting, the engine doused and the mainsail partway up. Mischa gave Alicia and Lennard a spirited embrace before they disembarked, the Quintrex idling alongside.

'Thank you for everything you've done for the brother here,' Lennard said. 'We've noticed the changes, all for the better, by crikey.'

'No problem... I've enjoyed every minute,' Mischa said.

They climbed into the Quintrex as Mischa led Stefan down into the cabin, closing the door behind her.

She clung to him for several minutes.

Her voice tender and fighting back tears, she said, 'I thought I was the tough one and you were too sensitive, Stefan. *Now* look at me, would you? You know your friendship means a lot to me. I'm so grateful you've given me the last two months to hang on to.' She stroked his cheek. 'Be glad when Tania comes back. Forgive her. What you feel for her is very special and very rare. So don't be thin-skinned. Take whatever she offers you with both hands. You've done it before. Do it again. *Grab it!*'

She shook her head wildly as if to clear herself of feeling. 'Just listen to this sentimental old lady, would you? Come on now, she's got a boat to sail.'

Stefan reached out and wrapped his arms around her. 'I feel... how can I put this?'

'Don't embarrass me now...'

'I don't know. Blest, I think,' he said. 'That's the word for it. Truly blest. You've restored in me a belief in the possibility of happiness.'

'That's nice,' she whispered as he released her. 'It's such a pity we don't have time for one for the road, don't you think?'

'Next time, perhaps,' Stefan smiled back at her as he mounted the companionway to the cockpit, 'let's make that a promise.'

'No perhaps about it,' she replied as she followed him out into the sun and watched him step into the waiting boat. 'Now you've lifted the prohibition, happiness is not just a possibility, Stefan. It's a certainty.' Her departing smile was enigmatic. 'A certainty for both of us.'

For both of us? Looking at her as she waved and the Quintrex gathered speed, Stefan realised something he hadn't before: that she had never talked about herself, about her own relationships and the grief she may have been experiencing if they'd broken down.

What was it she'd said the night she moved in? *I need replacements, and when I swim ashore for them there you two are. Was it more than crockery that needed replacing?* He turned away and, smiling, looked towards the shore. *We struck a bargain between friends even if I didn't know it at the time, and that's enough.*

PART II

PRINCIPAL CHARACTERS APPEARING IN PART II
Also found in *The Truth & Reconciliation Trilogy*

<u>Lennard Currie</u>: An Australian Aboriginal glass sculptor with an international reputation. He is a member of the Malgana nation from Shark Bay in Western Australia.

<u>Rosalie O'Sullivan</u>: The love of Lennard's life.

<u>Alicia Serrano</u>: A highly qualified Mexican linguist and global traveller, who joins Lennard to assist in preserving the endangered Malgana language. She has a brother Andrés, father Victor and grandfather Cerrildo.

<u>Stefan Novak</u>: A skilled glass technician, who works with Lennard on his glass sculpting projects and commissions.

<u>Tania Tibora</u>: Stefan's Australian Aboriginal partner and leading dancer with the Bangarra, Yajarlu and Wirruwana Dance Groups, with brothers Rex and Richie in Cairns.

<u>Gerrit de Waal</u>: A senior carpenter shipwright who survived the wreck of the *Zuytdorp* on the cliffs north of Kalbarri in June 1712, and lived among the Malgana people.

<u>Sunil Dewaraja</u>: A Ceylonese apprentice carpenter, who survived alongside Gerrit.

Tania's Secret

MELBOURNE, 24 DECEMBER 1997. Tania was halfway through the door that afternoon when Stefan returned with the last-minute shopping for the Christmas lunch he'd promised to cook for her. In his other hand, he held a bunch of her favourite carnations.

She was standing in the open doorway, her green Adidas sports bag in one hand and her favourite bonsai plant—a Moreton Bay Fig tree her mother had planted in 1970 to celebrate the day she was born—balanced in the crook of her other arm.

She stepped back to let him in. He saw that she'd been weeping.

'Hello, sweetie,' he said, surprised and concerned. 'You on your way out?'

Her eyes widened and slid away across his shoulder as she glanced into the corridor, before gazing back at him. 'I'm taking time out. I need some space,' she stammered hoarsely.

A burst of shock tore through him. 'You're *leaving*?'

His question hung unanswered as the charged silence lengthened between them.

Stunned, his mind raced. *Is she bored with me? Is she going walkabout to recover between Yajarlu dance assignments? If that's the case, she would have said so, surely.*

'Why?' he gasped as confusion overtook him. *Is it the failure of my crystal ware business? Is it the age difference between us? Is she leaving me for another man, younger maybe, with better prospects? Or a woman? Is it her Aboriginality and the unexpected disagreement I had with her brothers? Or perhaps my point-blank refusal for us to have the child she craves? Not right now, not while I'm facing bankruptcy.*

Her reply stunned him.

'I'm not sure when I'll be back,' she said. 'Or if... and there's no point explaining why. I've arranged for Alexa to pick up the rest of my gear on Boxing Day.'

'*Alexa* had a hand in this?' he snapped.

'No! This is my decision. Mine alone.'

He could barely breathe, the sense of dread at losing her overpowering. 'So you're leaving me for dead?'

'No. I'm leaving you for life.'

'What's that supposed to mean?'

She frowned and pursed her lips. 'Never mind.'

'It's a simple question.'

'With a complicated answer.'

Can I prevent her leaving? Force her back into the unit to fill me in and reconsider?

After a moment's charged silence, 'Does for life mean for good?' he asked.

'For my good, yes. You wouldn't understand.'

'Try me.'

'It's too personal.'

He lifted the bag of groceries and the carnations, which she hadn't acknowledged. His sudden gesture barely missed her face and she shuddered back with a sharp intake of breath as though he'd slapped her. The rich whiff of Lion's Christmas fruitcake added to the cinnamon fragrance of the flowers. 'Nice timing, Tan. It's Christmas Eve, for Christ's sake. We can't waste these.'

While her expression softened, her voice retained its scathing edge. 'I'm sorry it doesn't suit you.'

'My oath it doesn't suit me.'

'I'm not under house arrest,' she snapped, her tongue a scalpel now, her eyes alight and unflinching.

Then she leaned forward and kissed him on the cheek before stepping back and waiting expectantly for him to move aside. He hesitated before doing so, but she brushed past him.

'Look on the bright side,' she said, looking back from the passageway, 'now you're free and so am I. It's not your fault. It's mine.'

Her eyes brimmed. He dropped the flowers and groceries and moved towards her as if stumbling down an unseen step in pitch darkness, but she shied away and shook her head. 'Not now!'

Then she was gone, her sandals echoing down the stairwell.

Stung, he fought the urge to call her back. After several moments of shocked bewilderment, he checked the empty corridor before closing the door. He cursed himself for failing to read the signs. *What signs, for God's sake?*

Overcome with a sickening foreboding, he looked down at her from the balcony as she walked across the courtyard, the eccentric combination of her bonsai and gym bag lending her the forlorn appearance of someone homeless carting all she valued to the next night's shelter under a forgotten bridge.

'At least tell me where I can contact you,' he called out. 'Don't leave things like this.'

She didn't reply, but before she turned the corner, she slowed and glanced back. She nodded and he waved in return, a surge of hope racing through him.

In that frozen moment, he saw a Sikh couple hesitate at the courtyard entrance, alerted by his shout. Both glanced at Tania, then up at him. They stopped, then the man murmured something, and they resumed their walk, the woman's face framed in the cyan shimmer of her flower-patterned sari looking back at Tania.

For one dizzying instant, he imagined Tania reflected in her gaze and the crazy hope arose that she might turn and bar her way, prevent her departure and convince her to return to him.

But no, they disappeared in different directions among the passers-by.

A crushing weight descended as she vanished, and it dawned on him how much he was going to miss her, how much he relied on her being around. Two years of happiness had been snuffed out and he hadn't seen the writing on the wall.

Struggling to save his crystal ware business over the past few months, he hadn't given her the attention she deserved. Had he taken her so much for granted that now she'd turned her back on him?

He filled a vase from the kitchen tap, set it on the balcony table and stood the carnations in it, still bound by a twisted green rubber band. They'd be visible from the street.

That evening when he searched the flat, he found she'd sorted all her gear from his, down to their collection of tapes and CDs, to make it easy for Alexa. He noticed that she'd set aside the tape of one of their favourite films, *Three Colours: Blue*, for him. It was the last one they'd watched together. And she'd left him the exquisite mobile of blue crystals that he'd made for her, identical to the one in the film. It was still hanging in their bedroom. *At least she did that*, he thought resentfully.

On her dressing table, he discovered the crystal bird of paradise pendant he'd made for her when they'd first moved in together. He'd spent days designing and sculpting it and she'd raved over it, rarely going out without wearing it. It lay with the silver chain coiled beside it, as though dropped there as a hasty afterthought. Or was it? Wasn't it a clear signal she was done with him? Another deliberate gesture, like the bonsai, to drive the point home.

He hunted desperately for the charm bracelet he'd fashioned for her birthday a year before. It was his business stock in trade and he'd added elements to it month by month, twelve abstract shapes in shimmering glass combined with fragments of a range of precious and semi-precious stones, each charm commemorating meaningful moments in the progress of their lives together. *They're my speaking stones*, she'd told him, a memory behind each. It seemed she'd taken that with her.

Nor did he find a farewell note of explanation. *Did she write one? If I hadn't turned up when I did, was she going to slip it beneath the door as she closed it behind her?*

For several days, he contacted her family and friends without success, until at last her brother Richie rang to confirm that she'd arrived home in Cairns.

'She's decided to break off all ties with you,' he said. 'She's been invited to Brazil to work with the *Sapatos Alados* Dance Theatre in Belo Horizonte.'

'So *that's* the reason she walked out?' Stefan snapped. They had previously offered her a contract to work on a production before she met him and it had taken him an agonising week to change her mind and move in with him instead. 'When did they invite her back?'

'They called her yesterday. She's in two minds, but we're advising her to take the opportunity.'

'*Of course you are!*' Stefan shouted after a stunned pause. 'Thank you very much, Richie, I appreciate your interference.'

'Hey! Try me, why don't you? I swear I'll take out a restraining order on her behalf if you make a move in her direction—'

Shaking with rage, Stefan slammed down the phone.

Later, when he'd calmed down, he knew he must resign himself to her decision. Had she stayed it would have been against her will. Added to his financial troubles, her ill-timed desertion which, in his bitterness, he judged a betrayal, was unbearable, but he knew that worse was to come. When she moved to Brazil, she'd deliver the eighty-first blow, the most stinging of them all—and he'd know that their relationship was over.

Out on the balcony barbecue, he deep-fried some hash brown *latkes* and heated three doughnut *bimuelos* he'd found in the fridge, washing them down with a last half glass of wine before the reek of mozzarella and pepperoni scorching in the ovens of the pizzeria across the courtyard drove him indoors.

Later, when he cleared the debris from the balcony table, the central candle in the *menorah* candlestick waned, then flickered out. Had Tanya's love for him as well? She'd done a runner and wouldn't be back anytime soon. *If ever, for God's sake!*

He reached for the wilting carnations, shook the water from their stems and flung them into the bin.

Four years later, in the beachside cottage in Merimbula, Stefan woke to the shriek of gulls quarrelling over a chunk of bread thrown by a small girl walking along the embankment. She was towing a grizzled black-and-tan dachshund on a red lead.

He poured himself a coffee, walked out and sat at the table on the veranda, watching them pass, as other screeching gulls joined the aerial bombardment, until one more agile than the rest beat a retreat with the scrap in its beak, the flock in tumultuous pursuit.

He recalled the afternoon months ago when his glass sculptor friend Lennard had said he had a message for him. He'd guided him to the bench outside the glassworks on Bathers Beach in Fremantle, where Stefan had been assisting him since his bankruptcy.

'You may wanna hear this,' Lennard had said, 'or you may not. We've had word from Richie. Tania's back. She's been back for months. She's in Sydney, working on the opening ceremony for the Olympic Games.'

Stefan had taken a sharp breath, staring at him in silence before asking, 'Doing what exactly?'

'She's assisting Bangarra with the choreography of one of the segments. She may be appearing with the dancers, apparently. He didn't go into detail.'

'Why did he call you?'

'He knows you're working for me. He wanted to suss out how you're feeling about her these days.'

'What business is that of his?'

'Take it easy, bro. I guess he's concerned you'll find out she's back and may give her a hard time. He said he doesn't want you to contact her till after the ceremony... if you're going to.'

'Did he, now? Not much chance of that. Too much water under the bridge. I know where I stand. She's got my number and she hasn't called.' Then, after a moment's thought, 'Ah, good luck to her. Tell him I said that if he rings again.'

'No problem. So that's it?'

'That's it.'

'You sure?'

'Never been surer, even if it's taken me four years.' Then he'd conceded with a shrug, 'If she *does* call, I won't slam down the phone.'

Lennard had looked steadily at him with a bemused look. 'I'll pass that on when he rings back.'

Her call had come through to him a week after the Olympic Games closing ceremony and her terse first words echoed in his memory, 'It's me, Stefan. I'd like to see you. Are you open to that?'

'Of course,' he said, barely able to breathe.

'Can we meet on neutral ground?'

He struggled with the words. 'I'm going to Merimbula next week. To the cottage. I've booked it for a fortnight. I know it's not neutral ground—'

'That'll do,' she said, breaking in.

'So... shall I book you in?'

'No. I'll make the booking myself. I'll stay up in the boarding house. We can take things from there.'

'Let me know when you're arriving.'

'I will,' she said, and rang off

Tomorrow she'll be here, he thought, a tremor of excitement racing through him. *This time I have to make it work. How much has she changed? Is she on the rebound? How long will we spend treading on eggshells, feeling each other out?* He frowned at the thought of misreading the signs. *I can't lose her for the second time. Not again.*

His apprehension and excitement at meeting her again switched to a sudden, burning sense of outrage as the violent argument that erupted years ago with Tania's brothers the first time he met them in Cairns flashed across his mind.

Tania had warned him that past injustices were sensitive issues for many of her extended family, who still blamed their present deprivation and lack of opportunity on their forebears' dispossession and displacement during the past two centuries, and he ducked for cover when her brothers unexpectedly confronted him with their people's history a few days into his visit.

He couldn't share their indignation when it surfaced.

He and Tania had only recently moved in together in Melbourne and he didn't yet feel that he belonged. He was an outsider, and white, unfamiliar with the reasons for their deeply rooted resentment and deep down he felt it wasn't his concern.

Unsettled by the bluntness of their questions and alarmed by their rancour, he'd stifled his disquiet and tried unsuccessfully to deflect the grilling when they ambushed him—and then he'd done his best to conceal his embarrassment when they'd greeted his hesitant neutrality with uproarious hilarity, verging on insult.

'So you're not sure where you stand, my white brother,' Richie, the older of the two, snarled sarcastically, 'or what to believe? Is that why you're livin' in *our country* rent-free like you own the fuckin' place and never signed a lease?'

Disturbed by Richie's goading smile, Stefan responded, 'If it's land you're concerned about, you've won the rights to native title. Mabo's a step in that direction.'

'Not before time!' Richie fired back.

'That may be, but it is the right move, isn't it? Overturning the principle of *terra nullius* means a rewrite of our history and the law. What more can I say?'

Rex, the younger brother, gave a sardonic snort. 'More? I'll give you more.' His flinty stare was relentless. 'What about the rights to a longer life expectancy and better health? What about the rights to a treaty? Or better still, the rights to an apology and compensation to make up for what our people suffered in the past?'

Stefan, alarmed, had replied, 'It's the truth about the suffering in the past I'm not so sure about. I'll admit to my ignorance, not just about the facts, but more about how the hell you expect me to respond this late in the day.'

Richie braced his fisted knuckles on the table and leaned forward. 'That's big of you,' he growled. Their glances connected and the mix of derision and outrage Stefan had read there dismayed him. 'You admit you know next to nothin'. You don't know how to respond because it's all in the past, so you won't. That's weak as piss.'

'That's not what I said.'

'Well now, that's what I heard.' Richie stared him down with ill-disguised contempt. 'It's not your history, so why dwell on it? You're allergic to the facts like most of your mob or you just don't give a shit. It *is* your history, let me tell you. It's *our* history, you and me both. We share it. It's no good turnin' a blind eye. We need to own it, all us mob.'

'And own *up* to it bro, not forgettin' that,' Rex broke in.

'Too right. We need to acknowledge it and we're runnin' out of time. Besides,' Richie persisted with rising passion, 'we don't get a re-run so we can fix things up, more's the pity!'

'If you say so.'

'If *we* say so?' Richie's humourless smile held menace. 'Sittin' on the fence is dangerous, Stefan. Up there you're a target for two bullets.'

Stefan hadn't responded. He'd felt cornered, caught off guard, and the look that passed between the brothers told him they thought they'd sized him up and were about to hang him out to dry, scornful of his uncertainty. They took his ignorance for denial. Their sister's partner was another whitefella who refused to look Australia's history in the eye.

Then Tania had appeared at the door, four glasses and a frosted bottle of Kola Beer on a tray. She leaned against the door frame and clicked her tongue in defiant disapproval that silenced them all.

'This is no way to treat a guest in our house,' she said, 'talking so hot to him.'

She set the tray firmly on the table, gave Stefan a glance of reassurance and dived in spiritedly as she unscrewed the bottle cap. 'Who are you to think Stefan doesn't understand what youse are on about?' She put a protective arm around his shoulder as she poured the frothing drink, her voice calm at first, but her anger rising. 'You think he doesn't feel outrage at injustice? You think we're the only ones who've been through hard times? Don't think that for a moment. He's *Jewish*, for God's sake.'

She recapped the bottle and glanced keenly from one brother to the other as she slid full glasses across the table. 'Just because he doesn't see things our way doesn't mean he hasn't got a conscience and imagination. He has his convictions.' Then the tone of her voice lightened and her expression changed from suppressed fury to amusement, her eyes lighting up. 'He has his convictions, but unlike youse two bludgers, that doesn't mean he's done time in the Lotus Glen lockup.'

Both brothers looked sharply at her, smiled, and then burst into laughter.

'Don't you knock it, Tanny,' Rex conceded. 'We've got reservations in the Glen for whenever we need a break from the likes of you on your high horse givin' us a tongue lashing.'

'Oh yeah,' Richie added acerbically, 'us blackfella brothers, that's one of our privileges. We've got the penthouse fuckin' suite, with silk sheets in the fart sack and five-star service guaranteed.' He laughed again. 'Even a good screw when we need one.'

The tension subsided as the three erupted into laughter that Stefan, perplexed, hadn't shared. Mortified and thankful for Tania's support, he'd reached across to take the hand she offered him. She'd done the business, even though he felt that in his case she was a little wide of the mark.

'I'm Jewish, yes,' he broke in, 'but I'm second-generation true blue, born and bred in Geelong.' He waved a hand in a placatory gesture. 'I know I need to get a fix on all you've said. I don't think it hurts to admit I don't know enough to understand it yet. I need your stories. They'll give me the history.'

'No good runnin' before you can walk,' Rex commented. Then he'd grinned, sat down at the table and reached for his glass. He raised it towards Stefan and Tania, and then extended his forefinger, shaking it. 'You can count yourself lucky, with the sister here for backup. Welcome to this side of the fence where the grass is browner, the way we're used to it, the way you whitefellas think we deserve it when push comes to shove.' He gave a quick assertive nod, his dreadlocks swishing across his shoulders. '*Mi casa*, *su casa*, and that includes a private room in Lotus Glen. Give us the word. We'll book you in there with us and throw away the key. You'll find out how the other half lives.'

Stefan had later learned that neither brother had in fact been sentenced to the correctional centre. Tania had defused the argument by poking fun at their expense and they'd picked up on her cue and blindsided him.

From then on during the visit he'd sharpened his awareness, determined to read more clearly the freighted subtexts in their exchange of insults to allay his feelings of anxious disadvantage.

When he'd asked Tania if the vitriol they'd displayed had been genuine or a ploy to wind him up, she confirmed it was a bit of both. 'We may laugh a lot, but that doesn't always clean the slate. Like Richie says, we laugh at you whitefellas when you blame *us* for what *you've* done to us and then expect us to beg for your forgiveness, but that's one time our laughter's driven by our anger.'

Blaming the victim. It had taken Stefan a moment to unravel the irony in what she'd said and he'd never forgotten it.

The following day, the sound of the approaching plane roused Stefan, waiting on the steps to the airport arrival hall.

He leapt to his feet, his heart pounding. He shaded his eyes, scanning the sky as the Twin Otter swung low across the airport buildings before roaring in above the trees, the engine reaching a crescendo as it touched down and bounced into view at the far end of the runway.

It took an eternity to taxi to the apron and glide to a halt. The door swung down and the pilot climbed sideways down the stairs, followed by the first of the passengers.

Tania was the third to appear. Squinting in the sunlight, she raised a hand to shade her eyes, saw Stefan, waved and climbed down the steps. On the bitumen, she turned back to the doorway. She raised her arms to a dark-haired girl of three or four in a green t-shirt and denim dungarees. The child hesitated before reaching to grasp Tania's hands. She swung herself out and wrapped her legs around Tania's waist, her arms about her shoulders. Tania lowered her to the ground and walked towards Stefan, holding the child by the hand.

Stefan's heart lurched in his chest as they approached. Shock, surprise and the beginnings of elation raced through him. *My daughter?* The possibility was disorienting and electrifying. He sensed his life changing track as Tania reached the gate.

'Hello, Stefan,' she said as they embraced and broke apart. 'I'd like you to meet Kylie.' She looked down at the girl. 'Kylie, *este e Stefan, sui pai.*' Then she translated, 'This is Stefan, your papa.'

Kylie looked up at him, her dark brown eyes solemn and apprehensive, her black hair ribboned with green silk over each ear, ponytails hanging to her shoulders, her skin a deep olive gold.

'*Ola, Pai,*' she murmured, and when Tania nudged her, she gave a shy, gap-toothed smile. 'Hello, Papa.'

Speechless, Stefan squatted and took her in his arms before releasing her and holding her at arm's length so they could examine one another. He slowly shook his head as he gazed at her and she, confused and timid, looked up at Tania for reassurance.

'You are beautiful, just beautiful,' he whispered, and gently enfolded her in his arms once again.

'It's all right, Stefan. She won't break,' Tania said.

He felt his child's heartbeat against his own and, for one blinding moment, the thought occurred that had Tania hinted four years ago that this racing pulse was beginning to beat deep within her, he'd have passed sentence and insisted she extinguish it.

'Her Portuguese is better than her English at the moment,' Tania said. She placed a hand on his shoulder and he looked up. 'She's the only reason I left you when I did. Having her was a decision we couldn't agree on or forgive each other for at the time.' She gazed at him as though searching for the words. 'I know I should have told you about her. I shouldn't have kept her secret, but the timing never seemed right.' She gave him a quiet smile, a mix of apology and relief. 'Now you know.'

Stefan stood and put his arms about her, the confusing possibility striking him that she may have been aware of her situation the last time they'd been on holiday in Merimbula and kept it from him. Remorse and concern gripped him as he imagined what she must have gone through in the three months before Christmas.

He took both her hands. 'I can promise you this, Tan. Things are very different now.' He looked down, enthralled. 'My God! She's perfect.' He knelt and wrapped Kylie in his arms once more, fighting back tears. 'This has to be our happiest moment.'

Kylie folded into him and gave the lightest of smiles, which he took as her responding to the novelty of his closeness.

Now Tania had returned, bringing Kylie to him.

Their child, who had swum in his company that afternoon, her arms about his neck as he'd towed her through the water. She'd leapt from the end of the pontoon into his arms, her face shining with confidence, her body gleaming.

He stood and reached for the mobile of blue crystals that he, Tania and Kylie had spent time hanging in the cottage that evening. Once it was up, they'd left him to go back to the boarding house at the top of the dune behind him, where Tania had booked herself in.

He touched an outer string to set it swinging, its delicate tinkling accompanying the slap of wavelets on the beach. As he listened, the final scene of *Three Colours: Blue* came back to him, haunting and obsessive, the sounds of the chorale Julie had completed for her dead composer husband pouring through his mind.

He looked out across the sea as the memory of glorious voices in crescendo overwhelmed him, *Though I speak with the tongues of angels, if I have not love, I am become as hollow brass. Though I have the gift of prophecy and understand all mysteries and all knowledge, if I do not have love, I am nothing.*

Then he walked out to the pontoon and stood contemplating the water. True, Tania had brought Kylie to meet him. And she seemed pleased to see him, appeared comfortable in his presence, appreciative of his interaction with Kylie and her response to him. He saw that she was composed, self-contained and stronger than before. She still had a measure of reserve though, as if she was withholding something of herself from the world, something essential, waiting for her moment.

Has her love for me lessened? he wondered. *Has it leached away?*

The thought alarmed him. He turned and looked back up at the boarding house. Her second-storey window was lit, the curtains drawn. He saw a shadow move across the screen before the light went out.

Or did I imagine it?

He stood abandoned on the jetty in the darkness, momentarily disoriented.

Then, as he walked back to the cottage, his senses returned—the strong night scent of the Kiss Me Quick Brunfelsia bushes and the smoky hint of barbecues, the water shifting and bubbling against the jetty pylons, the play of cold air against his back so that he vigorously rubbed his arms to clear the gooseflesh.

And there, at the top of the dune, he saw a figure detach itself from the darkness and take the first careful step down towards him.

.

Welcome To Country

ROSALIE HAD NEVER BEEN further north than Gin Gin before, an hour's drive from Perth. She was amazed as the country first opened up and she and Lennard swept through it on the motorbike, but when they reached the rolling red sandplains of Eneabba and beyond, she found herself fighting her growing alarm at the emptiness, at the sweep of a cloudless sky in which the sun blazed. The landscape seemed somehow malevolent and hostile, the strangely twisted and stunted trees, blasted by the wind, growing parallel to the ground.

She felt vulnerable and estranged, as though she didn't belong, and she was uncharacteristically dispirited when they arrived at Wanamalu six hours later. But not for long. Lennard's mother, Mary, buxom, silver-haired and smiling, welcomed them both in a matriarchal embrace, while his father Andy stood back and watched her with a bemused and patient here-she-goes-again look on his face.

'Ah, Lennie, welcome home,' she said, before releasing him and turning to Rosalie, holding her at arm's length and gazing deep into her eyes as she bubbled with good humour. 'And *you*, Rosie, here at last and not a moment too soon. Now let this old girl take a real good look at you... *oh, yes*! *Now* I can see why you bowled my boy over. Everything Lennie boy has told us about you is right on the money.' She wrapped her arms around Rosalie and gave her a long-lasting, tight hug that left Rosalie peering in pleasurable surprise over her shoulder, giggling up at Lennard.

When she released her, Mary placed both hands on her shoulders, gazing at her once again as she shook her head and clicked her tongue. 'So what's our Lennie been feedin' you, girl? Birdseed? You're a skinny one and that won't do. Not out here in the country with the big sky, where the winds will blow you away given half a chance. We're goin' to have to put some flesh on your bones. Some *guga*. Some meat. Startin' right now.' She gave a burst of laughter. 'In all the right places of course. Come on into the house for a cuppa. I've got some fruitcake and damper I've baked for you both. Country style... never mind the calories.'

The rest of the afternoon and evening slipped quickly by. Rosalie was dazed as Mary submitted her and Lennard to a barrage of questions interspersed with good-hearted laughter that went on well into the night.

Lennard's father, Andy, was the quiet one, contributing a terse comment to the conversation every now and then. Rosalie observed him watching her with appreciative shrewdness through the evening as he turned kangaroo steaks sizzling on the smoky barbecue, giving her a knowing wink as the night wore on and Mary embarked on yet another anecdote that was news to Lennard.

The next day, at Mary's invitation, Rosalie rode one of the horses with her down to the largest of the freshwater pools beside the Hutt lagoon.

'I wanna welcome you to country, Rose,' she'd said the night before, and Rosalie had wondered if she'd sensed her feeling threatened and alienated during the journey north.

They stood on a rock platform at the water's edge, the wind gusting, Mary's unruly hair a whirling silver mane. 'This is my special place. It changed my life when I was very young. Let's you and me share my story.'

She sank to the rock, her legs crossed and her elbows on her knees. With a gesture of her right hand, she invited Rosalie to sit. 'But first,' she said, 'I'll introduce you to this place and let the ancestors know we're here. Pay them our respects.'

She looked up at the limestone bluff and then quietly sang for several minutes. Her voice was high-pitched and rhythmic, the melody shifting across two simple notes as though climbing and descending across an imaginary landscape. Rosalie found her chanting strangely soothing and the intonation other-worldly.

The song ended and, in the silence, Rosalie asked, 'Was that Malgana?'

'No, this is Nhanda country, girl, so that's the language here.' She pointed northwards. 'We sing the same song in Malgana over there when we're crossin' Andy's country. Country gives you your language and with it, your voice.'

'You mean the naming of ten thousand things?'

Mary smiled brightly, her eyes sparkling. 'That's it, girl. Our Dreamtime creator singin' the world into existence. We all need a voice to keep the land alive and talk to the ancestors in languages they understand. Even you.'

She held her right hand out, fingers clenched, before opening up each finger in turn as though revealing something hidden in her fist. Then she held it out, palm up, and with the forefinger of her left, she traced the line of a pale scar curving across it from the webbing to the wrist. She showed her other palm. It was diagonally scarred as well, a ridge that ran across the web of palm lines as though cancelling them out.

'Onslow Hospital,' she said simply. 'I was hidin' under there when I was twelve.' She rubbed her palms, flexed her fingers and then placed her hands on her knees. 'You shoulda seen me! I was hangin' on to them floorboards like a goanna up a tree! I wasn't givin' up without a fight. When they dragged me out, kickin' and screamin', I didn't know them nails were stickin' through. All these other lines here tell my fortune, but these two scars? Well, girl, they tell my *story*.'

In 1934, just after a devastating cyclone that all but flattened Onslow, she went on, she'd scuttled under the timber floors of the hospital to escape patrol officers who'd arrived to take her and her half-caste brothers away. She'd sprinted to the hospital from the Masonic Hall, where she'd sheltered with her mother and her brothers for three days until the winds blew themselves out.

'Our tents on the reserve, they were blown halfway to Africa,' she said. 'The jetty, it was gone, with half the buildings in the town. When it was all calmed down, the officers came for me and my two brothers. Out of nowhere, they came. We got no warnin' so we didn't expect them.

'When we saw the truck arrive, my mum and me, we knew what they were after. She sent me out the back way and I gave them the slip, but they tracked me down. They grabbed me by the ankles and dragged me out from under there. So I was taken away as well.' Then she giggled. 'You should have seen that one officer, though. That officer Amos. He was the one I'd always liked up till then. His clothes, his face, even his glasses so he could hardly see, they were covered with my blood. You shoulda seen me slappin' him around!'

She'd heard the screams of her mother mingle with her own as she was dragged into the blinding sunlight, her last jolting image of her mother glimpsed through the slats of the Reo cattle truck carrying her to the tender that would take them to the MV *Koolinda*, anchored beyond the remains of the jetty.

'When we got to Perth, I was one of the first put into Sister Kate's home. That was the year it opened.' She said that she and Lennard had found her name recorded in one of the archival ledgers there a few years ago, and he had photographed the entry.

'Lennard told me about the time you spent in Sister Kate's,' Rosalie said. 'He showed me that photo when we were looking through his album back in Fremantle.'

They'd been sitting on the back veranda looking out at

the ocean one afternoon a few days after she'd moved in with him. He had opened up the album on the table between them and had worked his way through the family shots, introducing Mary and Andy and his extended family of uncles, aunts and many cousins to her.

Towards the end, he'd come across the photo of Mary's ledger entry.

Name (Christened): Mary McDonnell.
Name (Aboriginal): Mary.
Arrival: 16 June 1934.
Registration Number: 0011.
Sex: Female.
Date of birth: Unknown, age twelve (approx.)
Language: Yamaji.
Origin: Onslow—arrived aboard *Koolinda*.
Health: Undernourished, sepsis in cuts on hands,
            stitches for removal.
Allocation: Myola Cottage.

Rosalie frowned as she struggled to recall the details. 'If I remember rightly, it said you spoke Yamaji? I thought Lennard said it should have been Malgana.'

'Hey, you're a smart one! No, they got my language wrong. Malgana, that's Andy's language. I spoke Yarnarri at the time. That's a dialect of Kurrama, but they wouldn't have had a clue about that, so we can forgive them.' She looked across the lagoon towards the Shoal Point dunes. 'They took me away so I wouldn't be brought up Aboriginal, but little did they know, I already *was* one. I was twelve, you see. I was older than the others, so they were too late.'

'How long were you in Sister Kate's?' Rosalie asked.

'Until I was fifteen; three years, but less if you count the times I ran away and was brought back. My brothers, they were sent to New Norcia. Things were different for them there. Things were harder. More discipline, more religion pumped into them poor little tackers by those Spanish monks with the cane in their hands.

'For all of us, speakin' language was forbidden, you know? After a while, I got real rusty, but my English was all right. What I did remember all that time was my memories of bein' happy in Onslow. Livin' on the reserve, sure, that had been hard, livin' in a tent and sometimes sleepin' down the beach in summer with the sandflies. It hadn't bothered me, but. They were good days, fishin' and crabbin' and all that. Maybe I didn't know any better, so who cared? Not me!'

'So what happened?' Rosalie reached out impulsively for Mary's hand and held it in both of hers.

'It all worked out. It always does when you've got patience, and me, I can be patient, girl. I'll hang in there till doomsday when I'm after something, doesn't matter what. Just watch me!' She gave an exuberant laugh, each exhalation succeeded by an asthmatic indrawn wheeze. 'What's that word describes it?'

'Tenacious?'

'Stubborn. I'm stubborn. Tenacious too, especially when I'm playin' cards. Never take me on, Rosie, let me tell you. With my talent, I'll whip you every time. You'll end up broke.'

'I'm broke already, but I'll keep that in mind.'

'Anyhow, the way it all turned out, I came back to Sister Kate's three years later to live there for the second time. A glutton for punishment, I was. I looked after those little kids while I was trainin' to become a teacher's aide at Claremont College. Those little *yamba*, those little ankle-biters, we used to scrub them in the bath with bars of Mitchell's wool fat soap. You ever hear of that?'

'No, it's new to me.'

'Well, it didn't sting like carbolic, so we used it on them. I can still smell the lanolin. And taste it! Oh yes, and I can taste the carbolic too! I remember that. There was this one house where the matron used to lather out my mouth with it every time I swore at her in Yarnarri. I never forgot the swear words! And you know what?' Her glance was mock-serious. 'That carbolic taste got me through my teacher training. I only had to think of it and my English was word-perfect.'

'So your memories of Sister Kate's, were they positive?'

She raised her eyebrows. 'You take the good with the bad, Rosie. Let's just say they weren't as bad as some people make out. But you know the worst? Apart from losin' my family, the worst was the shame I'd never felt before and couldn't understand. Why was I there? Had I done somethin' wrong? Had I broken some *wajbala* law? I felt like I was to blame, but I had no idea what for.'

Her voice rose. 'Look, don't get me wrong. I wasn't stupid. I knew 'bout the colour of my skin. I was old enough to know that. It wasn't anything I'd *done* that was wrong, it's what I *was*! I was white and I was black at the same time. My mother'd told me 'bout my father runnin' off from Yangkalinha Station, and he was white. I knew that. So the idea sank in that I wasn't white enough.'

She nudged Rosalie, her eyes twinkling, the lids almost closed and her face a riot of wrinkles cobwebbed every which way. 'You know somethin'? One time when they told me to scrub myself in the bath I asked if they wanted me to scrub out the black. I did! I was riled. "Then I will!" I screamed at them and I started scrubbin' and scrubbin' until I bled. And *that* upset them, I can tell you. They had to stop me.

'They expected a tame one, but I was wild. I was hangin' on to my dignity, showin' them the black was there for keeps.' She rocked back and forth. 'I took them on because I wouldn't let them break me, Rose. They thought they'd turn me into a housemaid tame enough to clean their houses in Nedlands and Peppermint Grove. Me? Wait on *them* hand and foot?

Never! They did help me get through the teacher training, but. And I'm grateful for that.'

'Did you see your mother again?' Rosalie asked.

'Oh, that was easy. I saw her every day.' She gave a secretive smile and tapped her forehead. 'In my mind, see. We never had nothin' in Onslow, but we did have this old car. It was a Buick, parked up in the Onslow dump. I can still remember it like it was yesterday. Paint peelin' off it. Dark red it was, but eaten through with rust, with just the engine block sittin' under the bonnet.'

'Did it go fast?' Rosalie asked, smiling.

Mary squeezed Rosalie's hand and bellowed with laughter. 'Eight straight, that engine, and let me tell you, girl, she was red so she went like the wind! On an empty tank and nothin' but three rims and one flat old worn-out, white-walled tyre!

'My mum used to take us kids down there and we'd squat on those mouldy purple leather seats with the redback spiders and the springs showin' through, my mother hangin' on the steerin' wheel and my brothers makin' engine noises in the dickey seat whenever we went ridin' down the highway to Perth or paid a visit to our family in the desert.'

Her laughter subsided. 'So, yes, girl, I saw my mother every day. Her and me and the boys, in that old wreck. And I talked to her, too, lookin' out through that cracked windscreen I told her everything. And every day I used to hear her promise me she'd start that car and come and fetch me.'

She was suddenly serious. 'That kept me goin' in Sister Kate's, knowin' I could tell her how I was, tell her what was happenin', share my secrets. That's one reason I survived. But don't get me wrong, girl. Sister Kate and her volunteers, they weren't *bad* people. I came to like some of them, once I got over bein' stuck in there. They did their best for me, for all the *yamba*, but they couldn't get rid of the insecurity we felt. How could they? *We* were the ones feelin' it, not *them*. It turned out a different story for my brothers, though.'

'So did you see your mother?' Rosalie asked again.

'No. She was passed away. I found that out after I left Sister Kate's when I was qualified. I went back to Onslow first. I found her grave there. Then I came down to Northampton to start teachin'. That's where I met Andy. He was workin' out on Wanamalu,' she said, with a spark of mischief, 'and here I am.'

'Yes, here you are.'

'Here *we* are, girl.' She pointed at the pools. 'Now then, this place. This place turned my life around. I came down here one day when I was twenty-one. I was livin' with Andy at the time and I was pregnant with Lennard, just a few weeks to go and I was huge! He was no bun in the oven, that boy, let me tell you, he was a damper cake bigger than a basketball. It was blindin' hot and we came down here for a swim.'

She described how she'd stripped and walked naked out into the water and when she'd looked down, she'd seen her reflection mirrored full length on its surface. She was transfixed. She was looking at herself from the inside out and the outside in, and she saw no shame there. She saw only her dark beauty, the swell of her belly and her body's intimacy.

She'd leaned forward and gradually immersed herself in the reflection beneath her. When she'd emerged, it was with a deep sense of joy, as if the spirit in her that had gone to ground was back in the light. She'd flung her hair about to wring the water from it and danced on the rocks like some wild, ecstatic water nymph in the hot sun in a fresh new world with Andy cavorting around her.

'I'd already decided to teach,' she said. 'No way wasn't I goin' to teach. I've spent the rest of my workin' life giving the *yamba* in Northampton some pride in being black and Aboriginal. I've taught those kids who walk the tightrope in two worlds to wear their skin like a flag of defiance,' she chuckled, 'and do they wave it, hey? Do they *what*!'

'I guess we all have those moments,' Rosalie said.

'Well, you're right, and this is one for you.' Still holding Rosalie's hand, she stood, reached out for her other hand and held them both. 'Come on, girl. Don't be afraid. There's no crocs in here, 'cept this old crock when I get in. It's time for you to get baptised.'

She pulled Rosalie to her feet and led her to the edge of the rock.

'You ready, girl?'

Rosalie nodded. They stepped in unison over the edge into breast-deep water, their blouses floating up around them, their feet raising a cloud of fine white sand that drifted to their knees. And again, in unison, they ducked beneath the surface and came up laughing.

'Welcome to Andy's country and mine,' Mary said. 'Welcome to our people's country and the country of our ancestors. Now we can share it together, you and me. Now you can make yourself at home.' She gave Rosalie a beaming smile. 'We've opened the door for you, girl, it's up to you to step through it. Do as I do when a new door opens… ask yourself why not? And risk it. Overcome your vulnerabilities by facing up to them. Be brave and become strong, little sister.'

Rosalie's Ashes

WHEN LENNARD ANNOUNCED HIS decision to spread Rosalie's ashes across the pool beside Jandamarra's rock in Windjana Gorge a month after her cremation, he received a mixed reception. He was prepared for it. He'd thought it through. He ignored friends who suggested it was too soon, that he should wait for the coroner's verdict, that another twenty-five-hundred-kilometre journey to the Kimberley aboard the Harley was risky in his present frame of mind.

When her brother Max surprised him with the warning the assassin might still be out there, Lennard said he had to stare down his demons. 'When you're down, you don't roll over. You get back up and you look your enemy in the eye.'

Max placed a hand on his shoulder and held it there. 'Nothing changes, Ace. She's still putting words in your mouth.'

'No, she's not, but if she does, I'll be listening.'

'You're still attentive to a fault. Now she's gone you really think you'll call the shots?'

'Bro, we were a team. Now the buck stops with me.'

Rosalie's mother Phyllis's gave Lennard her blessing, though.

Aware that Rosalie would have approved, she'd silenced her husband David's objections. 'We have to give this more thought,' David protested as they prepared for bed the night Phyllis told him. 'It's hardly rational under the circumstances.'

He slowly unknotted his tie, his eyes flashing. Phyllis felt him testing her resolve. 'It's a so-called Aboriginal sacred site, is it not? We won't be welcome, and I won't go near the place. So I'll have nowhere to mourn her. Have you thought of that?' He whipped the tie from around his neck. 'Why in

God's name return her ashes to the place she died? It makes no sense.'

Phyllis was having none of it. 'Because Rosie loved it there. That's where she went to recharge her batteries. It was her spiritual home. She told me so herself, with prophetic irony, now I come to think about it. "When I'm there I come *alive*, like there's no tomorrow." They were her exact words.'

She removed her emerald earrings and loosened her silver hair with an irritable shake of her head. 'And another thing, you can't continue censuring Rosalie's relationship with Lennard now she's dead. Let it go! You can't blame him for what's happened.' There was an explosive *clack* as she snapped shut the lid of the mother-of-pearl shell case where she dropped her earrings. 'Besides, she always said young Luke was conceived there.'

When Lennard told his son Luke about Rosalie's death, he spared him the details of the shooting. He could see that the eleven-year-old was unnerved and disbelieving at the loss of his mother; and he knew that his own despair and occasional bursts of outrage were confusing him, so he did his best to control them when they were together.

As the days passed, it was clear that Luke longed for reassurance and that he was distrustful of the sympathy shown to him by unfamiliar people among the gathering of friends and relatives in the house.

He kept a close eye on Luke when he appeared dazed and withdrawn. He imagined his feelings swerving between paralysing numbness and surges of grief he fought, with teeth clenched, just as he did himself. Until he was alone. Then his tears fell hot and uncontrolled, an unbearable admission against his will that Rosalie had been torn from his life for good—and he knew it would be no different for the boy.

They sat together at the funeral service. When Lennard felt Luke's occasional trembling, he placed an arm around his shoulder, sensing him disturbed by the touching eulogies and the scattered laughter that greeted stories of her humour and her sense of irony. Then he gripped him tighter when they were transfixed by the remorseless glide of the coffin towards the red velvet curtains that opened and then closed to the melancholy thrum of Lennard's recorded didgeridoo.

When Lennard invited Luke to ride pillion on the Harley for the journey north, the boy latched onto the prospect with unrestrained excitement. Lennard watched him unfold the well-worn road map dusted with red fingerprints to explore their route, running a finger along the highway and sidetracks, examining the stopovers that Rosalie had marked on it over the years, reading aloud to Lennard the barely legible notes she'd pencilled in—'*Look out for feral foxes*; *Fresh water in the gnamma hole on Grey's Road*; *Threadfin salmon in season.*'

His twelfth birthday fell on the day following the cremation and Lennard convinced him to postpone its celebration until after their return.

Lennard found him crying in his bedroom one morning when he'd failed to appear at breakfast. 'I don't mind waiting for my birthday,' he sobbed when Lennard consoled him. 'It's just that every time I think of Mum lighting my candles, I can't stop thinking of her being burned up by the furnace jets... I wish I'd never gone to the funeral.'

On the day of their departure, Lennard guided Luke down the passageway to the front door. Phyllis was there to open it for them. She was looking after the dogs until their return.

'You will take good care of her,' she said as she opened the door, before adding, 'I know you will.' She held the door open, allowing Lennard to cross the veranda carrying the rectangular jarrah urn with great care in both hands. She reached out to touch it as he passed. 'I wish I was coming with you.'

Lennard descended the limestone steps and strode to the carport, his riding boots crunching wet gravel. When he reached the Harley, he retrieved a beach towel draped across the seat. He wrapped it around the urn, then paused to feel its weight and his heart was wrenched as he recalled Phyllis's whisper the day they'd collected the ashes from the funeral parlour. 'Sweet Jesus,' she'd murmured, dry-eyed, her face drained, 'she weighs the same as she did the day she was born.'

He glanced up at Phyllis in the doorway with Luke still beside her, intertwined gold dragons breathing fire across her satin dressing gown. Her face was filled with concern, her eyes locked on his as though reading his thoughts.

Suppressing a surge of anguish, he secured the package upright within the pannier. His hand rested there a moment. *So it's come to this*, he thought, then shut the lid.

'Time to go, my beauty,' he said. 'Time to go.'

Overnight showers had fallen across the garden. Lennard glanced up at the line of clouds lifting. 'Like a row of can-can dancers showing off their blue knickers,' he imagined Rosalie saying. 'Stonewashed denim, no doubt, with everyone hoping for see-through lace.' It brought a wry smile.

A breath of wind rustled through the leaves of two olive trees lining the driveway, airbrushing sunlight across them. He'd raised a sweat twelve years ago, digging the holes, and Rosalie had planted the saplings into the reeking mulch he'd brought back from his father's stables. She'd ceremonially watered them in. 'Now you won't have to pee on them,' she'd joked.

'Why not? My magic formula's never failed. Ask the lemon tree.'

'So that's your secret? And here's me thinking it was your green thumb.'

Lennard straddled the bike and settled into the seat. He reached for his helmet propped on the fuel tank and adjusted the intercom built into it, before cramming his hair under its rim. He lifted the visor and looked round at Luke clattering down the steps after hugging Phyllis. He was unrecognisable in his brand-new black leathers and top-heavy in his helmet.

Lennard shifted his broad frame forward, allowing Luke to clamber aboard, then switched on the intercom. 'There's a stack of room for both of us,' he said. 'Lean into the backrest. Make yourself comfortable. Now try talking.'

'I can't see around you, Dad.' Luke's complaint crackled.

'Come on, Superman, power up your x-ray vision.'

Luke clicked his tongue twice, turning imaginary switches at each temple. 'That's better. Now I can see around corners.'

'No need for a periscope, then. You all set? Make sure you hang on tight.'

Phyllis raised a hand as the bike roared to life. It whined into gear and slid forward off its stand as Leonard manoeuvred it up the driveway. Beneath the olives, a stronger gust showered droplets on both riders in epaulettes of sunlit sparks.

Out on Bellevue Terrace Lennard turned right and slowed to a stop. He looked back and raised both hands, all ten digits extended. Then he pulled on his gloves and lowered the helmet visor before accelerating out of view.

It was a painful journey. Lennard imagined Rosalie with him, reliving shared moments as they visited her favourite places along the way—the empty sands of Sandalwood Bay and the reefs of Ningaloo. The pools beyond the railway bridge on the Fortescue River where flotillas of red-beaked black swans cruised effortlessly midstream until alarmed by pebbles Luke skipped across the surface. The gorges of Karijini, shaded streams deep within them icy. The night sea sweeping in towards the windswept dunes at Cape Keraudren.

It took some time for Lennard to get used to Luke's movements behind him, the weight of his body at his back when he slept, his waking now and then with a start, as Rosalie used to.

The sound of Luke's voice over the intercom disturbed him. He expected her voice, her lively commentary, her throaty laughter that set him alight.

At one point he caught the sound of Luke humming and the uncanny echo was reminiscent of Rosalie's favourite song, 'Warm Sweet Breath of Love'. Lennard loved to hear her sing it and he was overcome. He pulled over to the verge and parked for a minute to distract Luke, their arrival disturbing a mob of scrawny sheep that clattered across the gravel and vanished into the scrub.

They reached Windjana Gorge in five days.

It was late afternoon and the place was deserted. They set up camp, then waded barefoot across the river and climbed to the shelf on the rock. They sat there in the quiet till dusk, when the light took on the clarity Rosalie admired, turning the rock into polished marble and the pool a deep silver-green as the shadows lengthened on the cliffs of the gorge.

Lennard unscrewed the wooden urn and found the sealed plastic capsule inside. He had no idea how to open it. Screwdriver in one hand, container in the other, momentarily at a loss, he imagined Rosalie's gentle mockery. 'Same old story, Ace—it takes a woman. Here, it's a no-brainer.' He turned the urn over and, as though she'd pointed it out, he spotted the concealed line of the seal that he prised open.

He spilled a handful of her ashes into his palm, closed his fingers, kissed her farewell and stood. Luke followed his lead. They scattered her ashes across the pool and the finer particles drifted before settling in a circle that widened over the water, spreading around her, it seemed, as her hair used to, in a shawl of dark silk. He imagined her laugh as she'd invited him into the pool that last time, her slender sunburned body treading water green as glass beneath her.

He reached into his shirt pocket for a letter he had written to her while she'd been swimming the first time he'd brought her here, twelve years before. He'd watched her wade into the pool, easing into the deeper gulley at its centre. As the water had closed around her, he'd felt his hands on her, his fingers the water's caress, his palms the pool's liquid touch. He'd handed her the letter when she'd climbed out. She'd stood as she read it, pearls of water rolling down her skin, onto the paper and onto him.

Then she'd looked down at him, cross-legged on the sand. 'I'm flattered,' she'd said, nudging his lower ribs with her toe. 'This reads like a commitment, all the bells and whistles. And I have it in writing! Now you're really in the deep end. Sure you can handle it?'

Then she'd smiled. 'And I love the poem at the end,' she'd said, before reading it back to him:

> *'Some lines I have learned by heart,*
> *but the most beautiful among them*
> *are the lines of your body*
> *that my heart has learned,*
> *where everything is loveliness.*
> *And where the power of memory is such*
> *that I can run the fingers of my mind over them,*
> *over the lines of a remembered you,*
> *and feel such tenderness in the touch*
> *as to wonder in disbelief*
> *that I could ever feel so much.'*

He didn't know that she had kept it. She was no magpie, but when he'd sorted through her belongings, he'd found it in a drawer. The ink had blurred where the droplets falling from her face and hair had struck.

He unfolded the page and swam out to the circle of ashes, where he released it. The paper gathered globes of water and slipped beneath the surface, washing away his words as though erasing her epitaph.

When he climbed out, his body was streaked with ash.

Later, with Luke asleep and snoring gently beyond the firelight, Lennard felt for the first time reconciled to the fearful emptiness that had swept over him the night she'd died. He sat on his haunches before the embers, stirring them with a green stick, releasing a torrent of sparks. Magical sparks, he mused, stirred with a green wand, its smouldering end wisping like a stick of incense that smelled of citronella and kept the sandflies at bay. Beside him the rock, now black as obsidian, was glazed by the dying fire.

He remembered her with the letter in her hand, looking down at him that day, her eyes mischievous as she'd reached round to release the clasp on her bikini top. She'd removed it and held it out between thumb and forefinger as she'd patted the rock with her free hand. 'I think we should set this in stone, right here, right now. Don't you?'

Now, for the first time, he felt the cold. He stood and walked barefoot across the sand towards the overhang of trees to find more firewood. Partway there, the glint on the jagged stripes of a still, coiled shape caught his eye. Alert, he hesitated—a death adder.

He slowly backtracked and retrieved the folding shovel beside his sleeping bag. He locked the blade into place and, with both hands on the shaft, cautiously retraced his steps.

The snake was motionless and then, as though sensing his return, it raked back its head like a wound spring to strike across the thick coil of its body. He leaned forward, lifted the shovel, and then changed his mind. He took another step forward, inserted the shovel into the sand and lifted the snake. As it uncoiled to escape across the blade, he manoeuvred the shovel to hold it there and carried it to the tree line, where he flicked it into the undergrowth.

'Live, you little *thayadi*,' he said. 'Like I have to.'

He dragged a dry branch back to the fire, snapped it in two and laid both pieces on the embers. When the fire crackled into life, he reached for the empty urn and placed it among the flames that flared green and blue as they darted around its base, the lacquer smoking.

As he watched, the moon sailed free of cloud and bathed the gorge in uncanny light, turning the rock into a monument once again—a monument he'd visualised once before—a cenotaph he'd build in glass, commemorating all the fallen warriors during the frontier wars and now in memory of Rosalie as well.

He crossed the shallows and leaned against it, both arms outstretched for balance, the quartz still warm, the water freezing. He remained there for several minutes, spellbound.

At one point he imagined Rosalie calling out, 'Hey, Sisyphus! You may never shift it, but don't stop trying. And don't do your back in. I need you in good nick.'

He climbed to the shelf, where he sat and waited for the breaking dawn. It was not over. It would never be over. But it was done.

The Kite Flyer

Pour l'enfant, amoureux de cartes et d'estampes,
L'univers est égal à son vaste appétit.
Ah! que le monde est grand à la clarté des lampes!
Aux yeux du souvenir que le monde est petit!
Un matin nous partons, le cerveau plein de flame…
…Nous voulons, tant ce feu nous brûle le cerveau,
Plonger au fond du gouffre, Enfer o' Ciel, qu'importe?a
Au' fond de l'Inconnu pour trouver du nouveau.
To the child, enthralled by maps and sketches,
The boundaries of the universe extend to the limits of his
imaginative yearning.
Ah! How infinite the world appears, illuminated in the lamplight,
Yet how confined, when recalled in memory's review!
One morning we set out, our impassioned thoughts aflame…
…So fiercely does this fire burn in the mind, we are determined
To plunge into the void, however heavenly or hellish,
Into the abyss of the unknown, to discover something new.'
Charles Baudelaire, *'Le Voyage'—Fleurs du Mal*

I WATCHED MY PAPA Maarten board his ship, the Ridderschap van Holland, when I was eight years old. That gusty early dawn in Vlissingen, on Friday, 10 July 1693, is forever branded into my memory.

During the short time he had been home from the east this time, he had taught me to catch herring, ride a horse and only last month, how to make and fly a kite.

'Opa Laurens taught me to fly one, Gerrit,' he told me, 'just as his papa taught him. You never know when the skill will come in useful. Apart from the pleasure, the Chinese have used kites for signalling during their wars, and in some countries, they enjoy kite fighting.'

I remember sunlight streaming across the estuary, lighting up the waterfront and throwing my shadow onto the whitewashed bricks of the newly opened mill at the end of the dijk wall. As I stood beneath its unfurled sails, I watched them crank slowly into life. They quickened and I placed the green and scarlet silk kite I'd been struggling desperately to launch down on the grass, before walking across to the mill.

The drumbeat of the giant wooden cogs driving the grinding stones thudded through my hands when I placed them against the wall, prompting me to turn and lean back into the building, my head and chest vibrating. Laughing, I waved at the group gathered beside the outer breakwater thirty *roeden* to my right. Papa's tall figure stood out among them in his starched and laundered light blue officer's jacket, with its silver buttons and lace collar. I'd observed Mama sweating over it for an hour as she'd ironed it the evening before.

He raised an arm, summoning me back to join them.

With the westerly blowing directly in from the open sea, I lined myself up and held the kite at shoulder height before running forward and releasing it, only to see it lift overhead for several promising seconds before it slackened and zigzagged back to the grass. Determined to send a signal to the two ships on the horizon, I tried again, with the same frustrating result.

After my fifth unsuccessful attempt, a workman from the team loading bags of barley from the horse-drawn dray onto the mill hoist for de-husking walked across and offered to help. Embarrassed, but not defeated, I thanked him, and this time I sprinted into the wind with the kite soaring behind me, the string sliding out across my palm between thumb and forefinger.

I ran along the uneven brick path on the Oranjedijk sea wall towards Papa, hauling on the kite string as it rose, my shouts obscured by the crash of waves sweeping up the embankment. They ricocheted in bursts of spray the length of the waterfront, wrenching the moorings of boats in the inner harbour, sending them bumping and grinding together beneath jostling masts, snapping halliards and whistling stays. I remember pockets of herring gulls stirring and shuffling on the lip of the dijk. They lifted in succession to manoeuvre weightless on the gusts as I tore through them. I remember screaming encouragement at the gyrating kite swooping and swerving across the sky, tugging at my arm.

When I looked back, I saw the messenger-key Papa had attached to the cord spin slowly up towards the kite's thrashing tail. I followed its flash until it lodged hard against the split baleen of the cross splice. A stronger gust caught the kite and shook it violently, the panels flashing in the sun as though in flames. In my mind, the kite had reached the borders of the sky and sent a magical blessing to the ships, guaranteeing them a safe journey.

When it stilled again, as Papa had explained the month before, the key turned the lock and swung open a green and scarlet rhomboid door to the brightening blue, beckoning me into a world of exploration with infinite dimensions.

'You can go anywhere through it, Gerrit,' he'd told me. 'Anywhere you choose.'

'I want to go everywhere with you, Papa! *Everywhere*!' I'd shouted in reply.

Eyes streaming, I ran along the narrow path as though crossing a bridge to the horizon. When I reached Papa, I tripped and lay on the bricks at his feet, filled with joy and panting with laughter, the cord tugging at my outstretched right arm as though I'd hooked a struggling herring.

Papa leant across and caught the string. He lifted me to my feet and hugged me, the silver buttons on his officer's tunic digging into my ribs.

Out in the Wielingen channel lay the sunlit silhouettes of two ships bedecked in departure flags flickering blue, silver and orange—the *Lands Welvaren* and the *Ridderschap van Holland*, their sails unfurling.

In the inner harbour, the owner's yacht prepared to cast off, her bell sounding, the last group of officers boarding via her bouncing gangplank. I recognised the figure of *Schipper* Dirk de Lange shaking each by the hand as they boarded.

Papa lowered me to the grass. He cupped my face in his hands and bent to kiss my forehead, murmuring a farewell that I acknowledged before turning away to disentangle the kite string snagged painfully around my fingers.

Mama and Opa Laurens waited for me further along the path. I began winding in the kite, watching as Papa turned to board the yacht. He sent the three of us a final backward wave before he disappeared.

Mama's jaw was clamped, her eyes slits beneath a heavy frown. I could see that she was fighting back tears, ducking against the wind, shanks of dark hair whipping about her cheeks as she struggled to tuck them under her cap. She must have been steeling herself for the year's absence before hearing from Papa, who had promised her a bundle of letters from Cape Town sent home on a ship in the first return fleet. And worse than that, I knew she was preparing to see out a two or three-year wait until his return.

Looking back now, I realise Mama's expression spelled out her loathing for the sea. It had robbed her of Papa's companionship for most of their married life. She must have felt abandoned—and pregnant once again—left behind to care for the family and the household.

I never heard her complain, but she must have been overwhelmed by dread when he departed, the premonition that he would not return running through her mind. I imagined her expressing her terror to no one except her God in silent prayer as his departure grew imminent, believing that if she said anything to Papa or her friends, she'd place a curse on the voyage.

And Papa? He was free to take his place aboard his ship, a figure of authority in a tight-knit, structured society of two hundred men heading for the Indies.

Together, the three of us watched the yacht scud towards the anchored ships as the kite descended, rattling and bouncing away from me as it struck the bricks.

A year later, the batch of letters he'd promised Mama had been sent home from Cape Town in the care of Klaas Goelet, the carpenter aboard the *Karthago*. He was a friend of Opa's. We gathered around the dining table and Mama opened each letter in turn, reading them aloud to us, as was her practice.

In one of the letters. Papa indicated that the *Ridderschap* would be departing Batavia sometime in December 1694.

The vessel will arrive in Goeree in late July or August the following year, weather permitting, and always provided the VOC does not change the voyage schedules or allocate Ridderschap temporarily, or for longer, to the coastal trade across the Indies.

I am missing you more than I can express. I cannot wait to embrace you all once again.

Your loving husband,

Maarten.

'If Goeree is his home port this time,' Opa Laurens explained, 'considering the time taken to offload the cargo and travel south to Middelburg, it will take him at least a fortnight to get home. We can expect him in mid-September 1695, at the earliest.'

Opa's estimate of the timing of his expected arrival was accurate.

On the Tuesday of that week in September, the VOC Company carriage pulled up at the front door. I was in the back garden picking apples in the orchard when I heard the carriage wheels crunching on the gravel. I dropped my basket, and when I careened around the corner I saw the carriage at the end of the front pathway.

The door opened, but Papa did not descend. I froze when Ole Reineus appeared. I knew he was the schipper of the *Lands Welvaren* that had sailed with Papa's *Ridderschap*.

A black skull cap covered his shaven head and his snub-nosed and pugnacious round face was preoccupied. He balanced his corpulent body on the step before alighting gingerly between the flower beds, the carriage shaking. He raised a quick hand in greeting towards Mama, who stood expectantly between the two maids, Miranda and Adriana, on the front step.

He dusted down his blue velvet jacket and turned to assist the senior VOC administrative officer, Carel van Caerden, from the carriage, his aristocratic features sombre.

They turned and walked up the path.

Uncomprehending, I searched for Papa, peering towards the empty carriage, its door ajar. *Papa has not arrived!*

Mama blanched, consternation written across her features. It dawned on me they were about to deliver terrible news. It was a moment I knew she'd dreaded for years. I watched the scene unfold in horrified confusion, the visitors blurring as they approached the stationary women.

Mama let out a heart-wrenching wail and buckled at the knees, clutching at the nearest of the maids. My heart racing, I took several backward steps and collided with Opa Laurens, who responded to Mama's scream by breaking into a limping run to reach her. He grabbed me to steady himself, gave me a violent hug and leant down to hiss in my ear, 'It's all right, *mijn kleinzoon*. Go around the back and into the house. Go upstairs. I'll see you soon. I'll deal with this.'

Trembling, I could not move, and Opa signalled for Miranda to assist me. She ran across and, with an arm about my waist, led me to the back door, where I heard another harrowing scream. Mama's strangulated 'No! No! No! No!' was cut short when Miranda closed the door behind us.

We climbed the stairs to the mezzanine as the two visitors settled side by side onto the oak bench beneath the window in the *voorkamer*.

We paused at the top and I knelt to peer down through the railings.

Supporting Mama with his right arm, Opa Laurens eased her into the armchair that Adriana dragged across, before he sat beside her on the clavichord stool.

They contemplated one another before Ole Reineus cleared his throat. 'Anneka, believe me when I say how deeply sorry we are, but we must inform you that the *Ridderschap* did not reach Batavia after leaving Cape Town in February last year.' He placed a finger across his lips, as though unwilling to divulge what was coming next. 'Neither the ship nor any of the crew have been sighted since.'

There was deathly quiet. Then Mama, who had been staring at the floor, lifted her face to him. Distraught, but surprisingly self-controlled, she murmured, 'It's all right, Ole. I've prepared myself for this all my married life.'

There was a long silence, then Mama began to sob convulsively, her tears falling onto the black and white tiles until Adriana handed her a lace-trimmed handkerchief, bending to wipe the floor with a cloth before withdrawing.

Dazed, I stared blankly at the glass-fronted cupboard below, my mind drifting to the pressure of the silver buttons on Papa's blue coat against my ribs the day he'd left, the smell of fresh linen in his shirt, the feel of his fingers ruffling my hair, the kiss on the crown of my head, the kite striking the bricks as it fell.

With that image, the thought raced through my mind, *So much for my kite signal guaranteeing the ships a safe journey! My blessing has brought Papa misfortune.*

Years later, on 20 June, 1712, two weeks after our ship the *Zuytdorp* had been smashed apart at the base of the Eendrachtsland cliffs, *Opperstuurman* First Mate Joost de Vlieger squatted beside me to discuss our options. We were camped on the clifftop with the other survivors.

'There's been no sign of any passing ships, Gerrit, let alone our sailing partner, the *Kockengen*. I don't like to admit it, but she must have missed us days ago.' He gestured at the blazing fire. 'Even if she saw our signal during the night or the smoke during the day, knowing *Schipper* Hayman de Laver the way I do, I'm certain there is nothing on this earth that would convince him to come close enough inshore to check. If I was in his place I'd do the same—sail on!'

'Where does that leave us, then?'

'We have no option except to move the campsite north beyond the cliffs, and the sooner the better. The beaches opposite Dirk Hartog Island provide far better access to the open sea. The *Belvliet* is due here in a week or two, I think, if she hasn't already passed us. She should be in the company of the fleet that arrived in Cape Town before we left. Jan de Hei aboard the *Oosterstein* has the eyes of a hawk and the curiosity of a cat, my friend. If anyone's going to spot us and pick us up, it will be him.'

I raised my eyebrows. 'Curiosity won't get him far if he has no idea we're here.'

'True, but there's also Renier Hijpe commanding the *Zuiderbeek*.' He smiled drily, pointing a forefinger skywards. 'You know as well as I do he thinks that God created the sun to shine especially on him. I have no doubt he believes he could walk on water to get to us! All we need is a signal to blow his mind. Any suggestions?'

I gave him a smile that widened to a burst of laughter. '*Grote geesten denken hetzelfde*, great minds think alike, according to Father Cats!' I tapped my temple with a forefinger. 'I've had an idea up here for some time. A signal so surprising Renier will consider it a message sent to him directly from Paradise. They'll talk about it in Batavia and Middelburg for years to come. A gigantic kite! We send it aloft, and then we explode it.'

'Hah! That's brilliant!' Joost said, slowly nodding. 'A Chinese rocket. But how would you construct it? And launch it? And set the charges?'

I waved a hand around the campsite. 'We have the sailcloth. We have the ropes. We have the linseed oil. We have sufficient gunpowder left, and we have hands and time to spare.'

'Right, then we should get it done.'

Following my instructions, my Ceylonese apprentice carpenter, Sunil Dewaraja, and another two survivors spent the next three days preparing the necessary parts—intact sailcloth painstakingly cut to the traditional diamond shape, one *roede* long and half as wide; a strong but slender green tree trunk heated in the fire and straightened for the spine, its branches trimmed and bowed for the spars and lower reinforcing ribs; a three-line sheet unravelled for the ties and the cord, and a long shank of flayed rope for the tail.

They took a further day and a half to assemble the kite, before successfully testing it in flight at the clifftop on the strong afternoon breeze, to the raucous applause of the sceptical group of survivors. Then they applied linseed oil to the body and tail in preparation for impregnation with gunpowder before launching.

'All we need now are passing ships,' Joost said when he congratulated us on the outcome. 'Are you sure your ignition system is foolproof?'

'We can only use it once,' I replied, 'so it had better be. We'll know when we see any sails and launch it into action. We've bowed the spars, so the tail is superfluous for its balance in flight. It will make a perfect fuse once we light it. The kite will fly until the flame reaches it and then, guess what?' I violently clapped my hands. '*Kaboom!*'

'We hope.'

'We know.'

'You've done this before?'

'No.'

'I like your confidence.'

'Trust me. You have so far. I am your senior carpenter, after all.'

'All right then, we'll give it one more week. If the signal fails or we sight no ships in that time, we must move on.'

'Without me.'

'With you.'

'Without. We've discussed this.' I nodded at my leg and moved my injured foot a fraction. The pain was searing. The wounds above the ankle were oozing despite Sunil tending to them with heated saltwater. 'I can't be moved and I won't be carried and slow you down. You'll have your hands full carting that swivel cannon you're thinking of using as a signal.'

'Yes, but we're only taking one breech block, so we'll be carrying a lesser load. Why don't we fashion you a stretcher and you join us?'

I shook my head. 'Sunil says he's going to stay with me. I haven't been able to change his mind. Once I can walk, we'll overtake you.' I gave him a deliberately cheerful smile. 'In fact, we'll get to Batavia in time to greet you when you arrive.'

'That may take months.'

'So be it. I need to heal first or risk losing the leg. Or my life.'

'That's your final word?'

'It is.'

The week passed and, to our dismay, the expected ships did not appear.

On the elected deadline, Joost and the remaining survivors prepared to depart at sunset. They intended to travel under the full moon, he told me, to avoid the heat. He expected the walk to Dirk Hartog Island to take three days. They left a selection of supplies, including a bundle of prized biltong prepared from the drowned and bloated sheep we'd salvaged from the wreck, for which Sunil had developed a surprising craving.

They collected a huge pile of dead tree branches for us to replenish the signal fire, along with a large secondary supply of green branches left to dry out. They recovered some driftwood from the wreck as well, including one of Opa Laurens's carved statuettes of the Grecian Sphinx detached from between the rear transom windows. I asked them to leave it within view, partway up the cliff.

Baltheser Claasen, one of the German soldiers, presented Sunil and me with a pair of what he called 'sandal-moccasins worn by Roman soldiers' he'd made to measure from the sheepskins.

'You'd better agree they are a perfect fit,' he said as he handed Sunil his pair. 'Otherwise, I'll commit them here and now to the fire and you and your bunions can go barefoot.'

Sunil tried one on and then the other. 'They are perfect, Baltzer. You are an outstanding cordwainer, Eendrachtsland's best. How are you at making hats? I lost mine swimming ashore.'

'Feet are my speciality, Sunil, not heads.'

Sunil clambered to his feet and tested the shoes, hopping on alternate legs, raising both hands head-high and waving them in enthusiastic approval before looking down in mock surprise. 'They haven't fallen apart! I thank you for the gift, Baltzer. I will buy you a drink when we meet again in Batavia.'

Reclining against the trunk of a tree, I extended a hand to Joost.

'Till we meet again, Gerrit,' he said, 'and farewell to you, Sunil. May God be with you both.'

'Name the place in Batavia and we will be there to greet you when you arrive,' I said.

Joost looked down and grinned. 'That's easy. The Hotel Mauritius. Last time I was there they had a Chinese chef working in the Simon Stevin kitchens whose dishes were the envy of the colony.'

'I'll book us a table.'

'For twenty. I wonder, do they still serve biltong there these days?'

Sunil and I watched the group load up their sailcloth sacks, one survivor carrying glowing embers for future fires flickering in a tureen. Two at the rear hoisted the swivel cannon to their shoulders, a third assisting them.

They faded to shadows as the sun sank into the ocean, extinguished in a crimson blaze. The enormous moon rising above it glowed bright yellow in the haze, like an illusory lantern. It paled to white and shrank back to size as it rose among the emerging stars shimmering like shattered glass across the sky.

Three days later, late in the afternoon when I was asleep, Sunil sighted a sail on the horizon.

'Gerrit!' he shouted, waking me. 'There is a ship!'

I struggled to sit up and focus. The sail looked like an unearthly mirage, before another two followed closely, line abreast.

'Get the gunpowder!' I screamed. 'Prime the kite. We don't have long.'

Sunil splashed the remnants of the linseed oil across the sailcloth and soaked the tail, then he poured gunpowder across both. He unwound the cord to its full length, running it in a series of loops across an open area of heath between the campsite and the cliffs, its end bound to a boulder at the cliff edge.

He lifted the kite, walked to the lip of the cliff beside the fire, and waited for my signal. That took all of twenty minutes, as the ships came straight on before the wind, then jibed away to port to begin their broad reach to the north-west.

My shout was hoarse. '*Now*, Sunil. Now's the time. Fire away!'

'We need more wind.'

'It's strong enough. There's no time to waste. Let it fly!'

Holding the kite head high, its ribs bending as the wind caught it, Sunil manoeuvred the thrashing tail across the fire. It crackled into flame and he released the kite, allowing the cord to unravel across both palms, applying pressure as the kite lifted and dipped and shook violently, struggling for height, before soaring majestically across the campsite and powering upwards, gyrating to the left and then the right as he fought to manage it.

Dragged slowly towards me as the cord ran out, Sunil released it as the last loop hissed across the sand, giving out an ominous *thwack* as the boulder held. For several tense minutes, the cord hummed like a piano wire before it snapped, sending the kite cavorting wildly across the sky as though attempting to escape the flame ascending towards it.

Then the sailcloth exploded, spitting fire in orange and

yellow flames before plunging towards the ground, a trail of thick black smoke marking its descent like a streak of pitch across the sky's clear blue, while Sunil leapt and screamed along the lip of the cliff.

To my frustration, fury and despair, the ships sailed on.

Once again, my kite signal had failed. First the *Ridderschap* and now our rescuers.

Will there ever be an end to my bad luck? I wondered.

The next afternoon, Sunil took the empty water canister and made his way to the second pool in the gulley to the north. It hadn't rained for several days, and then only briefly. It was clear the seepages were drying up, so for the past week, he had been refilling the water canister more sparingly than usual.

At the pool, he half-filled the canister and then, on an impulse, he left it there and walked farther up the gulley in search of other pools. He found none, eventually reaching its end, its sides closing in and the floor sloping gently upwards.

He climbed to an exposed grassy clearing and stood among the green thickets at its edge, watching a mob of grey animals similar to those he'd sighted once or twice inland from the campsite. Alerted to his movement or his presence on the wind, they bounded away on their rear legs, their thick tails protruding. He was amazed at their hopping action and the length of each swerving leap.

He stepped out into the open to investigate what he took to be a depression at the centre of the clearing, perhaps a waterhole where the animals appeared to have been drinking. He found nothing but further patches of oat grass and scrub.

As he turned to make his way back to the gulley entrance, he heard voices behind him and froze. Two Indigenous tribesmen, one carrying three long spears across his shoulder and the other his water canister, were crossing towards him, conversing loudly enough to alert him to their arrival. They were naked, their hair and beards wild. Sunil noticed that the warrior carrying the water wore a cape of red animal skin hanging down his back and across his shoulders, strung at the neck.

He could not read their expressions. His first blinding reaction had him back on the Mannar beaches in Ceylon, bargaining with Indigenous Vedda tribesmen visiting the pearl divers to sell their carvings and bows and arrows, their moods unpredictable and their appearances as fierce as the two confronting him. Unable to restrain himself, he blurted a Tamil greeting. *'Vannakam! Vannakam!'*

He backed away as they approached.

They halted three *roeden* away. Sunil watched the warrior carrying the water canister place it carefully in a patch of sand beside him. He reached for a spear from his partner and held the shaft vertically, the glinting quartz barb downwards, barely touching the ground. *'Ngana nyinda?*

Is he asking who I am? Sunil wondered, expressionless.

The warrior seemed to deliberately avoid eye contact as he examined Sunil before calmly looking directly at him for several moments, then away.

Sunil took another involuntary backward step, alert to their every move, his heart racing as the silent standoff extended. A minute passed, then two. The warriors continued to look him up and down. Then the first warrior extended his arm and rotated the spear to the horizontal, the barb facing Sunil and the shaft across a shoulder. He gestured across the grassland, sweeping the spear through a half-circle before pointing eastward, his frown now menacing. *'Wanthala nyindangu barraja? Gagarrala?*

Sunil, confused and alarmed by the aggression he saw in the swing of his spear, stood dumbfounded. *He must think I've come from inland, from the east,* he thought.

The warrior nodded, before pointing at his chest and flicking a forefinger at his companion. '*Ngatha Malgana. Ngathangura nhaganha barraja. Nayiwu nyinda nala yaninyina?*'

Fearing the worst, Sunil ducked, turned and sprinted for the shelter of the closest thickets. As he did so, he heard a warning shout and the rattle of spears. '*Hoh! Nyinda wujarnu matharra! Wirra! Wirra!*'

Bent double and zigzagging in desperation, Sunil heard the hoarse warning, before he heard a second shout, fiercer than the first. '*Wirra! Gurra bajirri yana! Yugarri! Ngalingu nyindanha ngarrinmanha biladagurru!*'

In the menacing silence that followed, Sunil heard a final warning question ring out over the gasping of his breath as he sprinted on, '*Nyinda gulgathadi?*'

Then, within several *roeden* of the trees, a single spear whistled overhead, landed ahead of him and slid along the sand. Bracing for the second to pierce his back, Sunil reached the grounded spear, picked it up and turned to face his attackers. Shaking uncontrollably, his chest heaving, he held the spear horizontally in clenched fists in preparation for the confrontation.

The warriors, who had loped after him, took up the same position three *roeden* in front of him and then, in a simultaneous movement, they swung their spears to the vertical once again, the barbs just short of the ground. The first of them gestured impatiently for Sunil to do the same. Hesitant, he did so.

The first then grounded his spear, stepped forward and gestured to Sunil to follow suit. Suspicious that the other warrior had maintained his hold on his spear, Sunil waited. The first again raised a hand and pointed at the ground, glaring as he expressed a disapproving hiss. This time Sunil reluctantly grounded his spear.

He saw a nod of approval and the flash of teeth when he stood and, though still harbouring fearful distrust, it struck him that he may have misread their intentions, despite the apparent threat. They had carried his canister of water, after all, and the spear had missed him, though by a narrow margin. Besides, the other armed warrior now carried his spear casually across his shoulders once again, both his hands raised and relaxed across the shaft in the cruciform position, observing developments.

'*Gurra icithayi, ngatha gurra bumanha nyindanha,*' the warrior said, his voice calm but firm as he stepped forward and, as Sunil flinched for a blow, he reached out with both hands and gripped Sunil by the left shoulder and right bicep. He squeezed him as though in a gesture of reassurance or a demonstration of strength, before placing Sunil's forearm against his own for a full half-minute, seemingly examining the dark skin texture and colour contrast of both.

Apparently satisfied, he stepped back and inspected Sunil from head to toe once again, bemused. Then he reached up, ran a finger along Sunil's shaven jaw, and pointed at his groin. '*Nyinda wayabandi? Wurrinyu?*' he asked.

When he repeated the question and persisted in pointing at his groin, Sunil took off his shoes, undid the pewter buttons on his calico breeches and removed them.

'*Net als jij ben ik een man*, I am a man, like you,' he said.

Both warriors beamed before breaking into laughter.

'*T'i! Gutharra kuca warabadi! Nyinda ngugurnu wayabandi!*' the second warrior exclaimed, pointing at Sunil's genitals.

His laughter subsided into a wide grin as he stepped forward and took the trousers from Sunil on the point of his spear. '*Nayi naga! Nhanganha wurdbi thumanunyina manda galga wujarnugura!*' he exclaimed. He peered down at them in wonderment, before reaching out to touch them apprehensively. Then, gathering confidence, he released his spear and held them in both hands as he unfolded them, turned them inside out, checked the buttons and held them up to the sun as if to verify the weave. Satisfied, he gave his partner a triumphant and cheerful shout, '*Hoh! Nayi ngana!*'

Bemused, Sunil watched him sit down, stretch out a foot and insert it into the trouser leg. He stood and pulled the cloth to his thigh. Obviously wary of the feel and watching nervously as his leg disappeared, he hopped comically around them before tearing the breeches off, clearly so relieved to find his leg still intact that Sunil could not suppress a laugh.

Spurred on by Sunil's reaction and the ridicule of his partner, he inserted both feet and pulled the breeches to his waist, struggling with the buttons before Sunil stepped forward to assist him. '*Hier is hoe je het doet.* Here, this is how you do it,' he said, his voice relieved.

The breeches were too large and Sunil tightened the rope belt to hold them in place as the warrior, now highly pleased, leapt around them in a leg-stamping, arm-waving dance.

When he desisted, Sunil donned his shoes and they made their way back to the water canister. '*Baba nyindaguru,*' the senior warrior pointed as they approached it.

As Sunil took it by the handle, the warrior pointed at the cloudless sky and shook his head. '*Bundu bardiyalu gurra bunduthayimanha marugudu.*'

Then he sat and gestured for Sunil to join him.

When the three were comfortable, he pointed back at the water canister and then towards the east. '*Ngalingura maya bayirri yan, babamuthagurru. Ngatha ganmanha nyindanha babala barrangga.*

Sunil shook his head and shrugged, both hands palm up.

After pondering for several moments, the warrior said, '*Ngalingu nhanjanu wabagu warabadi wilithi gambanyu yuganga, garla gurrimutha. Nayi nhaga?*

When Sunil shook his head again, he repeated the question, illustrating his description with exaggerated arm and hand actions representing a flying bird and gesturing skywards, coupled with explosive sounds, '*Nganharra nangiyanu ngangguyanu yuganga marumaru!* Pockaa! Pock! Pock! Pock!'

'Ah, that was the kite,' Sunil responded, demonstrating in turn as he spoke. 'We set it on fire to signal the ships that passed us yesterday.'

He knew that neither warrior understood word or gesture and realised that they would have to return to the campsite for him to demonstrate. He pointed in that direction. 'Come back to our camp. I can show you.'

He stood and lifted the canister, again pointing towards the west. 'Come back with me. I can explain the kite. You can meet Gerrit.'

The warriors jumped to their feet, shouldering their spears. The senior shook his head, again pointing inland. '*Mirda. Ngali yanmanha warrbathu ngurrala.*'

The other, beaming and still wearing the breeches, told him, '*Marugudu nganharra nhanganha nyinda wilithi jinagabi ngurrala nyindangu.*'

Then he pointed at the late afternoon sun and slowly rotated his arm, first to the west, where he closed his fist, and then round to the east; and there, with the fingers and thumb of his right hand extended, he held his rising hand silhouetted against the sky just above the treeline. He held his position and gazed at Sunil with his eyebrows raised.

Sunil smiled and nodded. 'You'll visit us early tomorrow morning?' he asked, pointing westward.

'*I'i,*' the warrior said, '*i'i,*' before bending to pick up his spear and joining his companion.

Sunil stood beside the water canister, watching them walk away. They did not look back.

He slowly shook his head as they disappeared, a burst of relief coursing through him. Barely able to believe what had happened, he pictured once again the explosive image of Gerrit's eye-catching kite signal flaring against the sky, his thoughts racing. *Gerrit won't believe this! His kite has brought us the best of good fortune. Our rescue is coming from an unexpected quarter. We will survive after all.*

<u>Malgana Translation:</u>

Ngana nyinda? Who are you?

'*Wanthala nyindangu barraja? Gagarrala?* Where are you from, which country? To the east?

Ngatha Malgana. Ngathangura nhaganha barraja. Nayiwu nyinda nala yaninyina? I am Malgana. This is my country. Why are you trespassing here?

Hoh! Nyinda wujarnu matharra! Wirra! Wirra! Hey! You, black stranger! Stop! Wait!

Wirra! Gurra bajirri yana! Yugarri! Ngalingu nyindanha ngarrinmanha biladagurru! Stop! Don't run! Stand still! Or we will spear you!'

Nyinda gulgathadi? Are you deaf?

Gurra icithayi, ngatha gurra bumanha nyindanha. Don't worry, I will not hit you.

Nyinda wayabandi? Wurrinyu? Are you a man or a woman?

I'i! Gutharra kuca warabadi! Nyinda ngugurnu wayabandi! Yes! Two big testicles! You are truly a man!

Nayi naga! Nhanganha wurdbi thumanunyina manda galga wujarnugura!' Check this out! This is the skin that covers the stranger's backside and his legs!

Hoh! Nayi ngana! Hey! Watch me do this!

Baba nyindaguru, There's your water.

Bundu bardiyalu gurra bunduthayimanha marugudu. There's been no rain and it won't rain tomorrow or for some time.

Ngalingura maya bayirri yan, babamuthagurru. Ngatha ganmanha nyindanha babala barrangga. Our camp is way over there. We have a plentiful supply of water. I will take you to the water there later.

Ngalingu nhanjanu wabagu warabadi wilithi gambanyu yuganga, garla gurrimutha. Nayi nhaga? We saw the giant white sea-eagle yesterday. It caught fire, with lots of smoke. What was it?

Nganharra nangiyanu ngangguyanu yuganga marumaru! We all saw it and heard it yesterday afternoon. The burning sea eagle.

Mirda. Ngali yanmanha warrbathu ngurrala. No. We'll both get back to our camp right away.

Marugudu nganharra nhanganha nyinda wilithi jinagabi ngurrala nyindangu. Tomorrow we'll all come and see you and the white spirit at your camp.

Sunflowers On Mother's Day

Iᴺ Cᴇʀᴏᴄᴀʜᴜɪ, ʙᴇsɪᴅᴇ ᴛʜᴇ Copper Canyon in North Western Mexico, May 1967

My mother, Suré, died on 10 May 1960, a month after I was born. Although I have no memory of her, I've spent my life trying to recall her particular smell, her comforting touch, the beating of her heart against my own.

I have a tinted photograph showing me feeding at her right breast, taken a week before she died. I carry it with me everywhere. She held me in her arms for those thirty days and I treasure every moment of our imagined closeness.

The day she died is Mother's Day, of all days. Can you believe it?

When I was growing up and missing her, my father, Victor, used to reassure me the date proved I was so special Mamá made it her purpose in life to give birth to me, despite the risks. She was forty years old. He'd take me in his arms and give me a consoling embrace, often cradling my face in his hands—but in the secret corner of my mind, I'd wish it was Mamá comforting me. I'd feel confused and even more upset, and guilty too, for hurting Papá if he ever suspected how I felt.

Every year without fail, we used to visit Mamá's older sister, my *Tía* Ariché, on the anniversary of Mamá's death. We'd spend a week at her *ranchería* in Cerocahui, deep in the Sierra Madre Mountains among the canyons. We'd honour Mamá's memory, as though celebrating the *Día de los Muertos*, the Day of the Dead, six months early.

The first such visit I clearly remember occurred in May, 1967.

We drove up from our home in Saucillo the day before, in my Tarahumaran grandfather Cerrildo's 1956 Golden Hawk

Studebaker. It was a seven-hour journey, with short stopovers in Cuauhtemoc and Creel.

My older brother Andrés let me win four games of checkers out of seven during the drive, 'Because you're still a beginner and learning the moves.'

I went through Andrés's latest comics between games, reading and rereading the adventures of my favourite superhero, Kalimán, and his eleven-year-old apprentice, Solín, until I was car sick—just the once and fortunately outside the car. Papá bent me over at the roadside, an arm around my waist and his free hand holding back my hair, urging me not to soil his shoes. I slept the rest of the trip stretched out on the back seat with my feet up on Andrés's lap.

The next morning I woke early and found my *Tía* Ariché sitting in silence on the chilly patio, looking out across her grapevines. Andrés was out on his early morning training run, and Papá and Abu Cerrildo were still asleep.

Tía's feisty white miniature Schnauzers, Zipi and Zape, lay alert beside her, their muzzles on their paws, their eyes scanning the vineyard for any marauding thick-billed green parrots or other birds daring to feed on the grapes.

When I sat down, Zape lifted his overhanging eyebrows and met my gaze, the glint of warning in his bright, dark eyes letting me know he'd nip me if I got too close. I promptly lifted my bare feet to the seat of my chair and rested my chin on my raised knees, wrapping my arms around them, and he dismissed me and resumed his surveillance.

The green and gold leaves of the vines gleamed as the sun rose behind us. Clouds of tiny midges shimmered here and there in particles of light above the ripening purple bunches. The sun's rays slanting towards the rim of the Urique Canyon warmed my back and shoulders, melting away my icy dread at the thought of confronting Tía with the question I'd asked Papá and Abu Cerrildo countless times.

'Tía, please tell me the truth this time.'

No one else will and I'm sick of asking. The frustrating thought ran through my mind.

'What truth, sweetheart?'

'What happened to Mamá? Why did she die?'

Until now, Papá and Abu Cerrildo have not replied to me directly. They've diverted my attention. You're too young to understand. You barely knew her, if at all. All in good time. As if the cause of her death is a secret or they're shielding me from the distress of discovering something unbearable in her passing.

Tía's shrewd black eyes stared thoughtfully into mine for several long moments as she rearranged a loose strand of her thick black hair streaked with grey back into the bun coiled on top of her head.

I took a deep, determined breath and held her narrow-eyed look, unsure what she was thinking or what was coming next. She slowly nodded, rocking her body from the waist up in her creaky wicker chair, the gold Aztec Tree of Life pendant on her necklace swinging like a hypnotic pendulum across her black, loose-fitting linen blouse.

'An infection took her, Alicia,' she said at last, her voice an unexpected hiss. 'Septicaemia. After an emergency caesarean to bring you into the world.'

To bring me into the world? Uncertain what she meant, the words struck me like an accusation and I ducked my head as though she'd slapped me.

After a long pause, relaxing back in her chair, she continued, 'You are seven years old, going on seventeen. It's time you knew yours was a complicated breech birth. It took so much longer than we expected. It was never-ending and extremely painful for her. *Pero ella era estoica*, but she was stoical.'

Bewildered, I looked up and stared at her with hesitant defiance as she gathered her thoughts. Then my stubbornness gave way and I nodded, pretending with a thoughtful look that I understood her. She reached across with a calloused hand to pat my shoulder as though acknowledging my confusion.

'You arrived feet first. We couldn't turn you round,' she said, her voice now reassuring and matter-of-fact. She raised her eyebrows and showed her strong white teeth in a smile I guessed was sympathetic, 'as if you couldn't wait to meet the ground running. *Como la pequeña cabra montañosa*, like the little mountain goat you've become. But Suré had just turned forty. Very dangerous. Especially for a *mukí* of the Tarahumaran *Rarámuri*. And even though the pregnancy was unplanned, she didn't listen to our advice. As usual. *Ya mero, pero no*. Almost, but no. No. She was having none of it.' She gave a quick shake of her head. 'She was determined to have you, *mijita*. She always was the pig-headed one. Just like you. And the prettiest. How else did she snare your father from under my nose when we were young, while I was her *acompañante*, her chaperone?'

She leaned forward, wrapped her arms around me and squeezed before I could wriggle away, her smell earthy and her voice rasping as she spoke beside my ear. 'We wouldn't have it any other way, honey. She did us all a favour. You, especially you.'

When I broke free and ran, I heard her call out. 'Relax, *nenita*, relax, child. Now her spirit is *kiri-i-kiri huko*. At peace.' She cackled as if to emphasise the Tarahumaran phrase she'd shouted. One of the working mules in the paddock beside the house brayed in response, both silenced as the door slammed shut behind me.

The words she yelled again were faint, 'At peace, compared to the rest of us… me and you both.'

It took me many years to come to terms with the realisation that I was partly responsible for Mamá's agonising death and understand that she'd considered an abortion early in her pregnancy but decided against it. Even Tía Ariché, who hadn't realised she'd be fostering me when Mamá died, advised her to abort me.

Almost, but not quite. My life in exchange for hers.

Was that to be my ongoing story?

When I opened the curtains an hour later, Tía still sat alone, sunlight now igniting the blood-red climbing roses blooming on the trellis above her head.

A pine-scented breeze brushed across the vineyard, its minty fragrance reaching me through the open window, and there, beyond the nearby shadows of the canyons and the mauve silhouettes of distant mountains, a pale three-quarter moon hung like a fingernail in the brightening sky.

'What colour would you varnish it, Mamá?' I whispered, picturing us standing together at the window admiring the landscape, just as I'd fantasised about us doing at home in Saucillo, allowing her to share with me the experiences she'd missed. *'Oh, something golden, mijita, with the sun coming up,'* I imagined her saying. *'Something golden would be perfect.'*

The fact that I was speaking on her behalf did not diminish the authenticity of the shared moment. It seemed to me to add to it.

Before rejoining Tía, I took out Mamá's treasured brown leather beret from my chest of drawers. Papá gave it to me a month ago on my latest birthday, along with another two of her favourite things—a silver butterfly brooch embedded with garnet stones green as emeralds and a fringed sky-blue silk rebozo shawl he assured me she'd used as a child.

He explained that before she died, she'd insisted I should have them when old enough. She didn't want them buried with her in the coffin.

I hadn't yet worn any of them. I'd been afraid to. And

now I wasn't sure I deserved to, but I braced myself, put both hands inside the beret, held it open and placed it over my head. I tugged at my ponytail to adjust the beret there before tightening the leather thong running around the rim so it fitted me perfectly.

I stood for several minutes facing the mirror, arranging the beret with the bright green oak tree emblem on it front and centre. *It's shaped like Tía's Tree of Life*, I thought. *This is how Mamá must have worn it, checking her reflection as she adjusted it, just as I am.*

I felt uncannily connected to Mamá at that moment. I could not remember her, but now perhaps could get to know her by piecing together everything I was told about her and allowing my imagination to do the rest.

Perhaps.

It was a start.

What I wanted then more than anything was to have used the superpowers I'd learned from Kalimán and done a somersault in Mamá's womb seven years ago before moving headfirst down her birth canal, leaving us both intact and alive when I was born.

A surge of relief, almost of happiness, ran through me as the painful, unsettling sense of isolation and loneliness I usually experienced when I asked or thought about her fell away. I beamed at my image, as though her eyes were looking into mine and mine hers—and the unexpected idea flashed across my mind—*This is how I'd feel if Mamá was giving me the unconditional love I need to give myself.*

On my way out through the dining room, I surprised myself by using my fingertips to transfer a kiss to Mamá's charcoal portrait. Sketched when she was young, so long before she became my mamá, I'd always considered hers the face of a stranger. For the first time, however, I recognised myself in her. The high cheekbones with their shadows, though mine were not yet as pronounced. The wide-set eyes. The hint of creases at the edges of her smile.

The picture was propped up on the temporary *ofrenda* altar the maid Ofelia and I helped Tía construct, with its glass of water and bowl of Mamá's favourite salted cashews and peanuts, its five melting candles and incense sticks Ofelia had lit earlier for the day. The brightly coloured mandala of crepe paper flowers we'd made matched the two vases of brilliant orange and yellow *cempasúchil* marigolds I'd picked from the rows bordering the vegetable garden. Their distinct musky scent was designed to guide Mamá's spirit on her journey home to protect us, or away to the other world awaiting her.

Surrounding the offerings, Ofelia laid a semi-circle of her magic stones and crystals—a miniature dry-stone wall designed to protect Mamá from evil spirits and other *diablitos* who might want to cause her harm. Its centrepiece was a small white *calavera* sugar skull Ofelia made. She decorated it with rainbow-coloured icing and sequins.

By way of contrast, a copy of Filippino Lippi's *Adoration of the Magi* was hanging on the wall beside the altar. One of Tía Ariché's favourite religious illustrations, she believed its presence guaranteed Mamá good fortune in the afterlife.

When I walked out, Tía Ariché adjusted the empty wicker chair beside her without facing me. She patted its seat. 'Are you hungry, *mijita?*' she asked. 'After *desayuno* why don't we ride the horses down to Urique and leave some flowers on your mamá's grave like we did last year? Would you like that?'

Then she looked at me with her eyebrows raised and waited for me to nod.

'I know Suré would,' she went on. '*Nada mas segura*, nothing surer. What do you say? Some sunflowers again? Her favourites. Why don't you go and pick some? We can stay there overnight and come back up tomorrow. Oh, I like your beret. It suits you. You look as striking in it as your mamá did.'

I looked away as a warm glow rushed through me at her compliment and her mention of my similarity to Mamá.

When I stood to get the clippers, Andrés appeared on the path leading to the canyon edge. He'd removed his t-shirt and wrapped it around his head against the sun. The dark skin of his lithe torso gleamed above his faded blue running shorts.

His black mixed-breed Calupoh dog, Geronimo, sleek as a greyhound with a white flash down his chest, bounded past him, his long tongue extended, his tail a runaway metronome when he recognised me. He slurped at his water bowl before slumping with a heavy sigh beneath the table, where he stretched out, panting, just beyond kicking distance of Tía's sandalled feet and a respectable distance from Zipi and Zape, who acknowledged his arrival with a combined warning growl.

Andrés glided up to us, barely panting and looking as though he hadn't raised a sweat. He placed his metre-long snake-catching pole on the table and pressed the button on the stopwatch he wore on his left wrist. Ten years older than me at seventeen, I worshipped the ground he ran on, joining him for short stretches whenever he'd allow me to. Despite our teasing, he insisted he'd been training for the 1968 Olympics in Mexico City all his life. The Games were now a year away.

'*Una hora y veinte*, an hour and twenty,' he said. 'Same as yesterday. Halfway down to Lorenzo's lookout and back.' He glanced at me. 'You should have joined me, *floja*.' Then he noticed the beret. 'Or should I call you Che? All you need is his red star... and his beard.'

'I'm *not* a lazybones and I'm not Che, I'm *me*. Come with us to Urique after breakfast and I'll show you who can run.'

'I'll have a shower and breakfast first before we find out who shows who.'

As he walked away, I was reminded how much we looked alike, how closely we shared our looks with Mamá. A thrill ran through me. It gave me a new sense of belonging, a deep connection I was craving to offset the aloneness I sometimes experienced when I was mixing with girls my age who had their mothers.

Hours later, we laid the sunflowers across Mamá's horizontal ochre-painted grave in the Urique cemetery in the scanty shade of an alder tree.

'*Los girasoles simbolizan la adoración,*' Tía said. 'Sunflowers symbolise adoration, as I told you last time.' She squinted up through the leaves at the pale blue sun-scorched afternoon sky. 'They may not last long in this heat but our adoration will.' She hesitated, before adding, '*Mientras Dios esté feliz de sonreírnos.* For as long as God is happy to smile down on us.'

We paid our respects and left offerings of food and drink Tía had prepared, which we arranged on the grave.

We stood with bowed heads for a minute before Tía murmured her consent and Andrés and I chased each other in and out of the white-trunked sycamore trees encircling the cemetery—trees so pale and ghostly Andrés partly convinced me as we ran that they came out of the ground at the full moon and danced among the tombstones on their roots to the hooting of the giant owl roosting in their branches.

'That owl is La Lechuza,' he said as we ran, catching me unawares and giving me goosebumps. I knew the myth. She was the shape-shifting wicked old witch who swooped down, talons drawn, to seize unsuspecting children at night, ripping them apart with her beak and taking revenge on people who'd wronged her.

The goosebumps eased when he suggested Mamá was running unseen beside us. He said she'd loved to do so with him when she was alive, and suddenly I could sense her there, the eerie rustling of the breeze among the sycamore leaves no longer the beating of a giant owl's wings but the whisper of Mamá's breathing—a sound so soothing in that moment it struck me that Mamá was not dead to us. In a sudden rush of emotion I took his hand and squeezed it, aware he must be missing Mamá as much as I was. He allowed me to hold it for several privileged moments before releasing mine to sprint the last few metres to the gravesite.

Later, we sat for some time in the nearby sanctuary of Our Lady of Guadalupe, the cool, calm silence of the chapel occasionally shattered by the expanding corrugated iron roof cracking like a starter's pistol.

Tía reminded us to make the sign of the cross and kneel when we entered. As I did so, I looked up at the mural of the dark-skinned *la Virgen* on the wall behind the altar. She still wore the bright purple eyepatch someone crudely painted over her right eye during the Easter celebrations last year, protecting her from witnessing the suffering of her son on the cross, but allowing her to watch through her left eye the destruction and burning in hell of the papier mâché effigy of Judas—the climax to the ceremonies.

Before she settled into a pew, Tía Ariché adjusted her favourite cotton rebozo shawl embroidered in olive-green and gold snakeskin diamonds over her head and shoulders. Next, she removed my beret, replaced it with Mamá's rebozo and assured me I looked as fresh and untouched as la Virgen Purísima herself wearing it.

'So did your mamá when she was your age and as innocent,' she added as she adjusted it, before leaning forward with a meaningful glance. '*Pero sin tu rebeldía*, Alicia. But without your rebelliousness.'

My rebelliousness? How dare you? You're not my mother. You never will be! I forced a smile and bit my tongue, but my eyes gave me away and for a brief second I sent her a spark of defiance, quickly extinguished by the respect and fear I held for her uncertain temper.

'Oh, look at you, *mijita*. So fiery. So headstrong.' She shook her head. 'What are we to do with you?' Her expression softened and her voice changed as she reminded us as always that Mamá was far from dead and we should pray for her. Still alive in that other place, with spiritual access to our world, she was doubtless watching over us. '*Un milagro gracias a Dios, nada mas*,' she said.

A miracle? Thanks be to God? Nothing more?

Part of me wanted to believe her, and did, but in the following silence, perplexing questions flooded my mind. *Has Mamá forgiven me without me asking her to because she loves me and is my mother? Am I worthy of her sacrifice? Does she miss me as much as I miss her? Can I ever make it up to her?* And the question tormenting me above all: *If giving me life meant she'd died in accordance with some miraculous purpose, as Papá had suggested, what does it mean for my future? A future I was destined to spend without her.*

'*Un milagro?*' I asked.

'*Un milagro sin lugar a dudas, como tú.*' She patted my knee. 'A miracle for certain, just as you are.' She gave me her familiar enigmatic smile and contradictory look. 'On the other hand, only God truly knows.'

'And if God has his doubts, then we keep guessing—' Andrés broke in.

'Sssssssssssst! Not in this place,' Tía Ariché admonished him. She stretched across my back and delivered a sharp slap to the back of his head. 'You leave your scepticism at the door, and any other doubts you've got floating around in your empty skull, Andrés. In this place, our faith keeps hope alive, not questioned by your so-called logic and reason.'

I suppressed a laugh when I heard him grumble as he

flinched, '*Sí. Sí.* Okay, Tía.' He made a face and I saw him mouth under his breath, '*Pero no*, but no,' as he often did, reasserting his seventeen-year-old machismo Mexicano.

When we left the chapel, Andrés asked if we could race along the thousand-metre sandy circuit cleared of rocks beside the river. 'We don't have time,' Tía replied. 'It's getting late.'

Impulsively ignoring her, I took off my riding boots and laced on my made-to-measure huaraches. They'd been designed for running—with car tyre soles.

'Race you up the hill!' I shouted, and with a head start, I sprinted with Andrés and Geronimo over the rocks and slippery gravel up the slope to the tethered horses. I punched him several times on the arm when he said he'd let me win.

'Tía's right about your running.' He gazed intently at me, his dark brown eyes alight. 'You are a little mountain goat— and you look like one.'

'That makes two of us,' my tongue surprised me by replying before I'd thought of an answer. 'And you're ten years older so you're twice as ugly.'

My quick response caught him off-guard.

'*Tienes razón.* Touché!' he said, and we both laughed till the tears came, Andrés tickling my ribs with the bony fingers of his left hand while he held my upper arm with his right, careful to protect the long fingernails he'd grown for Papá and his good friend Tío Guillermo, who were teaching him to play new flamenco techniques on his guitar. Of course I'd grown mine as well, and when Andrés was practising after his lessons, he allowed me to sit beside him, joyfully tinkering with the child-size guitar Papá gave me when I'd complained about being left out.

Tía Ariché, beaming, struggled up the hill towards us. I could see her wondering what the fuss was all about. The two rebozos lay across her shoulders and in her right hand she held the little *hielera* cooler with our Lulú drinks on ice.

When she lifted the lid, she surprised us with an unexpected extra treat—a slice of her homemade *mazapan de cacahuate*, her peanut marzipan, left over from the plateful of pieces she'd placed on Mamá's grave, along with the paper cup of her favourite drink—crushed-ice mango licuado.

Before she handed us our rewards, she held out her arms, as always. *'Abrázame*, hug me,' she said. And I did, just as I'd have hugged Mamá if she'd lived. The smoky smell of sweat and camphor lingered when she let me go and I asked myself achingly, *Did Mamá feel and smell the same?*

Looking back on it now, when I was seated between Tía Ariché and Andrés in the chapel, her dark Rarámuri skin and his deep mestizo tan so distinctly contrasted to my paler fawn, I felt different—in some way blessed—and yet the same, and sensed emotions stirring within me I didn't yet understand. For the first time, I feared living in a mystifying world where I suspected my destiny was no longer of my choosing or my will, but more a matter of chance.

I learned on that Mother's Day that the world, for all its magic and mesmerising beauty, can turn and strike you quicker than a feral cat you're stroking in the street when it rubs against your leg. Shocked and bleeding, you stifle your scream and wonder, *Did I deserve the vicious clawing and the unexpected bite? And if so, why?*

Either way, you carry the scars as a lifelong reminder of your questions and the lessons you learn, and the confusing thought struck me, *If my relationship with Mamá—the most important of my life—lasted no longer than a month, are all my relationships only temporary and destined to end quickly?*

When we returned to Cerocahui the next day, Tía took me out to one of the ramshackle garden sheds. It was dark inside, the single cobwebbed window grimy. She reached up to a shelf where there was a row of lidded jars.

'Cup your hands together,' she said.

She shook the jar, unscrewed the rusty lid with some effort and poured a handful of small white sunflower seeds into my open palms. 'Now go, *mijita*. You know where to plant them. The early ones will be ready for you next year.'

Since then, I've taken a handful of seeds to plant in whatever flowerbeds are available wherever I am so that I'll have a bunch of sunflowers in full bloom on the following Mother's Day.

Caring for them as they grow, watching their buds develop and listening to stories told about Mamá over the years, have extended the one unremembered month we shared into decades, giving me a comforting, imaginary sense of bonding with the mother I never knew.

In ten short years, I'll be as old as she was when she died. It gives me an intense, uneasy awareness of my mortality, as if I'm living on borrowed time, and it reminds me—just as the growing sunflowers do each year—that mourning for her will never end.

What I learned that day I spent with Tía Ariché I've never forgotten. And although the memory can be mysteriously selective, fragmented and unreliable, I've often returned to those moments for insights into my own story, my coming of age and my quest for self-awareness, to better understand who I am and accept the person I've become.

There I am, my eager younger self, thrilled Tía has confirmed I looked so much like Mamá when she was younger, wearing her beret and rebozo and listening for further revelations to add to my growing picture of her. She took her stories with her when she died, but listening to Tía enabled me to imagine her retelling them.

There are times when I can still hear Tía describe the challenges Mamá dealt with during my birth and explain how she faced her demons with the courage, determination and resilient independence I like to think I've inherited.

A Strange Game Of Consequences

Alicia Serrano—in Saucillo, Northern Mexico, April 1968

I WAS EIGHT YEARS old when my papá, Victor, showed us his blue reinforced cardboard suitcase for the first time. I clearly recall him revealing its contents to us as he explained how he travelled from Spain to Mexico during the Spanish Civil War when he was twelve, and met Mamá by chance seven years later.

Andrés and I found him that day relaxed in his black leather armchair in the lounge. He was reading, his legs outstretched on a footstool, when we burst in from the garden. We'd been sprinting around the circuit in the backyard of Papá's house in Saucillo under Abu Cerrildo's coaching supervision and we were heading to the kitchen for a drink.

Andrés skidded to a halt beside him. 'Papá, *por favor*, please tell us how you and Mamá met,' he said.

Papá looked up. He closed his book and retrieved his distance glasses from his forehead. He put them on, sat motionless for a second, then raised his eyebrows.

'*Again?*' he asked.

'Yes, again. *Por favor.*'

'I've told you before. We met on the cathedral steps in Chihuahua City. We were both nineteen and members of the Children's Cultural Army. Teaching illiterate kids and adults to read and write.'

He rubbed his forehead as if to clear the horizontal furrows and allowed me to lift his feet from the footstool. I made myself comfortable on it and looked up at his long, thin sunburned face with its bony cheeks, Grecian profile and straight, high-bridged nose. I considered him more handsome than any *vaquero* in a Western on TV, especially considering his remarkable eyes. They were the same amber colour as mine, though in his, you could detect flecks of gold around the pupils. I leant forward with my elbows on my knees, my chin on my hands and stared into them.

'I joined Mamá's group that day,' he went on, before frowning for a moment as if collecting his thoughts. 'Later, we played chess during the breaks at school. We used a set Abu Cerrildo carved for her.'

'Like he does now? Using crystals from the Cave of Swords at the Naica mine?' I asked.

'The same.'

'And you liked her when you both played chess?'

'Yes, I did. We fell in love. You want me to go on?'

'That's not what I asked,' Andrés said. 'I want to know what happened *before* you came to Mexico. Before you met her. You've never told us the story. Not in full, anyway.'

'Because it's such a long one.'

'I want to know everything. Not just the bits and pieces you've told us so far.'

'Every detail?' He pointed at Andrés and shook his forefinger. 'You don't know what you're asking.'

'Yes, I do. It's our story too, don't forget.' Persistent as always, Andrés held both hands out, palms up. 'Your story will help Alicia and me understand.'

'Understand?'

'What you were like as a boy. How you came to *be* in Chihuahua City. Besides...' he seemed to search for the words, 'we want to know where *we* belong in the story. At least, I do.'

'Me too,' I said at once, supporting him as usual, but uncertain what he meant.

'Ah, I see.' Papá nodded, frowning. He rose abruptly to his feet and placed his open book face down on his chair. 'Very well. Come with me.'

We followed his tall, angular frame to the privacy of his darkened bedroom, where he pulled aside the curtains. Blazing sunlight filled the room as he lifted down a blue suitcase I'd never seen before, concealed on top of his wardrobe. He placed it on the bed, dusted it off with the back of his hand, flicked aside the rusty locks and slowly opened it, as though disclosing a mystery to us.

I was excited as he revealed its contents. It seemed he was bringing his past into our present at last, introducing us to the magic of his treasured boyhood memories lying in wait for us all our lives. Peering over his shoulder, I wondered what surprising stories each item held in store. I glimpsed a plastic bag of chipped, multicoloured glass marbles and steel ball bearings, a pair of battered yoyos, and a chess set in a net bag, its pieces intricately carved in light and dark wood. I saw crayons and several sketching pads, and a pair of black leather running shoes, cracked and twisted out of shape, their long spikes rusty. Two large, beige celluloid Philip Morris cigar boxes stood out beside a handful of comics and magazines, and beside them a photo album.

He took out the album, placed it on his lap, moved the open suitcase to one side and invited us to sit beside him.

'My papá Xavier, your other grandfather, was a professional photographer in Spain,' he said, opening the cover. 'He became a freelance photojournalist when the civil war broke out in 1936, over thirty years ago. He sold his pictures to the highest bidder or took assignments from the newspapers when they paid him enough to feed the family. Which wasn't often. Most of the pictures in here are his.'

He held the album open at the third page, his hand covering the right-hand page, fingers splayed. At the top of the left-hand page, written in neat white cursive, I read the words *Gernika—antes*, Guernica—before. Beneath it the date—26 April 1937.

It showed the peaceful scene of a small rural town in black and white that could be anywhere in Spain or parts of Mexico, taken at street level. Two and three-storey buildings with roman-tiled roofs, some inset with dormer attics. Arched front doors and whitewashed walls. Wooden windows framed with dark bricks and decorative cast iron grills. White-paved cobbled streets leading to a plaza filled with groups of people beneath the trees and a bandstand in the centre. Some animals—a handful of wide-horned cattle, and sheep, some black and others white. Beyond them, the tower of a church rose above the shadowy peaks of distant hills beneath a windswept sky streaked with clouds.

I leaned across and pointed at a flat-roofed single-storey building facing the square. It appeared to be a school, with a number of young children playing in the courtyard.

'What's that?' I asked. 'It looks like a school.'

'It is. A Basque school, an *ikastola euskadi*. See the name over the archway? The authorities set them up in smaller towns like Guernica and Durango during the civil war and moved as many children as possible into them, well away from the big cities like Bilbao and Madrid. To keep them safe from the fighting and the bombing.'

'They look happy.'

'They do. It looks like some of them are playing hide and seek. And you can see those three girls skipping, just like you do.'

'It's very peaceful, Papá,' Andrés said, 'with a civil war going on.'

'It was a quiet market day, even though open markets were forbidden at the time. You see the time on the Santa María belltower?'

'Half-past two,' Andrés replied.

Papá removed his right hand to reveal the other photograph. He held both pages up to us. 'By eight o'clock, it looked like this.'

Gernika—después, Guernica—afterwards, the other title read.

I peered at the apocalyptic scene of shattered buildings smouldering beneath a pall of smoke, flames raging here and there. The charred and grisly remains of limbs and body parts barely recognisable as animal or human lay scattered across piles of burning rubble beside multiple black bomb craters. Trenches and cellars lay blasted open, those who may have taken shelter in them buried alive.

I gasped at the ruins of the school, struck with horror as my heartbeat faltered. *Those poor children!* I looked away for a full minute, nauseated, fighting to calm myself, before glancing back.

The shadows of three firemen from a brigade unit stood pumping water at the conflagration. Fractured tubes the size of relay batons glinted in the blackened wreckage.

Andrés pointed them out. 'What are they?'

'They're the aluminium shells of phosphorus grenades. The bigger ones are thermite bombs,' Papá replied, 'used to create a firestorm across the town. Imagine the damage, especially when the people or animals caught fire.'

Andrés stared at the two photographs, shaking his head. He pointed at the earlier photo on the left-hand page. 'Is this one of Abu Xavier's photos too?'

'They both are. He was working in Bilbao at the time so he could have visited Guernica any day before the bombing. He showed my mamá, Marina, and me the pictures when he developed them back in Barcelona.'

'So it may not have been taken on the day before the bombing?'

'Knowing him, he'd have done everything to find a shot he'd taken as close to that date as possible.' He glanced at Andrés, frowning. 'I do remember one thing that concerned him. Some other world-famous photojournalists working in

Spain *staged* the photographs they sent out for publication. Breathtaking shots, full of drama. Prize winners, some of them. They looked authentic, but they weren't. They were posed many kilometres behind the front lines, using actors dressed for the part, complete with cartridge belts and rifles. They cheated, in other words.'

'Why?'

'Because they couldn't get close enough to the fighting. Or were afraid to. Or too lazy.'

'How could they get away with it?'

'Tricks of the trade, I once heard him tell Mamá. Blurring the background so the locations couldn't be verified. Your abuelo refused to do the same. All his shots were genuine. In the case of Guernica here, we know it was a market day, but they turned most of the farmers away. The town was already full of retreating Republican soldiers and refugees.' He circled the animals in the plaza with a forefinger. 'But it looks as if a few farmers got through the cordon anyway, as we Basques always will. We're a determined bunch, *cuando el empuje viene empujar*. When push comes to shove.'

Papá told Andrés the bombing had been carried out by German Luftwaffe pilots of the Condor Legion flying the latest Heinkel bombers, on loan from Hitler to General Franco's Nationalists.

'By eight o'clock the town was in ruins and up to a thousand people were dead,' he said. 'We don't know the exact number. Guernica didn't just change world opinion against the Nationalists, it also changed my life forever.'

'You came to Mexico?' Andrés asked.

'I did.'

'So we owe Guernica our lives, Alicia and me?'

Papá closed the album. He spread both hands across the cover, smoothing it out. 'You could say so. When Abu Xavier saw the extent of the carnage and took these photographs, he made up his mind to send me here. On my own. It happened as quickly as that.' He snapped his fingers; the piercing click beside my ear made me jump. 'A month later, I boarded the steamship *Mexique* in France, in Bordeaux, with the other selected children. We arrived in Veracruz in early June.'

'How old were you?' Andrés asked.

'Twelve.'

'Did Abuela Marina or Abuelo Xavier see you off?'

'Papá was working in Asturias, but Mamá came to the França station the day I left.' He drummed his fingers on the photo album for several long moments before he broke the silence. 'I never saw her again.' He pursed his lips as the silence lengthened. 'You don't have to ask. She died at the battle of Ebro River a year later. In July. Papá told me in a letter.'

'How?' Andrés asked.

Papá stared at Andrés, holding himself in check, it seemed to me. 'All right. She was evacuating three wounded volunteers from Benifallet and the ambulance received a direct hit. She's buried with them in the Rasquera cemetery in Tarragona. At least she had the dignity of a proper burial. Not a mass grave like many others.'

He shook his head. 'Before she died, she wrote to me whenever she could. Many postcards. Almost one a week. I lost count. They arrived every few months aboard the ships bringing them, in little bundles held together with rubber bands, sometimes with a letter from Papá.

'At the school in Morelia, we used to listen out for the postman every afternoon. Señor Arturo, on his red bicycle, with his pea whistle. Such an unmistakable sound! So shrill we'd hear him coming down the street and watch the *portero*, the gatekeeper, open the gates for him. A big fat man with a loud voice, he was. Always laughing. So loud we could hear his conversation from the classrooms even with the windows closed. It was exciting when he distributed the letters, but for me, almost always disappointing because the ships from Spain weren't frequent.'

Papá replaced the photo album in the suitcase and took out one of the beige cigar boxes. He placed it on his lap. He ran his fingertips over the two rampant lions facing off against each other in the logo embossed on its lid, as though reading them and its *veni vidi vici* motto in braille. He did not open it. He leant forward instead, placed it on the floor between his feet, and sat with his shoulders hunched.

And then, vigorously shaking his head, his fearful growl shattered the silence. '*Guernica!* This takes me back, damn it!'

I jerked sideways and glanced up at him, alarmed. Andrés placed a restraining hand on his forearm. Papá looked at each of us in turn, then closed his eyes and vigorously shook his head. He spread his arms across our shoulders and gradually tightened his grip, his fingers digging into my flesh until it hurt.

An icy foreboding rushed through me. I twisted around and loosened his fingers, then held his hand in both of mine on my lap. A rush of empathy overtook me. About to cry, I began stroking the back of his hand, desperate to comfort him, but unsure how. When I looked up at his tormented face it blurred through my welling tears and I looked away.

Thankfully, moments later, he relaxed. He opened his eyes and took a deep breath.

'Very well,' he said, 'since you want my story, why don't I begin on 29 April 1937? I am twelve years old. It's late in the afternoon during a thunderstorm in Barcelona. Imagine you're sitting beside me as you are now, in the little kitchen at the back of our house. Abuela Marina is opposite us, looking unusually serious. Abu Xavier has just developed the photos of Guernica I've shown you, as well as several others not in the album. We watch him put them down one at a time on

211

the mustard-yellow plastic tablecloth. Face up. In silence. We have no idea what he's going to say, but his expression is so stern and the photos so shocking we know it's going to be terrible.'

He held Andrés and me rapt in a long moment of shared suspense before he told us what happened next.

His storytelling, as always, held us spellbound.

Victor Serrano—in Barcelona, Spain, 29 April 1937

Mamá Marina and I stared at the freshly developed black and white photographs as Papá Xavier spread them across the kitchen table. He rapped the tabletop with the knuckles of his right fist several times and growled, '*Sobran las palabras.*' His face was so flushed it shocked me. 'Words are superfluous. Each picture speaks for itself.'

He scooped them up and looked across at me.

'Victor, I've added your name to those going to Mexico next month,' he said.

It took me a moment to understand what he'd said, before I reared back in my chair. 'What? *Me?* Going to Mexico?'

'It's either that or a choice between Great Britain, Belgium, France or the Soviet Union. You speak little French and no English or Russian, so Mexico is the obvious destination. Especially since their President Lázaro Cárdenas sympathises with our Republican Popular Front.'

He spoke so rapidly and the rain was drumming so loudly against the window I could hardly hear him.

'If the quota of those embarking on the steamship *Mexique* from Bordeaux for Veracruz on 26 May is full,' he went on, 'there are places available aboard the *Habana*, leaving the Santurtzi docks in Bilbao for Southampton on the twenty-first. Mexico or England. Either way, you are going. Mamá and I are agreed on this. I'm sorry. We have no choice.'

His warning frown and quick shake of his head as our eyes met discouraged me from interrupting him. 'It's for your own good, Victor. You're twelve years old. We will not have you sent to the front when you turn thirteen in July or *Dios no lo quiera*, God forbid, joining the siege in Madrid.'

He sat back, placed the photos on the table and crossed his arms.

'On my own?' I stammered.

'Yes,' Papá said.

Tense and breathless, I felt the world fall away beneath my feet. 'For how long?'

Mamá reached out and held my right hand in both of hers. 'Until the situation here is sorted out and things return to normal,' she said quietly.

'How long will that take?'

'*Quién sabe*, who knows? A year? Two?'

'Can't you come with me?'

'No,' Papá said. 'Mamá is needed here to run the ambulances.'

'Two years?' My eyes filled with tears I couldn't stop. '*Two years!*'

'"According to some, but I will not lie to you.' Papá picked up the top photograph. He tapped the ruins with a forefinger. 'I've told you before, General Franco has Hitler and Mussolini in his pocket. They're using the civil war as a testing ground for their latest weapons. It pains me to say so, but the Nationalists might win. We Republicans have the heart and the will for a fight, but without the firepower, we're on the back foot. The armaments Stalin and Cárdenas are sending us don't match theirs.' He shook his head. 'It's another case of might is right, in which case we could become the righteous losers.'

'How will I contact you?' I asked. My voice was shaking so much I could hardly speak, a feeling of helplessness overwhelming me.

'All in good time. Arrangements will be made.'

'Can't I stay here in Barcelona?'

'You risk being handed a rifle and drafted where the fighting is.'

'Others my age have done it. Even younger.'

'Yes, and come back dead or mutilated in the back of ambulances. Ask Mamá. She has seen them. I will not risk it. In Mexico, you'll have a future. They are setting up a special school in a city called Morelia for all the children selected to go. President Cárdenas himself lives there and he'll be taking a personal interest in the school. You can finish your education there if you're fortunate enough to be accepted for the voyage. Perhaps start a profession. In geology, maybe? I know you're interested—look at your rock collection—and you have the talent and the persistence for the study.' He stared at me, adding forcefully, 'Remember what I've always drummed into you. *Serás exitoso siempre que aproveche al máximo sus oportunidades*, you will succeed provided you make the most of your opportunities and don't waste them. Set your goals and work hard to achieve them, one step at a time.'

I was shocked. 'Finish my schooling there, Papá? Now you're saying it could be *longer* than two years?'

'We don't know for certain. We have to face the possibility.'

'Can't you change your mind?' I couldn't hold back my sobs as a rush of fear tore through me. I felt vulnerable, unprepared and utterly helpless. 'Please?'

'Our minds are made up.' Mamá handed me a handkerchief. 'Your safety comes first. Besides, Papá and I will join you as soon as the war is over.'

'Or I can come home?'

'Or you can come home.'

There was a tense silence. Flooded with disbelief, I found myself standing on the edge of an abyss. I looked at Mamá. 'How long before I leave, then? If I have to.'

'Three weeks,' she said. 'Whichever ship you're on, I'll come with you on the train, if I can. If not, I'll be at the station to see you off.'

'What about you, Papá?'

'I have to return to Bilbao to give these photographs to my friend, George Steer. He's a British reporter for the London *Times*... and the *New York Times*. I was negotiating with him in Guernica after the bombing. The quicker we communicate this atrocity to the world, the better.'

'So if I'm sent on the *Habana* you'll be there?'

'If I'm still in Bilbao. Otherwise, no. I'm sorry.'

He stood, walked round the table, took my hand and pulled me to my feet. He put his hands on my shoulders and looked intently at me. 'I know this comes as a shock. It is a big ask. You might believe you won't cope, Victor, but we know you better than that. You're young. You're adaptable. And even if you have no say in the changes in your life right now, you have control over your attitude towards them. You decide what actions you take. Only you. You understand?'

He gathered me in his arms. 'We're depending on you to put your best foot forward. How you handle every challenge in the future will tell you—and us—the person you are.'

When he released me, I sat back stunned, my mind in turmoil. *If I leave,* I thought, *my friends will consider me a coward for avoiding the military service most of them will be undergoing. If I stay, I will consider myself a coward for backing away from the challenges of a future lived alone in Mexico for who knows how long.*

Papá was right. The decision was not mine. I had to make the most of the situation.

A fortnight later, the Ibero-American Committee accepted my application to join roughly four hundred and fifty other Spanish and Basque children—'orphans' they called us—selected to travel to Mexico from Bordeaux aboard the SS *Mexique*. Of course we weren't all orphans, but the Cárdenas Government used the term to generate sympathy among the Mexican people when appealing for donations to assist in our rescue.

We caught the train for Bordeaux on 23 May.

I have never forgotten the final confusion when the train pulled out of the França station. The last-minute shouts and whistles, the slamming of doors as the train gained traction, steel screeching on steel, steam and smoke erupting across the platform enveloping the crowd blurred through tears I could not control.

I gazed at Mamá's tall figure in her grey ambulance driver's uniform and wide-brimmed black hat with its stiff white feather fading as the train glided away. It drifted into the right-hand bend, picking up speed, hauling the carriages out into a bleak and overcast day until Mamá was out of sight and the soot-blackened graffiti-covered brick walls beyond the station slid past, the carriages rocking from side to side to the clattering rattle of wheels on the rails.

I pulled the window halfway down and sat back, but the incoming hot windgust carried the sharp smell of smoke and soot into the compartment and I slammed it shut. I closed my eyes and surrendered to the train's vibrations, the distance between everything I was familiar with and the unimaginable future looming ahead widening relentlessly. The clacking of the wheels on the tracks echoed in the darkness of my mind as the train gathered speed. It seemed to be calling out to me, *There's no going back… there's no going back… there's no going back.*

It was awful. I'd never experienced such despair."

Alicia Serrano—in Saucillo, Northern Mexico, April 1968

Papá suddenly stopped. The silence lengthened and the atmosphere grew so tense it scared me, until Andrés looked up at Papá. 'Tell us about the train journey,' he said. 'How long did that take?'

'Well, Abuelo Xavier had calculated the journey to Bordeaux would take ten hours. Three to Portbou close to the border, where we had to change trains because of the narrower French railway gauge. Another three to Nanterre, where we were told we'd be staying overnight and changing trains again. Then on to the west coast and our ship.'

'Was he right?' Andrés asked. 'Did you get there on time?'

'We were a little late, with delays in changing trains. We arrived in the afternoon, in fact. In Bordeaux we reported to the National Evacuation Committee reception centre, wearing our name tags. I remember some Basque and Mexican officials checked us in... and then a tall Mexican lady in a yellow jacket introduced herself as *señora* Cortés. Her braided hair was dyed bright red—so bright you couldn't miss her. She called out our names through a megaphone, deafening us, while another Mexican *dama* handed us each one of these.' He smiled, reached out and patted the blue suitcase. 'It was packed with clothes and things for the voyage—even candy. I've kept it ever since. *Como un recuerdo*, as a reminder.'

Then he gave us a low chuckle. 'Once we had the suitcase, we had to kneel in front of a *sacerdote*, a priest—each of us in turn—who blessed us for the journey. I didn't mind so much, but all the older teenage Basque boys refused. Point blank. Every single one. They were having none of it. They were true socialists—maybe even communists—who had already been fighting in the front lines and they hated the Catholic Church for siding with Franco's Nationalists. When I saw that, I knew there'd be fireworks sometime in the future.'

'And were there?' Andrés asked.

'All in good time,' Papá replied quietly. 'That's another story for another time.'

'So what about the album and the photos? Weren't they still with Abuelo Xavier when you left?'

'Ah, yes. The photo album. A man called Kurt Lessing brought it to the school in Morelia three years later, along with some other things, when I was fifteen years old. He was one of Papá Xavier's closest friends.'

He gave a sideways shake of his head and a quick, sharp outbreath.

'I can remember that day as clearly as if it's happening right here, right now. The Principal called me from my class and showed me into his office. Kurt was in there and the Principal left us together. I thought at first he was Vladimir Lenin, the likeness was so striking. The same lean and bony face. The high round forehead and sweep of eyebrows over hypnotic Asian eyes, their piercing gaze screwed up against the light—or maybe it was short-sightedness. The same straight nose and goatee around his unsmiling mouth.

'Anyway, he sat me down, explained who he was, and then told me I had to be brave, because my papá Xavier was no longer of this world. He had faced a firing squad with other Republicans, and was shot against the wall of *La Modelo* prison in Barcelona, six months ago, on January 29.'

A crushing burst of shock rushed through my chest, and I heard Andrés gasp, 'No! You've never told us that before.'

'What he'd just announced seemed to deafen me,' Papá went on. 'I watched him mouth words I couldn't hear or understand. It was terrifying. I screamed at him to stop. The space between us turned black and the room spun. I felt like I'd fallen from a precipice. How long it lasted I have no idea.'

'So what did you do?' Andrés asked.

'Oh, I clung to my chair until my vision gradually cleared,' Papá said, 'and Kurt, seated in front of me, slowly reappeared. We stared at each other blankly for a full minute. It's as close to madness I think I've ever come. He gave me a glass of water, and then explained that Papá Xavier had been executed, not only for his sympathies with the Republican cause, but also for Mamá Marina's work with the International Brigades. His body was buried in the mass grave at the *Fossar de la Pedrera*, the Cemetery of the Quarry on Montjuïc hill in the suburbs.'

Then Papá reached for the photo album. 'I know everything I've told you today is a lot for you two to take in,' he said. 'But you must never think that Abuelo Xavier lost his life for nothing. I want to show you something Kurt Lessing brought with him.'

He opened the album to a plastic sachet at the back and withdrew a postcard sized photograph of a grey, black and white abstract cubist painting I had never seen before.

He held it out in front of us.

'This is a copy of one of the most famous anti-war paintings in the world,' he said. 'It's a mural showing the bombing of Guernica. See the screaming women, the gored horse and the flames? See that dismembered soldier and the bull's head?'

'And the dead baby,' I said, pointing.

'And the dead baby, of course. It was painted by a famous Spanish artist, Pablo Picasso, in 1937...' He hesitated. 'Have either of you heard of him?'

'I have,' Andrés said. 'We've got some posters of his work up in the art classroom at school.'

'Well, let me tell you, it was Abuelo Xavier's photos in the newspapers that inspired Picasso to paint his masterpiece. So you were right, Andrés. If not for the bombing of Guernica I wouldn't be in Mexico and would never have met your mamá.'

'In which case me and Alicia wouldn't exist,' Andrés said.

'And those three girls would still be skipping,' I said, as if participating in a strange game of Consequences whose rules I didn't yet understand. I sensed the strong beating of my heart, and added breathlessly, 'I wish they were.'

Yes

MELBOURNE, NEW YEAR'S DAY, 1997, several minutes after midnight. Stefan Novak was on the balcony of his third-storey unit leaning against the rail in partial shadow, alone and still. He peered up at rockets bursting into blazing spheres of red, green and blue beneath a cloud-streaked sky, before waning in a glitter of dust and smoke.

Dazzling showers of sparks lit up his face every now and then, its reflection flashing in the open windowpane beside him. His striking cheekbones and shadow of a beard gave him what he thought was a sombre, hawkish look, bitterness evident in the eyes.

The telephone shrilled over the clang of pots and pans and voices yahooing on the balconies below. He scrambled through the sliding door.

'Steve Novak?' The caller was barely audible.

'Yes. This is Stefan.'

'Stefan. You're still up. Good. I haven't dragged you outta bed.'

'No, I'm watching the fireworks.'

'Good onya. Look, I know the timing's lousy and I won't keep you, but I've got a favour to ask. Something for you to mull over before you give me the answer I want.'

Stefan hesitated, frowning. 'What answer?'

He was bewildered by an unexpected caller whose voice, though vaguely familiar, he failed to recognise.

'A simple yes will do me. That's all I'm after, bro. No argument.'

No argument from you perhaps, and bro? Why bro?

On guard, he replied, 'What's the question? A simple yes sounds complicated to me.' *Who am I dealing with? Some crank who's hacked my number?*

About to slam down the receiver, he thought better of it as the caller introduced himself. 'This is Lennard Currie, but you can call me Ace.'

Stefan was taken aback. While they'd never met, he knew Lennard's name and reputation. He had admired his work for years and now he recognised his voice—a resonant baritone with a characteristic outback intonation he'd heard for the first time last September when Lennard had taken part in the SBS television debate on Truth and Reconciliation. He'd spoken with passionate conviction that night, his powerful frame standing out among the panellists. Some friends had considered his point of view convincing, but Stefan was sceptical of his line of reasoning that raised more questions than it answered.

Where's he calling from? What's he after?

'I'm not expecting a snap decision,' Lennard continued. 'You've got three days to chew it over.'

'That's generous of you. So I do have a say.'

'Of course you do.'

'Glad we got that sorted. What am I agreeing to, then?'

'It's not so much a favour as a proposition; an offer too good to knock back. Hear me out. You'll get my drift.'

'Ask away.'

Lennard Currie! He'd been at the cutting edge of Australian art since the early 1970s—Aboriginal Australian art. He was a maestro whose glass sculptures were acknowledged worldwide, fetching five and six-figure prices. Several of his pieces were on show in London's Victoria and Albert and New York's Metropolitan and Corning Glass Museums.

A month ago, Stefan had visited his latest exhibition. He'd walked through the colonnades of the National Gallery into a breathtaking blaze of colour flashing through a forest of slender head-high glass sculptures radiating light. It seemed a liquid flame lit by the fiery desert sun glowed in the recesses of Lennard's imagination and by some magical sleight of hand and eye, he'd brought the quartz outcrops and scorched red dunes of the western desert indoors with him.

One sculpture, in particular, had caught Stefan's eye—the centrepiece was an exquisite, statuette of dichroic glass lit alternately from within and without, each flash lasting thirty seconds. It glowed in a magenta wash when light was transmitted from within, reflecting sensuous tones of aquamarine and turquoise when lit from without. The raw beauty of its colours and the patterns materialising like fiery hieroglyphs through its core in waves of light had enthralled him. How much colloidal silver and gold had Lennard used in the glass batch to create the effect? Or had he come up with an experimental chemical composition to achieve it?

Back on the street that afternoon, envy had speared through him as he'd compared the failure of his crystalware business with Lennard's success. He'd wondered bitterly how much of that success was attributable to Lennard's Aboriginality, singling him out for the approval and support of the art fraternity, then he acknowledged his thoughts were mean-spirited and regretted his prejudice. His sculptures were one of a kind; technical mastery and creative flair evident in their arresting brilliance. Lennard's streak of genius in combining glass and light the way he did deserved accolades.

About to tear up the exhibition catalogue, he'd changed his mind and folded it into his back pocket.

Now he looked down at the unopened letters scattered beside the telephone and rummaged through them to find it. On its cover, vermilion and scarlet patterns swirled through a glass figurine beneath the words *Earth and Fire*. On the back was a photograph of Lennard, masked and pouring a braid of red-hot light from a ladle brimming with molten glass. He had signed his Malgana name across it—*Malajarri*. Stefan read the translation and his smile was sardonic—*Thunder*.

'So what are you after?' He broke the silence.

'You and me, bro, we're glassworkers with all the experience we need. All the knowhow.'

'What for?'

Stefan was unprepared for his reply. 'We're gonna cast a monument—a replica of Jandamarra's Rock.'

'Jandamarra's Rock?'

'The one in Windjana Gorge. You ever seen it?'

'No.'

'Then I'll take you there, to the Kimberley. Like I say, we're gonna sculpt it in solid glass. It'll be the biggest thing since the Palomar telescope lens.'

'Big as Palomar?'

'Bigger. Half as big again.'

A brief silence was broken by Stefan's snort. 'Pull the other one, why don't you?'

'I've never been more dinkum in my life. I'm flying back to Perth tomorrow morning. If you're interested, why don't you meet me out at Tullamarine?'

The next morning, Stefan found the airport café packed. He saw Lennard through the plate glass door, seated at a table to the left. He was the picture of self-possessed relaxation. His long legs were stretched out beneath the table. He was absorbed in a book lying open on the tabletop. He appeared to be making notes, a silver pen in his left hand poised over its pages.

Lennard looked up and caught his eye. He closed the book, inserted the pen as a bookmark and stood. He was taller and broader than Stefan had imagined, the first signs of middle-aged spread evident under a sky-blue shirt. The sleeves were rolled up, a narrow armband of raised scars visible in a diagonal pattern above his left elbow. His skin was light brown, sinews of sheathed muscle gliding beneath it as he extended his right hand, the palm square and work-hardened, the calloused fingers powerful.

'Stefan Novak, I presume!' He flashed a radiant smile, all teeth.

'That's me.'

'G'day. I'm Ace.'

He waved Stefan to a chair and sat opposite, his elbows on the table, his chin balanced on the bridge formed by interlaced fingers. His face was broad and imperious, and although his eyes were shaded behind blue-tinted sunglasses, they were dark and expressive. The wiry strands of his black beard were streaked with silver and his hair was unruly.

He stretched and leaned back in his chair. 'You have any trouble picking me out?'

'You're hard to miss.'

'I'm the only Yamaji here?'

'The biggest, anyway.'

'And getting bigger, so I'm told.' The brass eagle on the Harley buckle of his belt of polished snakeskin glinted as he patted his stomach. 'If my *wilygu warabadi* is anything to go by.'

'The TV doesn't do you justice.'

'It does if you've still got black and white.' He smiled. 'You know what they say—the bigger they are, the harder they are to fell.'

'That I can believe.'

Around his neck, Stefan saw a leather thong. Hanging from it was an oval of worn abalone shell patterned in a lucent swirl of sea-blues and greens. When he looked closer, he saw the outline of a bird carved in cameo in the nacre. It appeared to be a sea eagle, its wings spread in cruciform flight.

'It's good to meet you at last, brudda,' Lennard said. 'It's time we crossed paths. We've got things of importance to see to.'

At last? Am I the celebrity here, Stefan wondered, *the one with familiar features? Hardly!* 'Secret men's business?' he asked.

'You could say that, long as nobody's listening and you're not about to grass.' Lennard glanced at his watch. 'I'm catching the early flight. That gives us forty minutes; long enough to give you the heads up.' He stood to buy the coffees. 'You take yours white?'

'White and one.'

'I'm with Henry Ford—any colour, long as it's black.'

When he returned with the tray, he took a deep, appreciative breath. 'Nothing beats that smell, that's for sure.'

Stefan was in unfamiliar territory, unused to the company of a national celebrity, unnerved at the prospect of conversing for the first time with a charismatic icon of Australia's Aboriginal community.

Lennard turned in his chair and, from an inside pocket of the worn leather jacket slung across its back, he withdrew a Kodak envelope. 'Let's kick-start this conversation and get down to business.'

He spilled several photographs onto his palm. He shuffled them, squared them up and spread them face down across the table as though dealing a hand in blackjack. He waved a hand across them. 'Pick a card,' he said. 'Any card.'

Stefan flipped the first photograph to his left. A woman looked up at him. Waves of dark copper hair framed her fine-boned face. Her skin was pale and lightly freckled. Beneath dark brows, her eyes were green and candid. He saw humour in them and, it seemed, a questioning; a fierce intelligence with a touch of... what? Mockery? *Who is she teasing?*

He cast a glance at Lennard, who was observing his reaction with a half-smile. He turned back to examine the backdrop—a wall of weathered rock, white and marbled and immense, encircled by a dark reflective pool on which it seemed to float.

'Whoever she is, she's drop-dead gorgeous, Ace. And bloody hell! If that's Jandamarra's Rock, you'll be working your ring off.'

'No doubts there, on both counts. That's my Rosie—Rosalie O'Sullivan. And that's Jandamarra's Rock. Top choice first up. The omens are good. Now check out the rest.'

Each photograph showed the rock from a different perspective as if the photographer had selected each new vantage point to show a different surface, an unexpected blend of sunburned colour, an unusual pattern of weathered angles and shadows. He noticed the photographer's footprints in the sand encircling the rock, as though he or she had walked around it many times, deliberating over the composition or the light.

The rock stood solitary in the centre of the gorge, solid and angular and timeless. The jade-green water surrounding it mirrored the background of soaring cliffs, their cave-pocked limestone walls so still it seemed you could walk across the water on their rust and sepia reflections. In one shot, Stefan noticed a narrow-snouted crocodile basking on the sand as if carved to scale in polished rosewood.

In the last photograph, he saw Rosalie for the second time. The rock jutted sun-bleached from the river and she was seated on an upper ledge, smiling down at the camera, her beauty bathed in sunlight. Her hair flowed across her shoulders. Her arms were wrapped around her knees, her feet bare. Below were multiple tidelines scoured by successive flooding of the river, which was shallow in the photograph, as though the wet season was recently over or yet to begin.

Stefan peered at the rock. He visualised a two-storey monument, a pyramidal iceberg in glass and splintered sunlight.

Sculpt that? In solid glass? He looked up, shaking his head. 'No... bloody... way.'

'*Yes way!*' Lennard cut him short. '*No way*, no way. It's a memorial we'll be casting, remember? A memorial to my people.' He paused. 'A cenotaph.'

'A cenotaph!' Stefan's heart sank.

'That's right! A cenotaph to commemorate our *wiyabandinugu murla*, our known and unknown fallen heroes who died during the Frontier Wars.' After a tense silence, he asked forcefully, 'Are you aware how many we're talking about here?'

'How many died?'

'Were massacred.'

'Since when?'

'Since the invasion.'

'You mean since settlement.'

'I mean since the invasion,' Lennard fired back. '*Nothing* was settled.'

'Oh, okay. If you say so. I'm not too sure, but I think I read somewhere it may have been around twenty thousand.'

'If not more.' Lennard leaned forward, adding tersely, 'Perhaps twice that. But we're not talking statistics here, bro, we're talking flesh and blood. We're talking *human beings*, by crikey. They lived. They died. And we're going to bring them back to the place where they belong.' He stared at Stefan. 'In this country's consciousness.'

Four years later in Fremantle, while switching out the lights, Lennard crossed the veranda to look across the city at the ocean. He inspected the night sky as he always did, bringing closure to his day.

The Rottnest Island light was partly obscured; a night mist rising from the ocean, he assumed. He counted the faintly pulsing flashes—eight each minute, as usual. But he was confused. An hour earlier when he'd glanced across the channel, the flashes had been clear and the stars pristine. This was no longer the case. If it was a mist, it had risen from nowhere and, with a blustery night breeze coming off the sea, it seemed unlikely.

As he turned to call his partner Alicia, a flash of light close inshore caught his eye, and then another. Someone signalling a passing boat? Or a barbecue lit on Bathers Beach? And then the flash recurred, brighter now, and it persisted.

He realised it was a fire.

'Alicia!' she shouted, startling her. 'We have a fire down near the glassworks.'

She joined him at the railing as the glow split into three distinct fiery vertical rectangles, casting a faint orange glow on the underside of a bank of rising smoke.

'That can't be the front windows of the glassworks, surely?' His voice filled with alarm. 'Was there an explosion? Call the brigade. I'll wake Stefan. We'd better get down there right away!'

When they reached the glassworks the stench of charred wood and smoke was choking, showers of sparks and ash raining down. The frames of the buckling windows were alight and through them, they saw flames raging along the jarrah beams in the roof, radiating wildly across to the lacquered panels between them. Thick smoke filled the workshop, fire engulfing the benches and furnishings. The other half of the building was also ablaze, the flames not yet as fierce.

Lennard directed Stefan, who had armed himself with an axe before leaving the house, to check the pottery next door. Its storeroom shelves were stacked with enamels, acrylic paints and cans of glaze and turpentine. Stefan shouted back that the wall between the workshops was glowing and the shelving smouldering. The blackened plate glass display window was cracked and threatening to explode.

Tenants in the units facing the glassworks were on their patios and in their gardens in the lurid orange glow, frantically hosing down showers of stinging embers that swirled like swarms of burning bees towards them on intermittent onshore gusts of wind.

Lennard sprinted through a cascade of flying debris to the gas mains, switching from hand to hand as he closed down the scorching tap. He knew they'd lose the furnace when the melt within it solidified and the latest exhibition piece annealing in the gas-fired mould would fracture. He had no alternative.

The cenotaph in the converted annealing room was separated from the workshops by a passageway protected by a solid wall. Months earlier, they'd removed the polycarbonate roofing sheets so it was temporarily safe unless the fire leapt the gap or the brickwork ignited.

He cursed at the thought of three hand-held extinguishers languishing on brackets inside the building, behind locked doors. Then he recalled the oxy-acetylene tanks on the welding trolley stored beside the back door that opened to the beach.

Shocked, he screamed at Stefan, 'The oxy tanks! If they go up, they'll take out this end of the building!'

The glass monument would be blasted with it, along with the dividing wall to the pottery workshop and the line of windows in the flats opposite. He closed his mind to the thought of injuries among the onlookers.

He leaned across Stefan's shoulder to shout instructions over the deafening roar and they sprinted around the building through the choking pall of smoke, with Alicia following behind them.

Lennard retrieved the lawn hose and struggled to disconnect the sprinkler, but it was corroded in place. Stefan hacked the hose apart with his axe and sprayed water over

Lennard, who struggled to undo the lock, the doors blazing on the inside, the heat unbearable.

The lock gave and Lennard hauled the left-hand door open, shielding himself behind it as a blast of flame roared out before swirling skywards in the violent updraft. A roof beam slammed to the floor, bringing down a wedge of corrugated iron with it, a volcanic column of fire and sparks erupting skyward through the gap in the roof.

Lennard retreated towards the others standing on the beach.

'No choice! No time!' he shouted at Stefan. 'They're inside the door. Hose me down again!'

'No, you don't!' Alicia yelled out as she grasped the situation, her face ashen. 'Leave it to the fireys.' She pointed towards two firemen unrolling a length of hose from the nearest hydrant across the railway.

'Hose me down, bro,' Lennard ordered again. 'We risk losing everything. And give me your shirt.'

Stefan did so and sprayed him as he bound the shirt across his nose and mouth, the garish *Ingga Thaaka Rocktoberfest* poster of a Munich barmaid offering overflowing steins of beer emblazoned across it.

Alicia stepped around him. 'Over my dead body!' she screamed, placing both hands on his shoulders. 'It's not worth it!'

He waved an arm towards the annealing room. 'We've got no choice, Alicia!'

He leaned forward to embrace her, then turned away. As he did so, her fingers caught the leather thong threaded around his neck. He ducked towards the blazing door, his first step faltering as his head jerked back and the thong snapped. She looked down in horror at the pendant dangling in her hand, then turned to watch him disappear into the roaring inferno, bent double, a twisted black and orange shadow melting into a blast furnace.

Moments later, he staggered from the flames and smoke, one hand gripping Stefan's smouldering shirt across his nose and mouth, the other extended behind him hauling the oxy-acetylene trolley down the single step and out onto the grass.

He flung the cylinders aside and fell prostrate.

They rushed forward to drag him away and hose him down, the hair on the back of his skull singed and sparking, tongues of flame writhing down the back of his t-shirt like the mane of a chestnut horse.

Lennard was in an induced coma for three days in the acute care burns unit in the Royal Perth Hospital, and preliminary surgery on his back, scalp and hands was undertaken as soon as feasible. Within a week, he received treatment with experimental spray-on skin cultured from his cells and the healing process began.

Days later, when Stefan was at last permitted to visit him, he marveled at Lennard's gutsy stoicism, the way he fought to bear the pain that was evidently excruciating and constant, despite the morphine.

It took a month before the spasms lessened as the surgery took gradual effect.

By then Stefan found Lennard returning to his irrepressible self. 'I'm gonna look like one of your mob from behind, bro, with a skullcap of new skin on the back of my head,' he said.

'Saint Francis reborn?'

'He'll do me.' Then he chuckled. 'Remember, bro, if I do look white from behind anytime soon, it's only skin deep.'

During another visit, Lennard told him he was determined to have the monument unveiled on time, despite his absence. 'I won't be out of here before the end of the year,' he said. 'You know the deadline we agreed. You and Alicia will have to do the honours. Any day will do, as long as it's before New Year's.'

'Trust me, Ace,' Stefan replied. 'We'll christen it before then, come hell or high water.'

The cenotaph survived the fire with minor staining and was quickly repaired. The Fremantle Council contractors cleared the wreckage of the glassworks from the site. They removed the annealing room walls and erected a temporary fence covered in hessian to conceal the sculpture.

Stefan spent his time in the charred shell of the building retrieving whatever he could salvage as jackhammers pounded at the concrete foundations and two bobcat operators weaved among the wreckage removing slabs and bricks.

'The fireys inspected the site,' he told Lennard. 'They've confirmed it was arson. Someone sprayed the place with kerosene. They must have used a pump of some sort before lighting it with a blowtorch, which was found in the wreckage, by the way. Whoever it was broke in through the pottery workshop.'

Later, when Stefan was about to leave, Lennard called him back. 'Hey bro, before you go, I've got an idea I want you to give some thought to.'

'I'm listening.'

'The glassworks. It's a write-off, isn't it?'

'Total, I'd say. The demolition crews are giving it a good going over.'

'Okay. So there'll be some vacant land to the right of the cenotaph?'

'Unless the council agree to put another building up.'

'That's exactly what we're gonna convince them to do.'

'For you to lease as another glassworks?'

'No. For a meeting place.'

'For a *what?*'

'A hall. A theatre. A place where plays can be performed.

And dances. Films can be shown. Stories told. Where people can debate and argue, get things off their chests.' He took a long breath. 'A *gathering* place, where we can get together to talk about the traumas in our history and iron things out. Blackfellas and whitefellas together.'

It took a moment for Stefan to grasp what Lennard was suggesting. 'Where people can let off steam? In a confined space? That sounds bloody risky.'

'Exactly that. We take a risk. Building the cenotaph was risky, but we've done it. Now we have to keep the spirit of the place *alive*. We both know there are two different stories— white and black. You especially; you know that.' He gave a knowing smile. 'I've watched you struggling to reconcile both versions and see our point of view for the last four frigging years.' His smile broadened. 'I think you still are, even though you're in denial.'

Stefan hesitated, uncomfortable with the observation. 'Knew I couldn't hide it from you.'

'No need to try.' He gazed at Stefan for several moments and then, as if to deliberately shock him, he said with quiet emphasis, 'There's not just one solution to resolve it, bro.'

'*What?*'

'It'll take a lot more than a cenotaph and good intentions.'

'Now you tell me!' Stefan threw up his hands. 'So what are you suggesting?'

'Like I said, we build a meeting place where both stories can be told. It'll be a game-changer. People will interact. They'll *perform*. Let's give the powerless a place where they'll have a voice. A real *voice*. Give them a chance to express what they're feeling face to face, and you'll get understanding. And respect. On both sides. We'll learn to work together. We'll form relationships. Have conversations.'

'Given time?'

'Of course given time. Think how powerful the reconciliation process will be as a result. It'll be a stepping stone to a treaty. To changes in the constitution recognising us at last, by crikey.'

'Change the constitution? That'll take a referendum.'

'So be it.'

Stefan looked at him for a thoughtful minute before nodding. 'It's possible, I guess, but it *is* ambitious. We're up against structural racism and prejudice. We'll have to move mountains to turn *that* around.'

'That's more like it, brudda!' Lennard smiled. 'And I like that "*we*". It's a start. It'll make the cenotaph the *living* monument we want, not one that people visit less and less.' Then he gave an unexpected burst of laughter, grimacing at the pain. 'I haven't been lying here on my *manda* doing nothing. I've even thought up a Nyungar name for the building—*Babanginy Koondarnangor*. Lightning and Thunder. We've got the cenotaph—that's the lightning. Now we need the thunder.'

'*Malajarri*?'

He smiled. '*Malajarri* in Malgana. Have a yarn with Alicia. See what she's got to say.'

'I'll be seeing her tonight. It should be interesting.'

Sunday, 10 December, 2000. The monument towered over them, surrounded by a shallow moat in which its diffracted colours shimmered. To the left of the passage through its centre, a single gas flame flared a brilliant orange in a bronze bowl on a pedestal of quartz. A Whadjuk Nyungar elder had lit it earlier with his *karlamarta* firestick.

Six senior Nyungar women dressed in ceremonial *bwoka* kangaroo skin cloaks wound their way through the invited spectators, waving the smouldering leaves of a *balga* grass tree in a smoking ceremony to prepare and cleanse the area. They were singing a Nyungar song of welcome prepared for the occasion.

'Time to go,' Stefan said when the smoking ended. He stood with his camera slung around his neck and gazed at Alicia. Elegant in a simple white caftan, she reached for the sea eagle pendant Lennard had insisted she wear for the opening. She lifted it to her lips. 'I wish he was here.'

'He's here. He'll be thinking of us,' Stefan replied, an arm around her shoulder.

He looked down at twelve-year-old Keisha Kuranha from Waroona standing between them, winner of a poetry contest held to select the first young Aboriginal Australian to walk through the cenotaph. She was carrying a saffron yellow spray of *mooja* tree flowers in one hand, a pair of scissors in the other.

They crossed the grass and the flagstone bridge to the entrance, accompanied by two of the senior Nyungar women, their *dwerta-dyer* headdresses resplendent with black and white *koolbardi* magpie feathers, with the sound of a didgeridoo echoing.

Keisha placed the flowers beside the flame and then, guided by Alicia, she cut the plaited red, black and gold ribbon draped across the entrance. It fell away and she followed the Nyungar women shyly into the canyon between the crystalline walls, coloured light pouring across her.

Alicia stepped forward to follow her and then hesitated, signalling for Stefan to precede her. He did so, running his fingers across the names of the fallen warriors glinting on the blue-grey panel to his left: *Yagan, Midgegooroo, Pemulwuy, Windradyne, Dundalli, Mosquito, Walyer, Multeggerah*, among others.

Following Keisha, Stefan saw her reflection deep within the sculpture, gathering and gliding apart and re-forming beyond the etched names like a ghostly image. When they were partway through, the music ended and in the sudden silence, Keisha glanced back. She caught Stefan's eye deep in the glass and it seemed to him that she was sharing with him for that instant the answer to a mystery familiar to her.

At the end of the passage, Stefan ran exploring fingers into the letters of the last warrior's name—*Calyute*. Then he walked out into the sun through swirling blue and aquamarine waves of light.

He and Keisha watched Alicia pause at the exit, the sea eagle glinting at her throat. He lifted his camera as she emerged.

Then he placed a hand on Keisha's shoulder. 'This is your heritage, Keisha. Never forget it.'

She looked up, smiling shyly. 'Yours too,' she said, before averting her gaze.

Later that evening, when the guests had dispersed, Stefan returned to Bathers Beach. He switched on the cenotaph floodlights and locked the gates. He sat on a bench and looked out over the darkly starlit sea, listening to the rhythmic scrunch of waves before they swished up the sand, the lingering smell of ceremonial smoke drifting.

The only other figure in the twilight was a barely discernible shadow stripped to the waist sweeping the sand with a metal detector, zigzagging up and down the slope of the beach with his dog a shadow at his heel. Stefan stifled a sardonic smile. *He must know what I know—life's a minefield and he's another searching for the Truth.*

He turned and contemplated the monument, thinking of its historical and symbolic significance, before looking out at the black ocean. He found himself fighting an unexpected surge of outrage and despair, then held his head in his hands.

Acts of racial violence! Will there never be an end to the division?

He looked back at the cenotaph and glimpsed beyond it the newly laid concrete pad for the meeting hall, the gathering place Lennard had conceived. A performance theatre. A powerful place for stories to be told and heard. A place for one-on-one conversations, for conflict resolution and a place for healing.

He tore off his shoes and walked to the sea's edge where he paced ankle-deep in the breaking waves before standing for several minutes, looking out at the light flashing strongly on Rottnest Island.

He recalled the first time he'd heard Lennard's voice over the telephone and had not recognised it, though it sounded familiar, and before he could ask who was calling, Lennard had said he had a question for him and wouldn't take no for an answer.

'Right now, I have the answer you want, bro, no questions asked.' Stefan's voice rang out across the dark water. 'The answer is *yes*, and yes again. Yes.'

Ebony and Ivory
—A Perfect Match

T HE YEAR 1701 SHAPED up to be a good one for Gerrit de Waal.

By mid-February, after five weeks working in the timberyard among the saw-windmills, he had changed. He felt strong. Fit. Broader in the shoulders and deeper in the voice and chest. His sixteenth birthday lay ahead in June and he was already able to hold his own in the teams in which he worked. Able to look his co-workers in the eye, respond to their teasing, give as good as, and often better than, he got.

All this without getting cocky and losing sight of the fact that he was an apprentice shipwright carpenter, recently indentured just after New Year, available at foreman Cain's beck and call and dependent on him for a good report back to Pieter Penne, the master shipwright in the *dokhavn* back in the city of Middelburg, twenty kilometres away.

While showing them around the yards just after dawn on the first day of their induction, Cain had pointed at several men in waders working knee-deep in the first of three log-bearing ponds, the surface of the water steaming in the cold. They appeared to be clearing sludge. They were mulattos, one very dark-skinned and others with skins of lighter shades.

'They're the hardest men you're ever going to meet, those blacks. And the least friendly,' Cain said. 'They'll drive you with fists of iron, *jongens*, so be prepared. Never take offence, not under any circumstances. Follow their instructions and their example and you can't go wrong. To the *letter*, now!' An unexpected wheeze gave way to a wracking cough until he turned, cleared his throat and spat a gob of phlegm across the gravel. 'They've been here for four generations, as you know, but the fear of exile is still in their blood. They stick together so that no privateer gets the wrong idea and tries to kidnap them again to ship them off to slavery in Brazil.' He sucked in his cheeks. 'On the other hand, if they do let you in and you get to know them, you'll find they have hearts of gold.'

Gerrit saw one, lighter-skinned than the rest, stand and look across at them, a hand raised to shade his eyes. His heart lurched when he recognised Sebastiao. He had met him once, many years ago, when he'd come to the house to talk to Miranda, one of his mother's maids in training. He was her father. Sebastiao raised his shovel in a wave, which Gerrit returned. When he saw Cain beside him wave back, he realised with some embarrassment he'd misread his signal.

Gerrit knew the mulattoes were descended from a shipment of Angolan slaves crammed aboard a Portuguese caravel from the island of Sao Tomé, captured by the Dutch privateer the *Golden Unicorn* over a century ago, while on its way to Brazil. The story was legendary. The ship had arived in Middelburg in 1596. As soon as the slaves had been baptised as Christians in the Reformed Church, they had been granted their tickets of leave.

Gerrit's beloved grandfather, Opa Laurens, had passed the story down to him. When he was a boy, Laurens had personally known the Dutch *schipper* who'd captured the caravel, but his name escaped him.

That was all Gerrit knew. The barest outline of their history. He was keen to learn more.

On the Monday of his fifth week, Cain directed Gerrit to work for the first time with the Afro-Zeelander group of eight senior lumbermen. When he joined them, their supervisor Sebastiao took him aside.

'No favours here, Gerrit,' he said, pointing across at the line of saw-windmills. 'I've assigned you to work with two of my lumbermen today, up on windmill number five. Lourenco and Marais. You'll help them remove the worn hemp sails and replace any rusted bolts connecting the sweep-spars to their stocks.' He looked sharply at Gerrit. 'Are you up for that?'

'I'm up for anything.'

'No trouble with heights?'

'Not so far.'

'Good. Keep it that way. You'll also repair sections of the lattices that have rotted through. It's dangerous work, so keep your wits about you.'

Gerrit found it exhilarating, perched high on the scaffolding, a safety rope about his waist. For seven glorious hours, he passed different tools, new bolts and fresh battens of larch to the lumbermen when they required them.

He had time to spare while they were working and, as he had on the third-storey window ledge in his bedroom at home when he was younger, he felt that he was sailing free across the oceans beneath the cobalt sky. He had a bird's eye view from up there. Beyond the ponds and against the distant southern fence was a cluster of wooden cottages, blue smoke spiralling into the still air from brick chimneys. They were the mulattoes' married quarters. An orchard of stone-fruit trees now bare of leaves stood beside them. Colourful washing hung from lines between them, and several small children were playing in the yards between rich green beds of vegetables.

Beyond the last saw-windmill to his left lay a spectacular wetland surrounded by reeds and willows, its shallows edged with thriving water plants, thin crusts of melting ice shimmering here and there between them. It was teeming with birds on the open stretches of water, wild ducks with iridescent green and burgundy feathers diving beneath the glassy surface and white-necked black moorhens scooting busily across it. Three years before, he and his best friend

Daniel had gone bird-nesting there, looking for eggs, until the gamekeeper had screamed a warning and fired two salt-packed shells from his *donderbus* over their heads as they ran for their lives. He had looked for the gamekeeper since working in the yards but had seen no sign of him.

Back in the mess hall that evening, Sebastiao turned to Gerrit. 'You've done well today, or so I'm told, boy. So you're welcome to join us at our table during dinner'

That stunned him. It was an unexpected privilege. 'Thank you... thanks, Sebastiao,' he stammered.'

'Just Seb. Seb will do.'

When the group looked up and welcomed him, shifting along the bench to make room for him, he was overwhelmed. But not for long. They treated him as though he belonged there, a brief nod from each sufficing for a communal greeting before they turned back to their lively conversations, while they enjoyed the stew piled high on their plates, washing it down with *roemers* of local *Drie Tonnen bier*—Three Barrels beer.

They spoke in Dutch, which surprised Gerrit. Earlier in the day, he'd heard them talking in a mixture of what he thought was Portuguese and a language he'd never heard, its intonations and pronunciation strangely musical. He sat listening in fascinated silence as he ate, amazed at what he took to be their tacit acceptance of him.

Or is it in acknowledgment of Mama's kindness in offering to train Sebastiao's teenage daughter Miranda? he wondered. *She is now a qualified domestic nurse and working in the Gasthuis Hospital, after all.*

After dinner, the darkest-skinned among them, who had introduced himself to Gerrit that morning as Serafino, *de Zwarte Prins*, the Black Prince, gave him a surprise sideways nod of invitation as they made their way to the end of the veranda, as they'd done each evening after dinner throughout the time he'd been there.

He trailed after them, despite his fatigue, and squatted outside the circle they formed. Several had thumb pianos with upturned tines they began to quietly twang, one had an empty metal canister he drummed with the fingers of both hands and, when the one-armed giant albino Otello later joined the group, he had a worn tambourine he rattled against his knee. Gerrit found the sounds and cadence hypnotic, its background hum and the occasional quietly singing voices accompanying rather than interfering with the talking.

Whenever the music stopped, there was a complementary silence, the conversation resuming as soon as it was taken up again.

I should have brought my two Queen Conch shell horns from Curaçao with me, he thought. *I wonder what they would have made of the sounds they produce.*

At one point in the evening, Serafino stepped across to join him. *'Je hebt het goed gedaan vandaag, jonge kerel,'* he said when he'd squatted, crossed his legs and leant back into the veranda railing. 'You did well today, young fellow.'

'I didn't know you were watching me.'

'I wasn't. Lourenco and Marais both vouched for you. They've asked for you to work with them again tomorrow.'

'Will that be that all right with Cain?'

'It will. Seb has influence and has arranged it.'

'Thank you. I'd like that.'

'Good. That's settled. Now, I have observed your interest in us.'

He looked sideways at Gerrit, eyebrows raised, as though wondering if he had anything to ask, leaving Gerrit uncertain whether he'd posed a question or made a statement.

Then Serafino broke the silence. *'Ebuê?'*

The expressive way he'd voiced this strange new word, accentuating it as though it was the musical sound of a question, prompted Gerrit to reply, 'You are right. I am curious.'

'About?'

'Well, you, to begin with. Are you a prince?'

His teeth flashed in the lantern light. 'No. But I am *ya akala*. I am black; the blackest here. I am *Muene ya Makala*, the Black Prince. And you see Otello over there? He's *Ndundu Dibanga*, Albino the Rock! You'll surprise him if you call him that.'

'What language is that?'

'*Kikongo ya munu kituba*. Kikongo is our language. Our *bambuta bampika*, our slave ancestors brought it with them a hundred years ago. None of us speaks it well now. Portuguese, a little. Dutch, yes. But Kikongo-kituba?' He shook his head, his mouth drawn down and his bottom lip protruding slightly in a grimace. 'We are third generation, as you know, so a few of us have only slight memories of it.'

He rubbed his palms together before giving Gerrit a keen look. 'You understand that the language you are born with ties you to your country and your people? Without it, you no longer belong. You cannot truly communicate. You are someone lost at sea. You are someone carried into slavery. As we are. Or were.'

He gave a thoughtful smile, coupled with what Gerrit sensed was sadness, but sadness tempered by what? Determination? Resoluteness in the face of ill-fortune?

'Imagine landing in a place where no one speaks your language and you have to learn theirs to communicate.' He gazed at Gerrit as though wondering if he could comprehend it. 'You lose part of yourself. You lose your spirit. It vanishes with every new word you have to learn. You become someone else.'

After a brief silence, he added emphatically, 'That may be us, but we are survivors and above all else, *free*.' He closed his fist and struck his chest above his heart. 'Free to choose not to brood over our history, *jonge*, but to acknowledge it and to use that knowledge to work towards a future that is safer and better for all of us.'

He gazed keenly at Gerrit as though ensuring he was following him. 'That way we keep hope alive, especially for our children.'

'You have children?'

'Not yet. Some others do.'

Then he opened up his palm and showed Gerrit his extended thumb fractionally separated from the tip of his forefinger. 'We may be partly Dutch, but only by *that* much. Just *one* drop of white blood. With me, it doesn't show! I am *Muene ya Makala*, a true Angolan man, a fisherman from the Kisolongo coast!'

His teeth flashed again as he broke into triumphant and ironic laughter. '*Eé!* I am *ya makala mulat*, married to a blonde and blue-eyed beauty from Friesland—my perfect Severine! *Beto ke ebene mpi ivuari*. Together we are ebony and ivory. A perfect match.'

When he'd gathered his breath, he asked abruptly, 'Anything else?'

Gerrit responded at once. 'Cain suggested you were all afraid of being sent back into slavery.'

'Ah! *Now* you are getting down to the heart of the matter. How much do you know about our history?'

He listened intently as Gerrit told him what he knew of his origins. Serafino did not comment for some minutes. He appeared to be concentrating on the music playing beside them, gathering himself, before he turned back towards him, his expression intense. Yes, everything Gerrit had said was true, he said. They *were* descended from slaves brought to Middelburg aboard a Portuguese caravel captured by a Dutch privateer in 1596, but that was only half the story.

'That was the *Golden Unicorn*,' he said, before draining his glass, 'and we haven't forgotten the name of the schipper.

It was Melchior van der Kerckhoven. And yes,' he went on, placing his glass carefully upside down on the floorboards beside him, 'there *were* one hundred and thirty of our ancestors led ashore—men, women and children, who were granted their freedom by the Zeeland courts after they were baptised Christians. What you clearly do *not* know is that the owner of the *Golden Unicorn*, Pieter van der Haegen, whose name we also remember only too well, appealed to the Supreme Court in The Hague. Three months later, the judges there tore up our tickets of leave and handed our ancestors back to him.' He threw up his hands. 'To do with as he pleased.'

He rocked back and forth against the railing, frowning. The lantern light caught the muscle in his jaw shifting as he appeared to grind his teeth. 'And what did he do? He rounded up our ancestors and shipped them off to Bahia in Brazil. He made his fortune after all, selling them, and slave trading for years after that!'

Gerrit waited for more, but Serafino had turned away again to listen to the single-thumb piano that was playing.

When it stopped, Gerrit pointed out, 'But all of *you* are still here.'

Serafino stood as the group started to disperse, then looked down at Gerrit, nodding. 'We are indeed, what's left of us. The people of Middelburg at the time insisted that the men who had already found work, along with the women and children who wanted to stay, should be allowed to remain in Zeeland. The local magistrates agreed. We've been working in this timber yard ever since.'

He hesitated as he turned to leave. 'Did you know that nine of our ancestors died when the decision to send them back into slavery was made, the week before they were due to be loaded back on the ship? They're buried in a mass grave in the corner of the cemetery, close to your house.'

Close to my house? Gerrit wondered. *He knows where I live?*

Serafino saw his surprise. 'Of course you didn't know. Why should you? We often visit the grave to pay our respects.' He looked the boy directly in the eye. 'They died within a week. *A week!* Was it suicide, do you think, or grief that killed them?' He gazed at Gerrit, his eyebrows raised. 'It was both, of course. When we gather there, we're meeting on African soil. *Angolan* soil. It's our special place. It's sacred to us.'

He reached down to pick up his empty *roemer*. 'We bring their bones back to life when we remember them, *jonge*. When we celebrate their act of defiance, their escape from a life in chains, we celebrate our own.'

Gerrit stood and dusted himself down, unable to respond.

As though sensing his discomfort, Serafino nodded. 'We used to see you sitting in your window when you were a boy.'

See me in my window? Sailing the house the way I used to as a boy? That was years ago. Ah, they must have been looking out for Miranda.

'I was sailing the house,' he said. 'Across the garden, which was the Indian Ocean. The orchard was the reef. I had to avoid it as I left the port and headed for the open sea.' He then asked, 'Do their graves have markers?'

'No, as I said they're buried in a common grave, so there's only one marker—a large piece of limestone carved by Lourenco's grandfather.'

'Is it shaped like a cross?'

'No. It's carved in the shape of an open book. The left-hand page lists their names, the right is blank. It's the book they carry when they go to meet *Nzambi a Mpungu*, the Divine Judge—the book that tells the story of their lives.' He began walking away down the veranda, following the group. 'In their case, that right-hand page is blank. It represents the life they were unable to live, the life that was stolen from them. Lourenco—the one you worked with today—he's the keeper of the grave. He does his best to preserve the carving and care for the site.'

He slowed and looked back at Gerrit. 'Reading their names brings them back to us,' he said as Gerrit caught up with him. 'You asked if I have children and I told you no, not yet.' He patted his stomach. 'I should have said I will, soon. My Severine is carrying. We expect our first in May.' He gave Gerrit a brilliant smile. 'With his or her birth, *Angola* will be reborn and in future, share the best of both our worlds!'

'Is that the name you're going to give him or her?'

'Angola? Of course, though Severine prefers Angela if she's a girl.'

'That's excellent,' Gerrit said as they reached the dormitory door. 'Thank you for talking to me. I have learned much.'

Serafino turned to descend the steps and join several others who were waiting for him to walk across to the married quarters.

'Thank you for listening,' he said, placing a hand on Gerrit's shoulder. 'We have a saying in Kikongo. See if you can memorise it. *Tosali menga mosi.*'

'*Tosali menga mosi.*'

'*Ya mboté,* very good.' He went down the steps. 'We may all be separate individuals, but *we zijn van één bloed.* We are of one blood. Think of that when you need to. It will confirm that you belong, but only after you acknowledge that you are white. I know I'm black. I know my black ancestry and I know our history, our place in the world. But you, Gerrit, you still have to learn that you are white, that you are privileged, that you can take your whiteness for granted. Think about it. We will see you tomorrow.'

'*Tosali menga mosi,*' Gerrit repeated as he opened the dormitory door, unsure what Serafino had just implied.

1712 shaped up as a terrible year for Gerrit.

On Friday, 3 June, during a wild storm, the VOC cargo ship *Zuytdorp*, aboard which he was sailing as the senor shipwright carpenter, was wrecked and split into three on the rocks at the base of the towering Eendrachtsland cliffs in New Holland. He was left lying on the clifftop beneath a stand of tea trees beside the signal fire after the shipwreck, his smashed left leg in splints and painfully healing.

The other twenty-two marooned survivors abandoned him after six weeks and trekked north in a vain attempt to reach Batavia, leaving only his Ceylonese friend Sunil Dewaraja to care for him.

They thought they were done for when they started running out of fresh water, but in early August, when Sunil was searching for water stored after the rains in local limestone gnamma holes, he came across a family group of Malgana Aborigines apparently travelling southwards. The meeting was confrontational at first, but Sunil was able to convince them he meant them no harm and their parting was friendly.

Two hours after sunrise on the morning after their meeting, a warrior appeared at the campsite on the clifftop. He stepped from the nearest coppice of trees, alone and unarmed, carrying three birds. He was naked, except for a red hide cloak tied at his throat and draped across a shoulder.

He strode into the camp and greeted Sunil, '*Nyinda ngugurnu?*'

Sunil bounded to his feet. 'Welcome,' he said. 'We were hoping you would come.'

'*Nyinda bulyarru?*' he asked, pointing at his open mouth and rubbing his stomach after depositing two white- and grey-banded birds the size of chickens and a large, brown-feathered carcass the size of a turkey beside the fire. '*Nhanganha gutharra thanindi barduda. Guga gambaniya.*'

Deliberately ignoring Gerrit, who was sitting with his back to a tree beneath the canvas strung across its branches and watching him keenly, he turned to look down the cliff at the shipwreck. Then he signalled towards the surrounding trees, summoning others Gerrit hadn't noticed in the shadows.

Several men joined him, also unarmed. Their discussion was boisterous and prolonged, until one of them, stepping below the lip of the cliff to the platform, saw the carved wooden statuette of the Grecian sphinx recovered from between the gallery windows at the ship's stern, propped against a rock halfway down.

Gerrit watched him rear back, apparently alarmed. He sprinted back up the slope, calling out to the others and pointing. They gathered around him staring in silence at the carving, before moving quickly back to the cover of the trees at the edge of the clearing. As they faded into the shadows. Gerrit assumed that they were superstitious and the statuette had spooked them.

How many others are concealed there? he wondered, the sound of several raised voices reaching him. *No one has so much as looked at me or acknowledged my presence.*

A short silence followed, and then he saw a tall old man emerge alone from the shadows, white-bearded, deeply wrinkled, his sharp eyes deep-set and barely visible beneath protruding bony brows and a sloping forehead. His back was remarkably straight, his carriage dignified. His legs were bone and sinew, his stride long. His nasal septum was pierced and parallel body scars were ridged like a stairway up his abdomen.

He walked directly across to Gerrit, where he squatted at his level beneath the tree and looked him over, avoiding eye contact except occasionally, when his glance was piercing but calm and authoritative, betraying no emotion.

He inspected Gerrit closely in silence, checked the weeping wounds and splints on his leg and showed surprise only when he saw the gin bottle half-filled with urine propped in the sand beside him. He stared at it—and then, before Gerrit could prevent it, he reached out his right hand and felt his genitals beneath his breeches, releasing them at once.

Wordless, he stood and stepped to the other side of the tree trunk against which Gerrit was leaning. There he also sat, facing inland, his back turned on Gerrit, looking directly ahead at the tea tree scrub during a tense silence lasting several minutes.

And then, in a baritone that shifted effortlessly now and again into a barely audible falsetto, the old man began to sing, his words sounding to Gerrit like a stream of musical sounds rather than comprehensible speech. The song lasted for ten minutes and fearing it may be a prelude to his execution, Gerrit struggled unsuccessfully to pick up cues from the intonation and emotional pitch as to how he should respond.

When the song ended, the old man was again silent for several minutes before he stood and resumed his position beside Gerrit.

For the first time, he smiled and gestured towards himself. *'Ngatha Kananggadi,'* he said. *'Kananggadi,'* he repeated with emphasis, then pointed at Gerrit, his eyebrows raised.

'I am Gerrit,' he responded. 'Gerrit de Waal.'

The old man's smile widened. *'Gayirrit! Gayirri! Nyinda gayirri yanmanu. Nyinda Gayirrigayirrit.'*

He spread his arms wide, gesturing inland as though indicating the surrounding bush, trees and gulleys, confusing Gerrit even further. *'Nhanganha Gathaagudu, ngurra Malganangu uthudujadawana,*

Then he nodded, as though assuming Gerrit had understood. *'Nyinda bardiyalu jinagabi wilithi, nyinda wiyabandi wilithi yanaangu gayirri wardandula.* He nodded again, more deliberately, before adding with slow emphasis, *'Nyinda nyinamanha narla barrajala ngathangu. Yuganga, maragudu. Nyinda wiyabandi Malgana… Garimarangu.'*

Then he reached across and placed his right hand on Gerrit's shoulder while patting his own with his left and repeated solemnly, '*Nyinda Malgana… ngatha Malgana. Nyinda Garimarangu.*'

He looked keenly at Gerrit as if expecting a reply.

'*Malgana?*' Gerrit tried. '*Garimarangu?*'

'*T'i,*' the old man beamed, before pointing at Sunil, seated at the edge of the cliff, observing them. '*Wiyabandi mathara bayirri, Malgana… Barungura.*'

Then he waved his right hand and shouted at the trees, '*Nhurra nyarlu, gaba warrbuthu, matka atkajadi wanyu. Maruthayinyina.*'

At his signal, two women emerged cautiously from the trees, the older carrying a hollow gourd of oil, the younger a teenage girl.

Gerrit was concerned when the old man held out a hand and pointed at his wounds. '*Wirda wujarnugura marrigudu, mambu ardandanu marrithayiniyan.*'

The two women knelt beside Gerrit, one on either side, and inspected the wound.

The older woman pointed at the urine bottle and whispered an instruction.

For a moment the girl looked apprehensive before she gingerly reached out for the bottle. She picked it up at last, scooped a hole in the sand a *roede* away and emptied it, before peering through the glass. She seemed mystified by its transparency.

She looked shyly over at Gerrit and tapped it with a fingernail '*Nayi nhanganhanu?*'

'It's glass. A glass bottle,' he said, then repeated the word 'glass' twice.

Her eyes lit up and she ducked her head before making her way down the cliff face. Within minutes she was back with the bottle filled with seawater, and they began gently cleaning the wound with it.

Then, when the girl applied the oily ointment, Gerrit flinched and bit the inside of his mouth to offset the stinging pain.

The girl saw him wince. '*Nyinda warniyanu?* she enquired, her voice empathic, looking briefly up at him.

Captivated by her glance, Gerrit saw a change come over her, her shyness evaporating as she spread the oil carefully across his wound, filling the air with the acrid scent of camphor. When she was satisfied, she looked back up and, with unexpected daring, reached out to touch the abalone shell necklace with an albatross carved into it, hanging on a leather thong around his neck. She pointed the albatross out to the other woman. '*Nayi naga nhanganha wilyara banduga.*' she said.

Glancing at Gerrit, she asked, '*Nayiwunga?*'

She looked expectantly up at him, but he shook his head.

After a moment she tapped her breast as though making a connection that Gerrit couldn't grasp. '*Ngathangura banduga,*' she murmured.

Then she reached for the empty bottle and held it up. 'Glass,' she said, before pointing again at the necklace pendant. She leant forward to touch the shell again and spoke the word, 'Wilyara,' then ran her forefinger across the albatross and repeated, 'Banduga.'

When Gerrit responded, 'Shell... and albatross,' and heard her correctly repeat the words, he was back in the timber yards, listening to Serafino. He was right. In losing your language, you lose your sense of self, but in sharing it, you experience the deepest sense of community.

At that moment he looked deep into the girl's dark brown eyes, and as she confidently held his gaze he heard the echo of Serafino's triumphant and ironic laughter. '*Eé!* I am *ya makala mulat*, married to a blonde and blue-eyed beauty from

Friesland—my perfect Severine! *Beto ke ebene mpi ivuari.* Together we are ebony and ivory. A perfect match.'

Gerrit smiled at the memory, and when the girl responded he wondered what the future held in store.

<u>Malgana Translation:</u>

Nyinda ngugurnu? Are you well?

Nyinda bulyarru? Are you hungry?

Nhanganha gutharra thanindi barduda. Guga gambaniya. Here are two malleefowl and a bush turkey. You can cook the meat.

Ngatha Kananggadi I am Kananggadi.

Gayirrit! Gayirri! Nyinda gayirri yanmanu. Nyinda Gayirrigayirrit. Gerrit! From far away! You've come from far away. You are Gayirrigayirrit, Gerrit-from-afar.

'Nhanganha Gathaagudu, ngurra Malganangu uthudujadawana, This is Shark Bay, home to the Malgana people, our much-beloved country.

Nyinda bardiyalu jinagabi wilithi, nyinda wiyabandi wilithi yanaangu gayirri wardandula. You, you're not the white spirit of an ancestor returned from the dead, but a white man who has come from far to the west.

Nyinda nyinamanha narla barrajala ngathangu. Yuganga, maragudu. Nyinda wiyabandi Malgana, Garimarangu. You are welcome to stay here in my country from now on. You are a young Malgana man now, of Garimara descent.

Wiyabandi mathara bayirri, Malgana, Barungura. The young black man over there, he is also now Malgana, of Barungu descent.

Nhanganha wiyabandi wilithi Gayirrigayirrit! Wiyabandi Malgana mardijithayimanha wurrinyu Banagara,' he said. 'This young white man is Gerrit-from-afar. He is Malgana now and may marry one of our Banaga women.

Gutiya, bugarra bugarra. Only one, and very, very old!

Nhurra nyarlu, gaba warrbuthu, matka atkajadi wanyu. Maruthayinyina. You women, get over here quickly. Bring the tea tree oil. It's getting late.

Wirda wujarnugura marrigudu, mambu ardandanu marrithayiniyan. The stranger's leg is injured. The bone is broken and has not set.

Nayi nhanganhanu? What is this?

Nyinda warniyanu? Did you fall?

Nayi naga nhanganha wilyara banduga. Look at this albatross carved in the shell.

Nayiwunga?' What's it for?

Ngathangura banduga. My totem is the albatross.

Song Of The Butcherbirds

IN THE PILBARA ON the Great Northern Highway, Western Australia, June 1990

I found it surprisingly hot for a midwinter's afternoon, but I had been warned. I was in the Pilbara for the first time, at the Exmouth turnoff in semi-desert country. Everywhere I looked, red sand spiked with tussocks of spinifex and feathered with clusters of pink and mauve Mulla Mulla flowers stretched to the horizon.

'You're hitch-hiking to Darwin on your own, my dear?' the wife of the driver of the last car to offer me a lift from Gin Gin asked. They were retired couple travelling around Australia and were heading north to Exmouth. 'Aren't you asking for trouble? A woman out there on your own?'

'Not if I can avoid it.'

'What about the heat?'

'Heat I'm used to. I'm originally from northern Mexico.'

'Well, I have to say you're a lot gutsier than I am,' she said. 'But you're young, I suppose. I wouldn't dare, myself... and I like my creature comforts.'

Fortunately, there was a stunted, solitary tree with a canopy of glossy leaves standing at the junction a few metres from the bitumen. I sat in the shade, leaning against its gnarly grey trunk, grateful for the rough bark digging into my back, keeping me awake. I couldn't afford to miss my next potential lift to Darwin. Since midday, they'd been few and far between.

I selected the black queen from Abu Cerrildo's travelling chess set lying open beside me. I was partway through a game. I held it up and inspected it—a copper-coloured Aztec queen with a headdress of feathers and a flowing gown intricately carved from silicate crystal. I held it up towards shafts of sunlight shimmering through the leaves and turned it this way and that, its facets glinting. *La Malinche*. I shook my head as I recalled Abu describing her to me. *A woman of words—interpreter between the Aztecs and the Spanish. A linguist. A woman after my own heart.*

I studied the remaining pieces. Three moves to mate. I replaced the queen, displacing the remaining white conquistador, the knight, before toppling the white king. So long, Hernán Cortés. Suck it up. Get down on your knees in front of Montezuma and take what's coming to you. A flayed heart, probably. Like mine.

I closed the set and glanced up through twisted branches and quivering leaves at glimpses of the cloudless sky awash with pale blue light.

How long before the sun arcs beneath the tree canopy and shines directly into my eyes? An hour perhaps, at most? It's already lighting up the white flowers dangling like lanterns in the scrawny Mexican Thornapple weed I recognise beyond my feet, identical to those in the Sierra Madre.

I gazed southwards down the empty road and groaned, banging the back of my head three times against the trunk of the tree. Just the three, I remember, because I laughed out loud and spoke to myself, as I sometimes do, 'Oh, come on now, girl. It takes time and patience. When you hit the reset button on your life, you've got to stay in the moment and adjust to the changes.'

I leaned back and closed my eyes, grateful for my sunglasses. Sunlight flaring red across my eyelids seemed to throw up shadowy images of the unforeseen, making me think I was watching black and white stills in the countdown before the start of an action film.

I wondered what was coming next.

Then I was alerted by the sound of a motorbike. I recognised the thump of a Harley Davidson. You can't mistake it. I sat bolt upright and saw the sun flash for an instant, perhaps on the rider's visor or a piece of chrome. I watched the intermittent reflections gliding closer along the road stretching southwards to Carnarvon. It looked like a diamond glittering on a ribbon of black silk.

I straightened up and took a deep breath to calm the pulse beating in my throat. I checked my watch—it was 4:15—and watched the rider's shadow distort and vanish and reappear in the heat haze rising from the road.

I walked out into the sun, dusting myself off, bending to flick a black and speckled grasshopper from the knee of my jeans. I stopped at the road's edge, hands on hips, before leaning forward and waving both hands as the motorbike swept past.

I assumed the rider was a man. He left me in a swirl of sound and I saw him glance over his shoulder. He slowed and circled back, red dust and gravel flung from the verge. He accelerated towards me before turning again towards the north, where the highway disappeared between the crests of low dunes on the distant horizon.

He switched off the engine, removed his helmet releasing a mop of wiry hair, and looked across at me through green-lensed Aviator sunglasses.

I took two steps back.

His eyes were hidden behind the Polaroid lenses and I was surprised to glimpse myself reflected in the curving sweep of the desert and the sky. I saw a tiny portrait of myself framed by his skin and, for the briefest moment, I imagined what he was seeing—my face pared to the bone with a new hardness to it I had lately found disconcerting. It was weird, as if I was someone else standing in the glare of the sun with a friendless arrogance about me. A stand-offish stranger I disliked. Which is not what I was like at all, in spite of everything I'd been through. It must have been a result of the grieving process and the mourning.

I took off my sunglasses and looked directly at him. For some reason, I was deeply self-protective. Unyielding. Speculative and on guard. With my right hand raised against the sun, I wondered if he sensed my defensiveness and I was annoyed he hadn't removed his sunglasses, as if he was keeping himself concealed from me.

Dark-skinned, his hair and coarse black beard were streaked with silver and dusted red, his bulk zipped up in a black leather riding suit with a white panel across his broad shoulders, powdered with grime and flecked with insect spatter.

'How're you going?' he said, his voice deep and resonant. 'I'm Lennard Currie. I almost missed you. You're the last thing I expected. Out here… in the middle of nowhere.'

I studied him in silence, my hand still raised. He tilted his head towards me as the silence lengthened. '*Nyinda wangginyina, malyu*? You do speak, sister?'

'Hi. I'm Alicia. Alicia Serrano. Thanks for stopping.'

'What're you doing? Did you fall out of the sky? Miss your bus?'

'Something like that.'

I looked at him, suddenly relieved. Clearly, he hadn't seen the TV programs or read the local newspaper reports five months ago. Or if he had, he didn't recognise my name or my face—and before I could suppress the memory—*Alain*. My mind was pierced by the vision of a pall of black smoke with lurid orange flames raging within it. For one dizzying moment, I was back in Guinea that dreadful night, waiting for Alain. Fighting for self-control, I looked back at the tree as if to check on my backpack. I hesitated for several moments before I clenched my jaw and turned back to face Lennard.

He waved a hand across the wide expanse of scrub. 'You look like a *wanamalu* waiting for the tide to turn.'

'I look like a what?' I heard my voice shake.

'Like a *wanamalu*. A shag. On a rock. *Nyinda wanamalu nyinangayi barldalyila.*'

I searched his face, refusing to smile, uncertain about his language.

'Cheer up,' he said. 'Now I'm here, you know you're not alone in the world. You and me, could be we're the only two left alive.' He balanced the helmet on the petrol tank and crossed his arms. 'You want a lift? Or have you called a cab?' He gave a quiet chuckle—I sensed it edged with sarcasm. 'Or maybe you're waiting for Godot?'

'How far are you going?' I asked.

As always, when I first start talking to an Australian I've only just met, I wonder if he or she may have misplaced my accent. *Perhaps he thinks I'm from the southern states rather than Mexico, and that's why he believes I may be wary of his dark skin.*

'I'm Mexican' I said. 'I've been in Australia since February.'

He squinted up at the sun before replying. 'I was wondering. That makes sense… so how far's far enough?'

I did not reply.

'I'm heading for Bandilngan Gorge—Windjana Gorge on the maps,' he said, and quietly added, 'I'm on a pilgrimage. To lay a ghost among the ghost gums. That's how my Rosalie would have put it.'

'You're on a pilgrimage?'

'On a walkabout, yes. It's personal. What about you?' he asked. '*Nyinda yanmanha yaburru*? You going the same way I'm going? Up north?'

His voice was expressive, his accent broad and the cadence clipped and foreign to me. His reference to Beckett surprised me. And the word *wanamalu*. To my mind, it sounded Samoan. Or was he Aboriginal?

'I'm on my way to Darwin,' I said. 'I've been told it's mango-picking season. There may be work available up there.'

'So you're looking for some easy pickings? Isn't the season

in October, but? Maybe they're coming in early this year, just for you, *malyu*. By about three months.'

There was an easy-going quality to him, yet I was suspicious of the apparent teasing in his grin, the way he looked sideways at me, inclining his head. I've seen black solitary eagles in the Sierra Madre Mountains do it before plummeting, claws drawn, towards a victim rattlesnake or ground squirrel deep in the canyon below.

'If so, I'll look for a teaching job when I get there. I teach Spanish,' I said, and when he waited for me to continue, 'among other languages.'

'How many do you speak?'

'Fluently?'

'For starters.'

'Five.'

'What, all at once?'

I granted him the ghost of a smile. 'Otherwise, I may head across Arnhem Land to Yirrkala. To study the *Yolngu* dialects spoken there.' I took a breath. 'I'm a linguist, you see. I have a PhD.'

He studied me coolly. 'Have you now? And you're going to Yirrkala to doctor with their languages? Now you're talking. So you want to see that good country?'

'Yes, I'll go there anyway.'

'In which case I can take you as far as Fitzroy Crossing. I'll be heading back to Perth from there.' He uncrossed his arms and ran his fingers through his beard. 'Listen, I can leave you at the Nanutarra roadhouse if you like. It's roughly two hours' ride away. I'll be staying there overnight. You're welcome to travel with me through the Karijini Mountains tomorrow, if you're game. I'll be taking a diversion through the national park. It's my mother's country and I have some special sites to visit. To pay my respects.'

So he was Aboriginal. I asked him what dialect he was speaking.

'It's Malgana. It's spoken around Gutharraguda—Shark Bay,' he pointed westwards with a wide sweep of his left hand, 'down that way, by the coast. *Was* spoken, I mean. It's almost extinct. Three old aunties in Northampton are the only ones left who remember it, and one of them is dying, of cancer. Annie Morgan. She's our last fluent speaker and she's helping us resurrect it, but we're running out of time.'

I looked at his broad face, his hair and beard sparsely wired with silver surrounding it. He was solid, thick-necked. Powerful. Dangerous, I thought. I noticed his strong-wristed hands now gripping the handlebars. A builder's hands. I recoiled from the striking image. *They could wield a bloodied machete!*

'Come on, take a risk,' he said. 'This may be the only chance of a lift you'll get for hours. *Ngayi bandi*? What's your worry? *Gurra wayangudhayinyina ngadhangu.* Don't let this face frighten you. I'm not Mad Max... and I won't eat you. Not enough *guga*, not enough meat, by crikey.'

I gave him a quick nod and turned to retrieve my backpack from the shade.

Three days later, we glided into the official campsite at the mouth of Windjana Gorge. We dismounted and Lennard stood the bike in the shade of a corrugated iron shed. He removed his sleeping bag and some netting from a pannier and shoved a can of insect repellent into his back pocket.

I slung my backpack and sleeping bag across my shoulder and followed him along the rocky track towards a gap between the one-hundred-metre-tall sandstone cliffs, the setting sun now burnishing their summits a deep red gold. I glimpsed the jade ribbon of the river to my left between the trunks of overarching paperbarks, fruit bats roosting among the upper branches like inverted black velvet bags.

Lennard stepped onto the spit of sand beside the river, disturbing a flock of white corellas. They erupted in a coordinated mass, the undersides of their wings flashing pale yellow and their complaining shrieks deafening until they settled on the opposite riverbank.

Jandamarra's rock stood in the middle of the river just as I'd imagined it when Lennard had described it to me—an imposing two-storey block of gleaming white quartz. It was so eye-catching I understood at once why he'd selected it as the model for the gigantic glass cenotaph he told me he intended to make. Dedicated to the twenty thousand Aboriginal warriors he told me died in the Frontier Wars, it was the next project he was going to undertake in his glassworks in Fremantle.

'There it is,' he said. 'The cenotaph. I've chosen it not only for its impressive shape and dimensions but also for its cultural significance to the Bunuba people.'

He selected a spot close to the water's edge and laid out his sleeping bag and roll of netting before walking back up to the trees and dragging back a dead branch. He broke it up for firewood and built a mini-pyramid, dry grass inserted as a firelighter at its base.

'It's against the rules,' he said, 'but there's no one here but us and the ranger won't be checking in until tomorrow. So we can make ourselves at home with the sandflies and the mozzies.' He pulled out the can of repellent and stood it on the sand. 'This'll help and the net will do the rest. I'll rig it up later, like I used to for Rosalie and me. You can park your sleeping bag next to mine to share the net,' he sent me a mischievous grin I was beginning to recognise, 'long as you don't snore or have any plans to molest me, *malyu*. Otherwise, you can hang out over there and let the wildlife carry you away.'

'Nor you me,' I said, 'but the snoring? I can't guarantee it.'

'No chance of either, for me. I'm here to mourn. It's an extra special place and I'll stay awake.'

'I guessed as much.' I unrolled my sleeping bag next to his and settled on it.

'I'll get the fire going later and we can share a can of Irish stew I've saved. And we've got the second bottle of spring water I filled in Dales Gorge to see us through. We can take off first thing tomorrow. At the crack of dawn. You'll be woken by the butcherbirds if they're singing.'

'The butcherbirds?'

'Best songbirds in the world. They're mesmerising. Then we can have breakfast at Fitzroy Crossing before I drop you off. How's that sound?'

'Fine,' I said, unsure what the night ahead held in store. While I'd got the better of my earlier fears and he'd surprised me with his consideration and gentleness until now, he was still an unpredictable man I had yet to get to know.

He removed his leather jacket and withdrew a plastic photograph holder from an inside pocket. He flicked it open and handed it across to me.

'Meet my Rosalie, Alicia. She was the love of my life, even if some people deny there's such a thing. She's sitting on the rock. She climbed it without realising she shouldn't. I hadn't warned her that the *muwayi*, the country here, is sacred to our Bunuba brothers. I didn't spot her climbing it in time to stop her. I took the shot of her anyway, before she came down.'

I gazed at Rosalie seated on an upper ledge. She was smiling down at Lennard. Her classic green-eyed beauty, striking cheekbones and tanned oval face was framed by auburn hair with copper tints to it, flowing across her shoulders. She was tall and slender, with a black pearl on a fine gold chain at her throat, her swimming costume white. Her arms were wrapped around her knees, her feet bare. She was bathed in mellow light similar to that filling the gorge around us, the cliffs behind her painted the same deep rust and ochre. Their reflections shimmering on the river's surface were so still you'd swear you could step across them.

She was beautiful and looked self-assured. And mysterious, I thought, but was there a hint of teasing mockery in her smile? A knowingness? Is that what had attracted him to her? Out of nowhere I thought of Alain and a rush of unexpected envy spread through me. I suppressed it.

'No wonder you loved her, Ace. You must have taken the shot around this time in the evening?'

'Yep, almost to the day and hour, twenty-seven years ago.'

'I'm glad I've met her,' I said, handing the wallet back to him. 'I can see why you brought her here. There is something special about this place.'

'It is special. Very.'

He turned away and stared at the rock in thoughtful silence for several minutes. I did not disturb him. When he turned back to me, his expression was so intense it shocked me. Our eyes met and I held his gaze, uncertain what he was about to tell me.

'Rosalie was shot here on 14 June 1987,' he said at last. He was talking fast, either because he wanted to get it over with, or he was struggling with the emotion. 'You won't remember the German tourist who went berserk up here at that time. I believe Rosalie was his sixth victim, but the police were doubtful at first. They didn't recover the bullet that killed her so they couldn't prove it.' He inhaled deeply and let out a heavy sigh. 'We were swimming in the deeper pool at the time.' He pointed, 'Over there, beside the rock.'

He raised his left fist to his mouth and exhaled a loud breath through his clenched fingers and thumb. 'So anyway, she was badly wounded. I carried her out across the river and tied her behind me on the bike for the ride to Derby Hospital. You can imagine how difficult that was, especially on the gravel.'

'It must have been horrendous.'

'It was. When I got to the bitumen, I came across a tourist

operator in a Toyota Land Cruiser, who took us the rest of the way. She died in the Emergency Department at ten that night.'

I squeezed his forearm. 'I'm so sorry, Ace.'

'Yes, well. Nothing else I could do, except bring her ashes up here a month after her funeral and spill them across the pool, which I figured she would have wanted.' He glanced sideways at me, sending me a wry smile. 'That was some trip. The grieving wasn't easy. In fact, it's never easy. It's a shapeshifter, varying its intensity, is all. Strikes when you least expect it.'

I felt a rush of empathy, recognising what I was experiencing with Alain's death. 'I know exactly what you mean.'

'I've come back each year ever since at this time, to mourn. This is my third pilgrimage. I'll never stop if I can help it.'

I realised how difficult it must have been for him to share so intimate a memory with me. 'Thanks for letting me share the privilege.'

I sensed him relaxing. 'If you feel like a swim, by the way, steer clear of the freshie Johnstone crocs in the water here,' he said.

'Freshwater crocodiles?' I sat bolt upright, shock settling in my gut like a block of ice. 'And you two swam here?'

'There are usually some around, but they're shy. Leave them alone and they'll do the same for you.'

'That's reassuring. Thanks for the warning.' I cut short a laugh. 'Swimming's definitely off my agenda.'

'I'll be going in. I always do.'

'Be my guest. Just don't expect to be rescued.'

I woke at two o'clock the next morning and sat up, immediately uneasy. Lennard was not in the sleeping bag beside me.

The gorge was awash with pale moonlight, the full moon past its zenith. Through the net, I saw the blue-black sky blazing with a brilliant trail of stars, as if someone had flung handfuls of shattered glass across it.

The fire was still lit, the crackling underside of a new log thrown across the glowing embers giving out wisps of smoke and the smell of burning resin.

I saw Lennard sitting motionless at the water's edge. He was facing the rock, cross-legged, straight-backed, his hands palms upwards on his knees, grounded in the scene. He was a dark brown lightning rod in that extraordinary light, his backdrop the rock, an iceberg of glass lit through by moonlight. The towering cliffs behind it glinted like obsidian.

To his left, not ten metres away, two dark shadows were outstretched on the sand. One made a barely perceptible movement and the bright red flash of a pair of eyes glowed in the firelight. Horrified, I froze, holding my breath. The freshwater Johnstone crocodiles he'd warned me about. Shy, he'd said, but aggressive if provoked.

For twenty nervous minutes, I sat and absorbed the scene, prepared to scream a warning at Lennard if I needed to.

Looking out through the net, I suddenly became eerily detached, as if I was someone other, separated from reality by the finest veil, as if a swirling, multi-dimensional hologram was transforming around me. I seemed to be on the verge of passing out, unable to grasp the mystery unfolding in front of me, as if losing my sense of self and descending into a fearful void. It was threatening. I thought I was milliseconds away from losing my mind and being enveloped in some terrifying ecstasy.

I lifted my right hand and struck my left shoulder hard to disperse the vertiginous sensation of disconnection from reality... or connection with something uncanny, infinite and unreal.

The sound of the slap must have disturbed Lennard.

Without looking round, he stood and walked barefoot knee-deep into the water, his jeans rolled up. The crocodiles, disturbed, spun around and hurtled towards the pool, one or both emitting low-pitched growls of warning. They splashed beneath the surface, their thrashing tails leaving a trail of foam and an expanding arrowhead of ripples, the triangular scales along their backs visible until they submerged and the pool resumed its calm.

I watched, disbelieving, as Lennard walked further out until only his head was showing and he swam towards the rock before disappearing behind it. He did not reappear. I waited for over half an hour before relaxing and sinking back into an uneasy sleep.

I woke late for once, the calls of the corellas disturbing me. When I opened my eyes and squinted, I discovered Lennard leaning over me, blocking out the sun. He nudged me with his toe.

'Time we were on the move, *malyu*,' he said, giving a dry chuckle. 'It's a wonder you slept through your snoring. You were like a steam train once you got going.'

'Thanks for the reminder,' I said, hauling myself out of the sleeping bag. 'I never heard the butcherbirds.'

'No. The corellas did the trick.'

I looked around and discovered he had removed the net and his sleeping bag and he'd cleared away all signs of our having spent the night there. 'You've been busy.'

'I got rid of the evidence while you were snoring.'

'What happened to you last night? The last I saw of you at two this morning you swam behind the rock and disappeared.'

'I do that sometimes.' He grinned. 'Vanish into thin air like a *kadaitcha* medicine man, leaving no trace. I was checking the proportions of the rock on the other side for the cenotaph. Took me a while before I came back. I got an extra couple of hours of sleep before dawn, would you believe, so I'm good to go. It's time we made tracks.'

An hour and a half later, we reached the bitumen of the Great Northern Highway.

'I usually turn right here and head south, back to Perth,' Lennard said, as he turned left instead, 'but I've promised you breakfast and I'm starving, so we'll head for Fitzroy Crossing. I can drop you off there once we've fed.'

'Sounds good to me.'

Forty minutes later we were enjoying Marty's Specialty of the Day in the Homestead Restaurant at the Crossing Inn—a thick omelette quiche with the lot, mushrooms and all, washed down with hot coffee. It was a meal to die for after last night's can of Irish stew.

The Fitzroy River—a wide brown slick of gliding water—was visible between the trunks of flowering river red gums, their discarded flowers a white carpet spread across the sparse lawns.

'So,' Lennard said, when we'd finished the meal, 'let's talk about the elephant in the room. Is there any point in me giving you one more pitch to join Annie Morgan and the others giving CPR to our endangered Malgana language?'

I glanced out across the river, my thoughts racing. Return to Perth within a week of leaving? After spending so long building up the determination to escape everything that reminded me of Alain's tragic death? No. Definitely not.

I turned back to him. 'Look, it's difficult for me, Ace. I appreciate the offer, I truly do.'

'Oh-oh, that's what you said before. Here we go. Here comes the Dear John.'

'I know we haven't talked about it since Broome, but I have given it a lot of thought. The idea of working on the language is extremely tempting and learning more about the Malgana songlines you mentioned is something I'm keen to do. But as

I explained, some things have happened this year I haven't yet come to terms with.'

I raised my hand to prevent him from responding. 'I have to pick myself up and get myself motivated. I have to turn what's happened to me into something positive. I told you that's why I'm on this journey and doing it the hard way, hitchhiking. Testing myself by travelling to Darwin and Yirrkala. They're my goals right now. My mind is set, and the best way for me to keep going *is* to keep going. I need to be sure I'm coping and back in the world of the living before I settle on anything else.'

'So that's it?' He raised his eyebrows, thoughtful disappointment reflected in his eyes. 'I can't convince you there's testing and there's testing, and you've done well to get this far? I can't get you to come back with me and take the next step up from the bottom rung in Fremantle?'

'I don't think I can compromise, Ace.'

'You don't think or you can't?'

'I can't.'

He leaned across and patted my shoulder as he rose. 'All right. Like I said, there's no hard feelings, *malyu*. Make sure you visit me if you're ever back in Perth. And I know the Geraldton language centre will always welcome someone with your expertise.'

'Of course I will.'

'Make sure you do.' He gave me a wide, frank smile. 'You know what they say, drink the water up here and you'll never leave, and last night you drank the water from Dales Gorge. Now you're a goner. You'll be back. I simply have to count the days, by crikey.'

We rode through the town and he stopped beside a coppice of towering ghost gums three hundred metres north of the outskirts.

'This looks the goods,' he said. 'You've got some shade and it's a long straight stretch, so you'll stick out like a dog's.'

'That's one Australian slang phrase I do know,' I said, laughing as we dismounted, 'but I wish I'd never heard it. It reminds me of my brother Andrés's dog, Geronimo, and it's completely changed my image of him.'

'Sorry about that,' he said, flicking the motorbike stand out with his boot and propping it up. He shook his head, his expression filled with regret. 'So this is it, Alicia. Mission only half-accomplished, as far as I'm concerned. But at least you're on your way.'

He stepped forward, put a hand on my forearm and attempted to kiss me, but I dropped my backpack and turned my face away. His beard grazed my neck and ear as he took a quick backward step. When I looked at him, I realised I'd both surprised and hurt him. I felt terrible.

'Please don't get me wrong, Ace,' I said. 'That's not how we Tarahumara farewell each other. I showed you how we do it. Remember?' We held out our right hands and our fingers stroked our palms. 'Now we're bound to meet again.'

'Sooner the better,' he said. 'If you do come back to Perth, you'll find me in the glassworks on Bathers Beach in Freo. You got that? Bathers Beach.'

'Goodbye, Ace. Thanks for the lift. And everything else. I appreciate all you've done for me.'

He mounted the bike and turned southwards, towards the town. He lowered his visor. 'See you when I see you,' he said. 'Hopefully sooner than that, to be honest.'

He accelerated down the road and didn't look back.

As he disappeared, somewhere in the tree above me an unseen bird broke into bursts of song and an electric jolt of excitement raced through me. A butcherbird? It has to be! Others in the nearby trees echoed the fluted trills and calls. I listened, spellbound, as a wave of grief welled through me and I was back in Windjana Gorge, looking through the net at Lennard meditating at the water's edge. He was so integral to the landscape I experienced the pain of my exclusion from it.

And from him, I suddenly realised.

I'd rarely felt so isolated, my deepest vulnerabilities exposed. I had an aching need to connect with the sense of mystery in the world around me that Lennard seemed somehow to be in touch with. I had so much to learn... and so much to give linguistically.

Before I could stop myself, I sprinted across the road and ran along the verge, following him, waving desperately and screaming at him in the growing distance. He didn't respond at first, and then I saw him bend to peer into his rear-view mirror, before coming to a stop and twisting around to look back at me.

He turned the bike and rode back, the thumping of the engine changing tone as he approached, sunlight flashing from his visor—a diamond glittering on a ribbon of black silk once again.

I took a deep breath to calm the pulse beating in my throat and I was unexpectedly conflicted, my excitement tempered by sadness close to deep despair at seemingly betraying Alain's memory so soon.

It wasn't until I met Annie Morgan two days later that I forgave myself and was filled with gratitude as I anticipated the changes in my life's direction.

Lennard introduced us when we passed through Northampton.

She was sitting with two friends on her front veranda beneath sprays of purple bougainvillea. Their animated conversation reached us when Lennard switched off his Harley and we dismounted. It sounded as though they were bickering and squabbling good-humouredly at the tops of their voices, intermittent bursts of laughter carrying to us as we approached.

They were silent as we climbed the steps. The whirring of their battered Panasonic tape recorder greeted our arrival, before one of them—Susie Kelly, I soon discovered—switched it off and the rollers squealed to a stop.

'Afternoon, Aunties,' Lennard said. 'Let me introduce Alicia Serrano.'

With an extended forefinger he pointed out Annie Morgan, Susie Kelly and Molly Sanderson in turn, before explaining, 'I picked Alicia up on the side of the road at Exmouth, hitch-hiking to Darwin—'

'*Darwin?*' Molly interrupted him. 'You lost your bearin's, sister? Aren't you headin' in the wrong direction?'

'No, Aunty Mol. I've convinced her to join us. This is where she belongs right now. Where she's needed. Alicia is the linguist we've been looking for.' Then he grinned. 'With a PhD.'

In the silence that followed, the three old ladies looked up at me bright-eyed, dawning appreciation evident in their collective, '*Aaaah.*'

'Just what the doctor ordered,' Annie Morgan said, patting the seat beside her. 'Never mind Darwin. Make yourself at home right here, 'Leesh. Next to me. Tell us all about yourself.'

Although her sunken eyes were bright and her strong, dark face appeared cheerful beneath a red-chequered scarf that concealed her skull, her wheezing cough told a different story.

When I sat beside her she took my right hand in both of hers and stroked it, without a further word. An unexpected rush of warmth overwhelmed me. Deep in the heart's core, I knew I had come home. I had found my place and understood for certain, like never before, that I had a new sense of purpose and a deep connection to others.

Expect The Unexpected

ON JANUARY 10, 1989, on the last evening before our arrival in Conakry aboard the cargo ship *Louis Maersk*, Alain and I were sitting together on the starboard open deck beside the lifeboat. Bare feet on the rails, we were admiring the sunset, the tin-foil surface of the ocean burnished in every shade of orange from vermilion to fire.

I found it hard to believe we'd be in Guinea at last, after months of preparation in Spain for our expedition kayaking down the Niger River from the source to the sea—a feat never performed before and fraught with danger... but at that moment I felt especially fortunate and carefree, and was thrilled when Alain surprised me with a gold-chain pendant hung with a sparkling solitare diamond on a gold clasp.

'A late Christmas present,' he said, smiling. 'Your birth stone. I bought it for you when I was doing the banking in Algeciras, when you were waiting for me in the café.'

Before I could thank him for it, Tony surprised us there. 'Ah, *there* you lovebirds are,' he said. 'Been looking for you everywhere. It's good to see you fitting together like pieces in a jigsaw.' He swung his camera in my direction, and surprised me with, '*Smil... sige "appelsin"* as the Danish say. Smile... say "orange", Alicia.'

Keeping a straight face, I pointed at the ocean. 'Orange,' I said, as Alain clipped the necklace round my neck and I stroked his hand and kissed his cheek.

Tony had been filming the sunset from the monkey island above the bridge, he told us, the shadow of West Africa a serrated purple smear on the port horizon.

'That shot will make an interesting segue to our arrival in Conakry tomorrow,' he said, his voice as passionate as ever when discussing his documentary of our expedition.

I knew how much it meant to him. 'Creative filming gives my existence real meaning,' he'd told me one evening when he showed me the workings of his camera. 'I don't know what I'd do without it.'

At dawn the next morning, we skirted the Îles de Los, a compact circle of lush green islands off the peninsula of Conakry, and moored alongside the container terminal at nine o'clock.

One of the first Guinean officials aboard was Abdoulaye Camara, the liaison 'fixer' Alain had hired to accompany us on the eight-hour journey upcountry to Faranah.

Tall, straight-backed and solid, his skin a light mahogany, he had at first glance the appearance of a determined boxer. His eyes were faintly bloodshot beneath his initial frown and his lips were compressed, but his expression lit up and he displayed an appealing, pugnacious mix of smiling aggression as he picked us out waiting for him on the deck. Bareheaded, his beard white at his chin, he was dressed in a smart, dark blue, short-sleeved safari suit. A gold medallion on a silver chain hung around his muscular neck, and a gold-winged badge, similar to a pilot's, was attached to the left-hand pocket of his shirt. I read 'GFC' embroidered on it.

He exuded reassuring authority. *He's someone with his finger on the pulse*, I thought.

He shook Alain's hand, 'Good morning gentlemans from Australia, and Mexican lady,' he said, his voice gravelly and his English slightly accented. 'Abdoulaye Camara, *à* votre service. I represent the Guinean Film Corporation. I am pleased to make your acquaintances.'

We've hired a smiling assassin. He may be just what we need, was my next thought as Alain introduced us, Abdoulaye's smile all flashing white teeth.

Alain led us to the officers' day room, which he'd arranged for a conference. He handed Abdoulaye all our paperwork. It took him some time to go through it—the passports and *Laissez-Passer* permits, the yellow fever and typhoid inoculation certificates, bills of lading, ownership papers and licenses for the car and kayaks, and the letter of permission from the Guinean Ambassador in Paris to film the documentary.

He also had an outline of Tony's documentary and read through it. At one point he raised his eyebrows with a sceptical shake of his head, 'The River of Dreams? An expedition kayaking down the Niger River from the source to the sea? C'est trés, trés ambitieux,' he muttered, before gazing at Tony and raising his voice, 'You must be aware several have failed and others died trying—'

'Of course. We've done our research,' Tony snapped.

'So isn't it evident the river is cursed? The spirits guarding it are trés mauvais. They are evil and malevolent.'

Tony smiled dismissively, 'We'll take care. We'll keep our fingers crossed and touch wood,' he said, tapping his temple.

Abdoulaye gave him a direct stare. 'You may smile, but remember, you have been warned,' he said, nodding and pursing his lips. 'In this country, you must expect the unexpected. Especially since you will be travelling close to the Sierra Leone border when you go to the source of the river. It is an unmarked no man's land.'

He went on to explain that there'd been reports of raiding parties of disgruntled striking Sierra Leonians rebelling against the financial crisis in their country crossing into Guinea and pillaging the local farms. In one case Liberian mercenaries who'd crossed the Sierra Leone border to stir up the simmering civil war in that country were among them.'

A rush of dread uncoiled deep in my gut as a sudden premonition of disaster overwhelmed me. I am rarely wrong, so I gritted my teeth as Abdoulaye reached for the other documents and reread them. 'Two days only or perhaps three,' he said at last, leaning back in his chair, 'to offload the car and your canoes. To arrange the official stamps and, naturellement, to pay the customs and other duties. It will cost you, but I will fix it so you pay the minimum.'

He gave us a quick, knowing grin and a sage nod. I caught what I took for a cunning glint in his eye and wondered for a moment if he was being ironic; he'd been educated by the French, after all. And if he was, how were we to judge? 'That is why I am here. A man with much experience, I have my ways and means. You will not regret it. Meanwhile, I will take you to the Novotel Ghi hotel,' he pointed vaguely through the door, 'just over there. Very new and very close. After immigrations.'

Despite my misgivings, Abdoulaye—soon Abdou to us— was as good as his word.

Within two days, Alain had all the necessary paperwork in hand, including receipts suggesting he'd been fairly taxed the right amounts. We also had the car and kayaks in the Novotel compound, adjacent to the container terminal at the end of the peninsula and facing the ocean. When we checked the four hatches in the kayaks—the two smaller hatches in the long, narrow foredeck and the two larger in the wide rear deck behind the seat—we were relieved to find that the camping gear and other equipment for the expedition packed inside them were intact.

Alain had been with Abdoulaye to visit the Rio Tinto minerals exploration office in the city to reconfirm their sponsorship of the project, prearranged in Perth. They agreed to allow us to share rooms for a week in the mining camp up country at Faranah and, critically and generously, for the company helicopter to ferry us for one flight to and from Foroconia. It was the closest village to the Tembakounda spring at the source of the Niger.

They had also visited the principal of *Lycée francais* Albert Camus—the LAC—an international secondary school, to which Alain had decided to donate the Toyota and trailer for their water sports program, once we were on our way down the Niger aboard the kayaks. They agreed to the handover in a fortnight, with Abdoulaye assigned to drive the vehicle back to the school from Faranah when the time came.

On the third and final afternoon, Abdoulaye drove us around Conakry and we watched Tony film two successive scenes.

The first was a sweeping pan of the waterfront Boulbinet fish market. He captured its teeming stalls and barrows glittering with the red and silver fish scales of the day's catch, its bustling and colourful crowds, and the dockside lined with an uncountable number of gaudily painted, high-prowed wooden fishing boats. Some were dragged up onto the narrow beach, others moored in the murky, rubbish-strewn shallows, and everywhere, the tangy sea smell turning rancid. By way of contrast at the end of the shot, he focused on the blue hull and superstructure of the *Louis Maersk*, still moored alongside the container wharves in the distance.

The second was a deep-focus, wide-angle shot of Alain outside the sprawling Madina market in the centre of the city. He was surrounded by eight or nine ragged and rowdy beggars, none more than ten years old. I stood back with Abdoulaye and other locals attending to the smoky street food stalls lining the red gravel walkway behind us, watching the drama play out.

Alain had bought a plastic bag of boiled sweets and he handed them out into outstretched open palms, the beggars clamouring for more until the bag was almost empty.

Suddenly, as if materialising out of the bare ground, a dusty, runny-nosed child of about six appeared, his twisted, crippled legs curled beneath his backside. He shuffled forward for his share, using both long arms to drag himself to Alain's feet. When Alain handed him the last sweet, he took it in one hand and wrapped his other arm around Alain's calf. He pocketed the sweet and asked for another. When Alain showed him the empty packet, shaking it and holding it upside down, the child screeched and showed his temper, reaching out to clutch his leg with both arms, catching him off-balance.

I was horrified as Alain staggered backwards for six or seven steps, dragging the boy across the gravel. When he regained his balance, he shook his leg, before taking several further steps, this time forwards, with the same unfortunate result. The child clung to him with a vice-like grip as he was yanked along, his crippled legs now trailing out behind him.

I heard a ripple of laughter running through the watching crowd.

When Alain at last stood still and looked down, I could see how agitated and perplexed he was. Abdoulaye and I both took a step towards him. Before we could reach him, he went down on his haunches, sat back on the ground, forcibly unlatched the beggar's hands and stood, still holding his wrists. He lifted the child from the ground by his arms and held him against his chest, cradled in his right elbow. With the boy's skinny black arms now gripped around his neck and his legs dangling, Alain murmured what I took for reassurances to him as I followed them from one street food stall to the next. When the boy pointed excitedly, they stopped beside the corncob brazier, where the pungent, smoky smell of charcoal embers and roasting maize filled the air. There Alain lifted him to the ground, selected a cob and bought it for him.

'It's hot,' he said, blowing on it before handing it down, 'don't burn yourself.'

He leant down and held out his fist, and the boy fist-pumped him as Abdoulaye translated, patting the boy on the head.

I watched, deeply moved, as Alain took out his handkerchief and wiped the boy's face clean.

'Nicely done, mate,' Tony said as he shut down the camera. 'That'll make an interesting addition to the doco. I got a decent tracking shot of you both. Every step you took and both your expressions.'

'The last shot with the young fella staring straight down the barrel of the lens must have seemed uncanny,' Alain said.

'You're telling me. He looked like a little jungle alien interrogating me. Made me squirm, especially when I stalked in for a close-up and he didn't bat an eyelid. He was looking straight into my soul, to be honest. My viewers are going to feel the same. It'll stir them up, give them a new slant on their perception of reality. They won't know what to feel about things they've never seen before or been too preoccupied to notice.'

'His image will show them something of themselves?'

'Exactly. They'll find the boy cross-examining and observing *them*, rather than the other way around.'

'They will believe the boy is justifiably questioning the white man's presence in Africa,' Abdoulaye suggested, before adding with a sharp, ironic glance at Tony, 'and warning him about his disbelief in its primitive superstitions.'

It was Abdoulaye who told me the villagers around Faranah spoke the Yalunka dialect and not Malinké, when I showed him my Malinké textbook. '*Now* you tell me,' I said, dismayed and annoyed with myself for not researching the Guinean dialects more thoroughly.

'There is a little similarity,' he said, and when he saw how confused and concerned I was, he added, 'but fear not, madame. I'm sure you will find one or two Malinké speakers among them. There is intermarriage everywhere among the tribes, and many wives. And besides, most speak French. You are aware it is the second language.'

We left Conakry at nine the next morning, with Abdoulaye at the wheel. It was the dry season, the dusty, corrugated and potholed gravel sections between stretches of bitumen barely slowing us down.

During the journey, armed soldiers stopped us at three separate checkpoints. Our papers were scrutinised with shows of overplayed officialdom, before a toll was demanded, and Alain paid. Abdoulaye had warned us about the practice. 'My advice is to pay without argument. Refusing will not be productive. It will result in a hold up,' he'd chuckled at his play on words. 'I will make sure you are not charged more than three thousand francs each, so four or five American dollars at the most. Twenty for all four of us.'

Seven hours later we passed beneath the white wooden archway welcoming us to Faranah, a kilometre from the town. *Bienvenue à Faranah* it read, with the Guinean red, yellow and green striped flag freshly painted on its crown.

When we crossed a cast iron bridge and sighted the Niger for the first time, Alain couldn't control his excitement. 'Stop, Abdou!' he shouted, and Abdoulaye pulled over to the right, on the upstream side of the deck.

Forty metres across, the river was chocolate brown and looked, I thought, deceptively deep and surly, the swirling current breaking the surface in irregular threatening surges as though showing its muscle.

An icy terror ran through me again and for a moment I shivered uncontrollably.

'There must have been a recent thunderstorm up in the headwaters,' Alain said, as he scrambled out, 'though it's partway through the dry season.' He threw his wallet and papers on the passenger seat he'd vacated, handed me his sunglasses, climbed onto the railing and with a triumphant yell, leapt into the river fully clothed, his arms flailing above his head.

Without a thought for his safety or the possibility of crocodiles or hippos, Tony wasn't far behind, and if anything, louder.

They were two crazies out of control, shouting and laughing like teenage boys in their element. I held my breath when they were swept by the current beneath the bridge and into a wild and rocky rush of white water a hundred metres downstream on the other side, where they were able to stagger ashore.

I loaded the camera as they jogged back along the path on the bank, and filmed them as they repeated the leap, this time Alain shouting, 'Beware the candiru! Better safe than sorry!' before he struck the water and disappeared beneath its surface.

'The candiru?' I had asked him when we were aboard the *Louis Maersk* and he was listing the many dangers we faced on the journey.

'The toothpick fish. It's supposed to be able to swim up a man's penis and hook itself into his urethra,' he told me.

'Ouch!'

'Ouch, for sure. I believe it's only found in the Amazon, and its ability to attach itself to a man's private parts is probably a myth—but Tony and I will take no chances. We'll keep our clothes on all the time.'

'That was some christening, by Jeez,' Alain said, shaking the water from his blond hair before he and Tony climbed back into the car, soaking wet.

'Sure was,' Tony agreed.

'It's in the can,' I told Tony. 'All the action of the second jump.'

Half an hour later we registered into the mining camp. It was a collection of six white modular transportable huts, which Alain told me were called "dongas" in Australia. One of them housed the showers and toilets, another the mess hall and the kitchens. After a well-deserved long hot shower, I found the self-serve rice and spicy goat stews satisfyingly filling.

When I settled down for the night, Abdoulaye's foreboding warning, "Expect the unexpected," echoed in my apprehensive mind. I could not shake my dread. My only consolation was the thought that whatever terrifying or deadly challenges lay ahead, Alain and I would be facing them together. I fell asleep spooning him, hoping his pragmatic and cheerful Australian optimism would prove my premonitions wrong… and woke the next morning wondering uneasily what destiny held in store.

The True Meaning Of Tragic Irony

In Saucillo, Northern Mexico, 1967-8

OUR GRANDFATHER CERRILDO'S 1956 Golden Hawk Studebaker was a sight to behold. It was his pride and joy. I can still see the excitement in his unusual almond-shaped dark brown eyes, his wide smile with its single silver canine crown standing out, the creases in his leathery skin deepening as he pushed back the brim of his sweat-stained white Stetson and ran through the car's mechanical qualities for anyone prepared to listen, 'Four gears and overdrive on the steering column gearshift,' he loved to boast, 'and she's powered by a *trescientos cincuanta y dos pulgada cúbica*, a 352 cubic-inch, OHV Packard V8. Would you like to take a look?'

He'd have the bonnet up and open before you could refuse him the opportunity to show it off, the engine block cracking like a shotgun as it cooled. 'Here she is, *mi bestia gruñona*, my growling beast. Naught to sixty in eight seconds. What do you think?'

When we were kids, my older brother Andrés and me, his little sister, used to sweat alongside him in the driveway of the house in Saucillo, hosing down and polishing the two-tone orange and cream bodywork and steam-cleaning the engine and chassis.

Especially after Andrés's monthly marathon training runs in preparation for the 1968 Mexico City Olympic trials. They were now a year away. He used to run alongside the car for three or four hours over forty-two dusty kilometres on the gravel road from the right-hand turnoff at the Conchos overpass, westwards to the Naica mine where Papá and Abuelo Cerrildo worked; or south towards Camargo on Highway 45D, the bitumen cutting through shady pistachio and apple orchards, and past green fields of cotton, maize and groundnuts.

I distinctly remember one Saturday in October, 1967, when Abuelo first pushed back his seat and made room for me to sit in front of him and learn to steer while he changed gears and worked the pedals. I was seven years old. I fought to suppress my giggling excitement as my arms struggled to manage the car's unaccustomed weight. Such responsibility. Such trust.

He had the windows down and rhythmic mariachi music blaring as he shouted instructions at Andrés right beside my ear, deafening me. '*Glide, boy! Glide!* Keep your feet close to the ground. Elbows in, and hands in line with your hips... until you're sprinting. Then you wait for my instructions!'

It took me several kilometres to get the knack with the steering wheel, and then, whenever a distant cloud of rising dust signalled oncoming traffic, I resumed my seat and became Andrés's helper again, passing a water bottle or one of Tía Ariché's special chia energy bars out through the passenger window when he needed them as he slipped along, his hands held low, his feet barely leaving the ground as though he was skating on ice, his clipped stride quick but deceptive in its length.

'Just under two metres, *nieto*,' Abuelo had told him earlier that month, after measuring both our strides as we'd loped around the circuit lined with pencil pines in our backyard in Saucillo. 'You'll have to build up your stride length when you're sprinting. That will come. You're only sixteen.'

'Almost seventeen,' Andrés corrected him.

'I beg your pardon, seventeen next month. You are filling out, I grant you that. The weights and gymnastics are doing you good. That, and kayaking with Alicia on the Conchos River and Rosetilla dam.'

'Not to mention his favourite food he scoffs down when we're running up at Cerocahui,' I added, thinking of Aunty Tía Ariché's mouth-watering tortilla, beans and squash and her chiles rellenos with three eggs and tomato salsa.

'Yes, her recipes are to *die* for,' Abuelo said, closing his eyes and sucking in his lips to kiss the four fingertips of his right hand. 'Like her second-to-none goat meat tacos *de cabeza* I can't resist.'

'They're all so filling, but greedy guts here, he always goes back for seconds. Even for *chica* Camila's cooking here in Saucillo,' I added with a grin, referring to the basic but always tasty meals our housemaid was teaching me to cook after school.

'And thirds,' Andrés said.

'*Comes lo suficiente para engordar una palanca.* You eat enough to fatten a crowbar,' Abuelo commented, patting him on the back.

Andrés often seemed lost in a meditative daydream as he ran those longer distances beside the car. I used to wonder what he was thinking about. Was his mind blank as he counted the kilometres slipping by? Was he noticing changes in the passing scenery? The clouds changing shape in the upper winds? The sun climbing through the big sky, rendering it a paler blue?

Or was he concentrating on enduring the pain he was experiencing until it became second nature? Or maybe imagining creative new floor plans and designs for the houses and buildings I'd watched him drafting in his room at home now that he'd enrolled in Architecture as a compulsory Arts option to his Physical Education degree at the National Polytechnic Institute in Mexico City next year?

From that day on, when I wasn't busy steering, I'd look out for a change in his expression signalling he was about to accelerate to a light canter or an occasional sprint, before easing back after a minute or two. He'd give a sudden, determined smile as he rose to the challenge, fluently lengthening stride, his arms driving his legs to a higher knee-lift. Then he seemed to float across the ground, his upper body perfectly balanced, his black Calupoh dog, Geronimo, looking up with an occasional approving bark as he raced along beside him like his shadow.

'What do you think about when you're running faster?' I asked him once. 'What goes through your mind?'

'I have to decide in a split second whether I'm a frightened hare caught in the headlights of anyone who's going to chase me down when I overtake them on the back straight... or an Olympic champion, like Billy Mills, with the killer instinct nobody's going to catch once I kick in and take the lead. I'm training myself to feel I'm fit and strong enough to grind them into the dust after turning into the home straight.'

He gave the characteristic burst of laughter I loved to hear and always shared, even though I may not laugh out loud. 'The other thing I do once I've changed gears is recite a poem to myself. It has the perfect rhythm for running hard and its meaning speaks to me. The school coach found it for the athletics team. It's called *If*, by an English poet, Rudyard Kipling. He was a runner too, so he knew what he was writing about. You want to hear the last verse?'

'Of course.'

'"*Si puedes llenar el minuto implacable*
Con sesenta segundos de distancia recorrida,
Tuya es la Tierra y todo lo que hay en ella,
Y—lo que es más—serás un Hombre, hijo mío!
If you can fill the unforgiving minute
With sixty seconds' worth of distance run,
Yours is the Earth and everything that's in it,
And—which is more—you'll be a Man, my son!"

He nodded. 'Once I'm up and running, with overdrive still in reserve, I keep repeating, "*Serás un Hombre, hijo mío, Serás un Hombre, hijo mío!*" as I race towards a target at the side of the road—a tree, a light pole or a sign a hundred or a hundred and fifty metres away. Then, before I reach it, I switch on the turbochargers and sprint the last thirty or forty metres flat out until I dip through the tape.'

When I heard that, the first time he raised his pace that day I teased him by shouting the refrain through the window, using words of my own, "*Serás un Hombre, mi hermano!* You'll be a man, my brother! *Serás un Hombre, pero no por un tiempo todavía*, but not for some time yet."

'*Dices tú, ardilla*. Says you, chipmunk,' he shouted back.

There were times when he slowed his pace to recharge his batteries, as he put it. Then he'd signal to me with his left hand and I'd open the door and join him, jogging for anything up to a kilometre, careful not to trip over Geronimo as he bounded up to lick me a welcome before they both picked up the pace once more and left me struggling in their wake.

I loved it. So much so that running became my other passion, after words and language. I knew I had a talent for both, as both came naturally to me. I spoke both Tarahumaran and Spanish by the time I was five and I was learning English at school and extending my Basque vocabulary with Papá when he had time to respond to my pestering.

As well as running with Andrés whenever he allowed me to, I also ran in teams with other Tarahumaran girls my age and older, chasing a wooden *ariweta* hoop rolled between us with our sticks beside the river at Urique, or through the scrubby pines and oaks along the crest of the Copper Canyon at Cerocahui for as long as we enjoyed the game, never conscious of the time, but revelling in the sheer exhilaration of the sport.

We learnt to perfect our skills, moving as lightly and efficiently across the rocky ground as our developing bodies allowed. We were aware, when we watched the older women also running, that we'd be doing so for a lifetime—perfecting the art of running and living up to our preferred indigenous name of Rarámuri, the light-footed ones.

And uncannily, through it all, I was vividly conscious of my dead Mamá, wondering if she was watching me and appreciating everything I did, as though I was doing it all as much for her as for myself.

Which of course I was.

On a hot Sunday afternoon in early December, 1967, in the foothills of the Paso de Cortés, in Zoquiapan National Park near Mexico City, I clutched Papá's hand, my heart thumping, as the leading group of runners pounded past us for the second time. They'd reached the halfway point in the eight-kilometre cross country course.

Andrés was still among them, running third or fourth. I caught our pre-agreed signal—a forefinger lifted quickly to his right eyebrow told us he was feeling good, with plenty in the tank, all high-octane fuel waiting for the spark, as he described it.

I checked the stopwatch—thirteen minutes, thirty-five seconds and counting. Just under national record pace for Mexican junior boys, aged eighteen and below.

From the slope overlooking the course, we could see the line of runners as they laboured up the next hill, some now falling back, several walking at the rear, a handful stretching away at the front. Andrés was in the mix in his blue and white Saucillo High School colours, before he disappeared over the top and into the pine plantations.

Clouds were spilling across the crests of the two nearby volcanoes, Iztaccíhuatl and Popocatépetl, the sky a blinding sunlit blue. Stratospheric winds were wiping away the chalky trail of a barely visible silver aircraft streaking across from east to west. *Has it just taken off from Benito Juárez airport in Mexico City?* I wondered. *Are others lined up on the runway about to follow? Will their white trails entertain me with a heavenly game of* tres en raya, *noughts and crosses, emblazoned across the sky?*

I began imagining where I'd place my marks.

'Here they come,' Papá yelled, peering through his binoculars. 'Just two of them.'

I craned my neck to see, then fought my way to the front as the spectators stood, their conversations rising to a crescendo of cheers, my screams among them. Andrés and a taller runner, dressed in black, powered down the long slope beyond the trees towards us, shoulder to shoulder. A third runner was struggling a distant thirty metres behind them.

A hundred and fifty metres from the finish, as though propelled by an invisible rubber cord stretched between my willing mind and his, Andrés took a step to his right, and within several arm-pumping, smoothly accelerating strides, he gained a five-metre lead and slowly extended it, before he ducked through the tape.

In the last thirty metres of the race, the number 11 on his chest flapped upwards in his slipstream, and I saw beneath it through my excitement and my tears the Saucillo High School badge on full display—*el correcamino*, the roadrunner. Andrés was a roadrunner, but he was no Mexican chicken. *Eso es tan irónico*—that was so ironic, I thought. Irony was a fascinating new abstract word in my vocabulary whose meaning Papá had taught me recently and I was trying to understand it. Particularly tragic irony.

Then I checked the stopwatch in my sweaty hand and realised I'd forgotten to press the button. I quickly did so, only to discover I'd added half a minute to Andrés's time when the official timekeeper later confirmed before the medal presentation that he'd run the course in a new national junior record of twenty-seven minutes and five-point-four seconds.

'It was Billy Mills who helped me win,' Andrés confided to us on the journey home. 'He coached me all the way.'

'What? Was he speaking to you in Oglala Lakota with someone translating for you into Tarahumaran?' I asked.

Papá gave a burst of laughter. 'Trust you to know he was speaking Oglala Lakota.'

'It says so on Andrés's poster,' I replied defensively. 'And Jim Thorpe on the other poster is a Sac and Fox. He speaks Algonquin.'

Papá turned back to Andrés. 'So what advice did Billy give you?'

'When we came down the slope to the finishing line, it was like I was running with him on the last lap in Tokyo, when that Tunisian, Mohammed Gammoudi, shoved his way through the gap between him and the Australian Ron Clarke to take the lead, and he chased them both around the turn into the home straight. Then he stepped to the right, just like I did today, and blasted past to win the gold.'

'Just like you did,' I said admiringly.

'You recall all that from the film of the race?' Papá asked.

'Remember I told you about Señor Valentin, the Russian coach who's visiting us this week during the Cultural Olympiad? He showed us the film at school. That last lap. Three times. He was pointing out how rough it can get on the track, how we have to avoid getting boxed in, and what to do if we are.'

'You did well today,' Papá said. 'We're proud of you. The Olympic trials are next. Will you compete if your win today qualifies you?'

'If I get an invitation, maybe yes.'

'No maybes,' I broke in. 'Just a yes.'

Two weeks later, we learned that his win, along with other times he'd recorded, had earned him an invitation to run in the ten thousand metres at the Mexican Olympic Trials.

Late evening, Sunday, 21 April, 1968, a week after the Easter celebrations in Saucillo, the Olympic trials were televised.

I carried the loose wiring and the aerial while Abuelo Cerrildo lifted the black and white television out to his worktable on the back veranda. I climbed up into the pistachio tree and hoisted the aerial into its upper branches above the roofline of the house. I lashed it in position and Abuelo, fiddling with the controls, shouted that reception was as clear as he could manage.

I climbed down as he adjusted the volume, the *Telesistema Mexicano* sports announcer's voice commenting on a track event that was underway. I leapt to the ground and rushed to Abuelo's side to check—the one hundred and ten metres hurdles for men had just finished. I glanced at the program. We had an hour to wait before Andrés ran the most important race of his young life.

He had enrolled for the February intake of students at the IPN, the *Instituto Polytécnico Nacional* in Mexico City, and we hadn't seen him since his departure. Papá had taken a week's leave to support him, even though he was not allowed to enter the Olympic stadium to watch the race.

Abuelo, the housemaid Camila and I settled into our chairs when the ten thousand metre runners were called to their marks. It was impossible to distinguish them in the growing twilight and on the steady long shot taken, I guessed, through a camera stationed on the stadium roof. Earlier events had involved closer cameras strategically placed around the stadium, so that we'd watched the muscles twitch in a tangle of sprinting legs one minute, a high jumper's distorted features as he sailed over the bar the next, or tracked a discus spinning high through the air across the stadium.

I was tense, searching for Andrés but not recognising him, as twenty or so small, shadowy figures shuffled into a curved line at the start. A short delay, before the crack of the pistol set them off, the bunched pack rocketing into the back straight, runners jostling for position before settling into pairs and single file down the back straight for the first time, the pace easing into a fluid stride as they reached the end of the first lap. The field official turned the arm of the lap counter down to a number it was impossible to read, but I knew it was twenty-three.

Who is who? Where is Andrés?

Multiple bulbs in the four floodlight towers overhead were glowing but refusing to fire up. For three laps the camera angle didn't change and the shell of the stadium darkened further... until the floodlights flared alight, each with a startling explosive crackle, the runners now standing out as brilliant as day.

Andrés—*there* he was—running freely in tenth position, looking comfortable, the floodlights on his body throwing four shadows across the lanes, tracking every footfall.

José Garcia, who I'd seen in one of Andrés's *World Sports* magazines, was six or seven metres in the lead.

I imagined Papá following the race on his colour television in his hotel, the white lines clear against the reddish tan of the rubberised tartan track, the deep green of the infield grass, the state colours of the runners' vests and shorts—Sinaloa scarlet, Jalisco orange, Chiapas black and yellow, Yucatán green, and Andrés running well, still in the middle of the field, in his Chihuahua silken blue.

With ten laps to go, Andrés was holding his midfield position. A leading group, including Garcia, Juan Martínez and Pablo Garrido, was playing a game of catch me if you can, threatening to draw away.

And then the camera angle switched to a bird's eye view, and the distant figures circling the track were too small and mesmerising for me to follow. My attention was drawn instead to the stairway leading up to the Olympic cauldron. I decided to count the steps and imagined running up them, carrying the Olympic torch—ten grey steps between iridescent pink banisters per lap, ten laps to go. Each time the leader passed the halfway point down the back straight, I'd sprint up another ten, like scaling an Aztec or Mayan pyramid, to see how close to the cauldron I'd be at the finish, when I'd climb the rest and light the flame to celebrate Andrés winning.

After ninety-three steps, my stomach churning and gasping for breath in my imagination, I'd reached the summit. I stood beside the angled cauldron, panting, the torch raised in my right hand.

I watched the final lap, the camera angle switching back to close-up. I had a trackside view as it followed Juan Martínez, leading, with four runners chasing him at the bell. Mario Saldivar was his closest challenger... and Andrés was still in eighth position, the length of the home straight behind him.

I was overwhelmed as Andrés passed the bell. *Does it sound to him as it does to me, like the Chihuahua cathedral bell striking twelve for Mamá and Papá, when they were nineteen and met for the first time on the cathedral steps in 1943?*

He ran the bend into the last lap, digging deep, his stride long but not yet at full sprint. He was beautiful to watch, so smooth, so fluent as he cruised past another runner in the back straight and then another as he turned for home, holding his form and gathering gazelle-like speed over the last thirty metres in a controlled sprint, dipping through the finish in sixth position.

Then I leaned across to light the cauldron for him, sobbing with delight and pride.

Was it Billy Mills whispering to him in Oglala Lakota that had inspired him to run so well, or Jim Thorpe in Algonquin this time?

Either way, it was a North American Indian sharing his secrets with a Central American Rarámuri Indian.

'*Sexto*,' Abuelo shouted. 'Sixth!' He sat shaking his head, looking down at the stopwatch in his trembling hand, and then, after a deep breath, 'In thirty minutes and forty-eight point four seconds by this watch. And he was making ground on Martínez and the others in the last lap. He gained at least ten metres. Did you see that?'

'He was brilliant.'

'He may have missed out on a place in the team this time, but you wait till Munich.' He gave me a hug that choked the breath out of me, before releasing me with a lopsided grin, his eyebrows arched upwards, his silver tooth flashing, 'He wouldn't have done it without our coaching would he, *nieta*? You and me both.'

'You and me and Geronimo, Abuelo,' I said, 'and the Studebaker, of course.'

'Ah, *mi bestia gruñona*. We must not forget her.'

'And Camila's special nutritious diet,' I added, placing my arm across her plump shoulders as she ducked away, a blush rising beneath her olive skin to the silver coronet of her unruly hair.

I did not tell them that I'd climbed the steps to light the cauldron, striving upwards with one goal in mind—to reach the top, determined to succeed without a backward step.

To do it on my own and please Mamá.

I'd known for certain then that I'd concentrate on a *two*-lap race from now on. Just the two. No further. One lap cruising to the bell, the next a sprint to reach the finish. *Another twenty-two laps? Out of the question. The eight hundred metres.* Eso me viendría bien, muchísimas gracias, *that will suit me, thank you very much.*

In Mexico City, October 1968

Papá and I flew to Mexico City at the beginning of October

for the Olympic Games, due to start in twelve days. We stayed with Papá's friend Tío Guillermo in his unit in the Chihuahua Building, beside the Tlatelolco Plaza.

During late afternoon on Wednesday, 2 October, 1968, Andrés, Tío Guillermo and I joined the crowd of students and others who were gathering on the Plaza to listen to speeches from their political leadership. Mexico had been embroiled in sometimes violent student unrest for months, but with the Games in jeopardy we understood the students' Council was about to declare a truce.

I had convinced Andrés to join us. He was enjoying a rest day between training sessions.

'No, it's my day off—and *nothing* comes between me and my running,' Andrés said, when I first asked him. 'Nothing. You above all people know that,'

'*Please*, please, please, please… I want to finish the film in my camera,' I begged him.

'Alright, I'll come, but only for an hour or so,' he reluctantly agreed. 'And only for you. I wouldn't do it for anyone else.'

Tío Guillermo, also unwilling at first, showed his displeasure as we joined the crowd. 'We're not going to enjoy this,' he said with a thin smile. 'There must be ten or fifteen thousand people here already.'

I held up the camera and snapped his expression just as I was jostled sideways. 'At least let me use up this film,' I said. 'There are now only twenty-three exposures left.'

'*Only* twenty-three? You'd better make it quick.'

We worked our way to the back edge of the crowd close to the church, the voice on the speakers clearer now. A group of schoolboys in maroon and khaki uniforms in front of me restricted my view, even though one of them, whose features I recognised as Tepehuán Indian, flashed me a brief smile and stepped to one side when he saw my dilemma.

When I raised both arms above my head to take a hopeful

random shot, Tío Guillermo took me by the armpits and effortlessly lifted me to his broad shoulders without so much as asking. I almost dropped the camera, but the position was perfect. I had a bird's eye view across the plaza and was able to balance my elbows on his bald head. He was rock solid each time I said I was about to take another shot.

I ranged the camera across the crowd and took several shots in quick succession. The first was the pregnant lady with the black pram, standing stock-still and listening intently, with her two little kids—*are they twin girls?*—squatting on the paving beside her, playing what looked like cat's cradle with a web of black string. I was delighted when the nearest of them stuck out her tongue when she saw the camera.

Another was a broad view of the Chihuahua building. A central balcony window on the third floor was wide open, a border of white sheets drawing attention to it, a pair of black loudspeakers at each end of the window ledge. I took it to be the hallway beside the lift shaft. There were several figures in the window, one of them speaking into a microphone.

'The Strike Committee,' Andrés said as I took the shots. 'Just as I thought. They want to call the demonstrations off. They're concerned about the number of granaderos and riot police already here. They must be able to see something from up there we can't.'

'Clearly, they know something we don't,' Tío Guillermo agreed.

The reaction from some rowdy groups in the crowd to their announcement shocked me. They began shouting in unison, others joining them, '*No queremos Olimpiadas, queremos revolución*. We don't want the Olympics, we want a revolution.'

The chant became deafening, drowning out whatever warning the student was shouting down at us.

'*Malditos extremistos*, bloody extremists,' Andrés yelled at us. 'I should have known they'd be here.'

I was surprised to see a single line of helmeted soldiers placed an arm's length apart at the base of the building, facing the crowd. They were standing at ease beneath the concrete overhang, bayonets fixed, as though guarding the entrances to the stairwells and the line of shopfront windows. An officer stood at the centre, his uniform immaculate and his polished epaulettes shining, a large orange megaphone in his right hand.

'It's the presidential guard, by the look of the uniforms,' Andrés said.

I photographed the officer, before raising the camera to focus on two helicopters that appeared out of the growing dusk high above us, one painted in dark blue police colours, the other in army grey camouflage.

The crowd quietened as they circled for several minutes, seemingly observing us, until two brilliant red flares were fired from the top floor of the Foreign Affairs skyscraper to our right. I took a dramatic shot of the flares falling against the darkening sky, trailing what looked like flames. They exploded on the paving between the church and the Chihuahua building, people beneath the line of their descent screaming as they fought to escape the shower of sparks.

The church bell unexpectedly rang out, tolling six and silencing the crowd. People close to me looked up at the bell tower, some laughing, others clearly counting out the chimes. I held my breath, the eeriness of the moment leading me to suspect it was a warning signal.

For several minutes the student's voice crackling over the loudspeakers urged the crowd to disperse, before falling silent as the police helicopter swooped directly at us. Tension rippled through the crowd as it also fired two flares aimed at the plaza, this time one red, one green, with the same incendiary descent and explosive result. The crowd scattered as they struck the ground. The helicopter skimmed low across the buildings, before soaring up and hovering over us, alongside the army helicopter once again.

The stunned silence lengthened, underscored by the consistent *whup whup whup* of helicopter blades.

Then a group of helmeted soldiers carrying rifles with bayonets fixed burst from behind the church wall to our right. They charged forward and took up positions in front of the church, facing the crowd. In a strange, dreamlike sequence, a side door of the church opened and I photographed a large number of men in plain clothes pouring down the steps, the door slamming shut behind them. The first of them showed a sheet of paper to the surrounding soldiers, who let them through. Wearing white gloves on one hand and carrying black pistols in the other, they melted purposefully into the crowd.

One of them passed so close to Andrés he could have reached out and touched him.

Andrés looked up at me. 'The Olympic Battalion. And they're armed. It means trouble.'

As he spoke, I heard the sharp crack of a gunshot, followed by several others. I ducked when I heard their terrifying echoes. I raised the camera again, fighting to control my shaking hands, to capture a soldier in the line beneath the eaves of the Chihuahua building, who had slumped to his knees and toppled forward at the feet of the others.

The officer raised his megaphone and spoke into it, his voice screeching until he adjusted the instrument and yelled at the crowd to leave at once. When he repeated the order, there was another sharp sequence of gunshots coming either from the roof of the church above us or from an upper floor of the Foreign Affairs skyscraper beyond it.

The officer was flung backwards against a shopfront window, hurling aside the megaphone. He slid down the glass, a smear of red marking his descent. He sat on the paving rocking himself, his legs outstretched, clutching at his chest, his mouth wide open coughing gouts of blood across his uniform.

In a shocking otherworldly moment, I read the name of the shop above his head in bold black print—*Fotos Exprés*.

I rushed to take the shot as Tío Guillermo lifted me down. He took hold of my hand, and we turned to run for the lift well at the far end of the building. The panicked crowd surrounding us rushed with one mind towards the same exit, their screams and shouts incoherent, trampling over those who'd fallen, papers flying as they threw aside the pamphlets and leaflets distributed among them earlier. An older man tore off his white shirt and waved it overhead in surrender. He staggered across our path before Tío brushed him aside. Others were scrambling for cover behind the vehicles in the carpark and crawling beneath them.

When I looked around for Andrés, he wasn't with us. I screamed a warning at Tío Guillermo. We slowed and he leaned down to shout in my ear, 'He must be ahead of us. Did you see him go?'

Seized with a terrifying degree of dread I screamed at the top of my lungs, 'No. He must be back there.'

We fought our way back through the chaos of running and falling bodies, kicking aside an overturned black pram, slipping on abandoned shoes and sandals, a handbag, paper cups, a scattering of empty food cartons.

We found Andrés lying face down beside the outstretched body of the blond-haired teenage schoolboy who'd been standing in front of me moments before beside the Tepehuán Indian. A bullet had smashed through the base of the schoolboy's skull and blood was seeping from beneath his body, spreading across the slate tiles on each side of him like a pair of wings with red and black-tipped feathers.

Andrés was groaning, his left calf bleeding into his jeans, shredded where a bullet had torn through them. Tío Guillermo turned him over, a grazed contusion evident beneath his hairline and across his nose where he'd struck the tiles. His eyes were glazed and unfocused.

As I looked down at him the world swirled around me, leaving me frozen with shock. For a moment I had no idea where I was. I doubled over and heard myself scream as though I was someone else, before I heard Tío's voice calling for the camera case. Barely comprehending, I handed it to him. He unclipped the strap, tore off the carnation and bound Andrés's leg above the knee.

Below the wound, his left foot protruded at a grotesque angle.

Tío stood, took me by my upper arms and shook me, before taking my face in both his hands. He leaned down to look into my eyes with unforgettable intensity. 'Listen, cariño. We have no time. You have to get away from here. Run. Run as fast as you can. I will take Andrés to the Green Cross Hospital. *To the Green Cross Hospital.* Remember that. Now Go. *Go!*'

He turned me around and pushed me away so violently that I almost fell. I regained my footing and stooped to pick up the camera. I stood unmoving in another moment of indecision, watching Tío use his teeth to tighten the knot on a white handkerchief he wrapped around his left hand before lifting Andrés across his back and right shoulder. He manoeuvred Andrés's arms around his neck and gripped both his hands in his right.

'Go,' he shouted again, leaning forward and balancing Andrés on his hip, his trailing legs off the ground. He took his first lunging step towards the exit, his left hand a cloth-bound white fist raised for balance. 'Go. Run like you've never run before.'

Helpless, I could not budge. The world spun around me, my terror-stricken mind a void as I lost all sense of time and watched a formation of soldiers advancing like black spectres across the plaza towards the pandemonium of screaming people, trapped by armoured vehicles and soldiers at the exit to my left. Some were firing from the shoulder, some kneeling before advancing again and others sliding into prone positions, one or two with their rifles balanced on the bodies of the fallen.

Closer, in stark black outline, the pregnant woman was crawling away from her pram. She was pinned as if paralysed in the blazing beam of a spotlight directed at the plaza from the police helicopter.

Is she searching for her children among the wounded? Did they try to run? Were they trampled in the stampede? And the horrifying question struck me, *Will the spotlight focus next on me?*

I tore my gaze away and my mind cleared as though I'd received an electric shock.

I had seven exposures left. I levered rapidly through them on automatic focus to the end of the film, before packing the camera back in its case and snapping it shut. I sprinted along the parapet beside the Aztec excavations.

When I reached a flight of steps leading down into the ruins, I swerved to leap down them, three at a time, looking for shelter between the pyramidal platforms. It wasn't until I ducked for cover behind the brickwork and knelt to gather my breath that the full force of what had just occurred struck me... and with a sickening sense of shock and despair I heard Andrés tell me once again that nothing—but *nothing*—came between him and his running.

PART III

Three Short Pieces

The Birth Of Medika

THE TWO WOMEN HE was searching for were squatting beyond the hill, hidden from the encampment. They were barely visible, huddled in the sun-flecked shade of the mooja tree, its canopy thick with golden blooms. Blue-grey smoke spiralled skyward from a pile of dried leaves smouldering beside them.

Crouching and hidden from view, he watched them move closer together.

He saw the older woman look down at the squirm of a pale infant, the new-born *bilyunu* in the leaf-lined hollow of the earth cradle she had prepared.

Jayarra, the younger woman, leant back against the rough bark of the tree trunk. Her legs were spread wide, straddling the hollow, her hands gripped across her breasts. He made out the blue and scarlet lifeline of the placenta uncoiling from her bloodied vagina to the child's centre, a sunlit sinew in the flickering light.

Tense, he watched the older woman reach for the newborn child. *Is she female? Yes! She is,* he realised, as she licked clean the mouth and the eyes and the quick pulsing curve of rib and stomach, a warm-tongued welcome to this world, its first plaintive cry barely reaching him.

Then, teeth bared, she clamped the cord and chewed, separating the child and lifting her in ancient hands away from the earth-scooped cradle-grave. He saw her stand and hold the infant to her withered breasts as if to feel the heartbeat, the *wurduru* of another life fluttering against her own, and to breathe the awareness of this new existence deep into herself.

He saw her anoint the child with a smear of *atkajadi* oil and hold her momentarily in the cleansing wisp of smoke before leaning down to pat a free hand in the warm ash, the *thalaaba* of the fire, using it to powder the child. Then she handed her to her mother, her *ngangga* Jayarra, soaked in sweat but smiling weakly at the pitch of the infant's cry that now carried louder to him as she cradled her in an elbow-crook and offered her a dark nipple. The child rubbed her ash-covered cheek against it, before fastening her lips round it with a sudden, sure jerk of her head.

The older woman retrieved the expelled afterbirth. She selected a length she retained and, with the side of her foot, she filled the birth hollow to bury the rest, scooping back the red earth that he knew would have suffocated the quivering infant had she, the *bugarra*, the old midwife, so decided.

He acknowledged with elation that the child had been allowed to live and he saw Jayarra marvelling at the gold of her skin she must know would darken, and the finest blonde threads of her sparse hair.

The older woman reached up to pick a bunch of crocus flowers from the golden canopy above them, and then another, placing them in the curved wooden *yandi*, ready for Jayarra to lie the infant within it for their return to the campsite. In the flowers, he had been told, was the infant's name, Medika, and in her body was her spirit, recalled from its dreaming by the *wilithi jinagabi wiyabandi*, the white spirit, who was no spirit returned from the dead, but a man and her father.

He watched the older woman split the length of the placenta and plait it into a necklace of ash-covered sinew for the infant; a reminder bracelet linking her spirit past to her living present. The infant would wear it, he had been advised, as a charm during the first weeks of her life, as the others of the Malgana family welcomed her into their circle of awareness in this beloved place of their dreaming, edged by the western ocean and the sleeping of the sun.

They walked back up the hillside towards the campsite, where he, her father, *Gayirrigayirrit*, Gerrit-from-afar, stood and welcomed her into his sunburned arms.

'*Bilyunu Medika bardiyalu ngathinyina.*' Jayarra smiled as she handed her across to him. 'Our baby Medika is no longer crying.'

He gazed down at the infant in wonder for several moments, waves of emotion rushing through him. 'Medika,' he whispered at last, before glancing back at Jayarra. '*Nganuralu nguba gutiya.* We are of one blood, Jayarra.'

He adjusted Medika into the crook of his left arm, reached out and drew Jayarra into him, his right arm about her waist. 'I know I'm white,' he said, 'but together we are ebony and ivory. A perfect match!'

Otello Ferreira

FRIDAY JANUARY 7, 1701. A day I will never forget. I was fifteen years old.

The twins, Cain and Abel, each wearing a cardboard label bearing their names, met us at the gates when we arrived at the saw windmill timberyards south of Middelburg. We three had signed on as apprentice carpenters in the dockyard the week before, and we were starting our six months' induction there.

They introduced themselves, took us to the dormitory and then led us up the steps to the communal dining room lined with pinewood tables and benches. I ducked as we entered to avoid the iron ring and striker hanging on a chain beside the door. I took it to be the timberyard bell.

Abel held up his label. 'In case you think our names are a practical joke, that's how we were baptised, Cain and I, by our Papa Adam, and our Mama Evelyn,' he said. 'We're Puritan English gentlemen. As you can hear, our Dutch is rudimentary, but we do our best to get the message across. We're retired professionals from Norwich. And I'm the chef here, as you'll learn to appreciate or you go hungry.'

He snapped a finger several times and the door beside the servery hatch opened.

An extraordinary figure appeared, one I'd seen many times around Middelburg with the other African-Zeelanders, had stared at and commented on among my friends but had been too fearful to approach.

'Meet Otello,' Abel continued, smiling as he observed our surprise. 'If you want to eat well, he's the one person in the camp you want to show special respect. He is the chief steward and helps me around the kitchens.'

Otello was a tall, broad-shouldered, white-skinned

and heavily freckled albino African-Zeelander mulat. His receding, tightly curled hair, caught in parallel shafts of winter sunlight slanting through the slatted window, was tinged a fiery orange. His eyes were pale blue, so pale I noticed that his irises had a faint pink colour at certain angles, as he turned to look at each of us in turn. He had a massively muscular right arm, the tendons and sinews writhing like snakes beneath his skin as he moved. His left was missing at the shoulder, a stump evident, the sleeve of his white jacket pinned to his chest.

He stepped forward. 'Otello Ferreira,' he growled.

He reached forward and offered Nikolaas his broad hand. 'Welcome,' he said, and I saw Nikolaas wince as he took it. He turned to me and did the same. 'Welcome,' he repeated, crushing the bones in my fingers, and 'Welcome to you too,' he said to Axel, who wrung his hand when Otello released it.

'Now then,' Abel said, 'before you start work, we have a small test for you. Follow me.' He led us towards the kitchen door, stopping at a red line painted across the floorboards, dividing the room in two.

'You see this line? No one—but no one—crosses it. It's as close as you come to the servery hatch at mealtimes.' He pointed down with dramatic emphasis. 'This side—your territory. That side—Otello's and mine. And never the twain shall meet!'

Then he gave us a mysterious smile. 'Unless of course, you can get past Otello here. You have two chances to try. Once now and once again the day you leave. That way we measure the progress you've made. How much stronger you've become in six months.

'Let me explain. When he was younger, Otello was taken to Dejima Island in Nagasaki to work as a family cook for the VOC administrator in Japan. He was there for seven years and, during that time, he learned how to arm grapple the Japanese way. Show them, Otello.'

Giving each of us a curt bow, in turn, Otello stepped up to the line. He turned sideways to face us, feet apart, his left braced against the wall, his right pointed along the line. Then he extended his arm, cocked slightly at the elbow, tensed the muscles and tendons, and cupped his hand with the fingers together.

I found the suggestion of threat and obvious power in his posture alarming.

Abel chuckled as he placed a small hourglass on the servery ledge. 'Now I'll give each of you one measure on the timer to shift that arm and claim some of our territory. Like this.'

He stepped forward, took up an identical stance facing Otello, and placed his right hand in Otello's fist. For several moments he strained unsuccessfully to shift Otello's arm towards the kitchen, before relaxing with a frustrated gasp.

Otello's face was impassive.

Abel stood panting, gathering his breath, before pointing at Axel. 'You're the smallest,' he said. 'So you try first.'

'But I'm left-handed.'

'Then we'll handicap Otello. You can use both hands and take up any position you choose.'

Axel walked up, placed his left hand in Otello's extended hand and his right on Otello's forearm. When Abel turned the timer, Axel stretched forward and struggled to push the arm, his feet scrabbling on the floorboards until Abel eventually called for him to stop. The arm did not budge.

It was my turn next. I positioned myself as Abel had done. Otello's fist closed over mine and I tensed, waiting for Abel's call. When it came, my body convulsed from head to toe as I exerted all the strength I had, leaning forcefully in, my shoulders rotating awkwardly into the thrust. I gave a long, grunting outbreath. Gasping for another, I felt my face reddening, the veins in my neck pulsing, before I groaned again. And then again, with another desperate and violent effort. It was like pushing against a rock, against a statue, while time seemed to extend unbearably. The longer I struggled, anxious that my energy was deserting me, the more agonising it became.

When Abel at last called 'Time!' I glanced up at Otello, breathless. His face was expressionless or was that a glimmer of quiet satisfaction in his eyes?

'Now I know how Sisyphus felt,' I murmured, rubbing my hands together.

Abel smiled in surprise at my comment. 'That is a commendable reference indeed, coming from an apprentice. Sisyphus. He personified the idea of persistence. You boys can learn a valuable lesson from him.'

Nikolaas was the last to face the test and the result was no different.

'As I said, you get to try again before you leave,' Abel reminded us as he pocketed the hourglass and walked back to the kitchen with Otello. 'We'll see you boys when you come back in for lunch

Cain then took us down the dining hall steps and into the yards. Carrying a rake, with which he occasionally levelled the pebbly gravel on the pathway, he led us down the line of seven saw windmills, describing each in turn. Four of them were operating, the sails slowly turning, the saws rasping and grinding, an occasional metallic shriek making the hair on the back of my neck stand up.

Twenty minutes later we reached the seventh windmill at the end of the row, smaller than the others. It was also slowly turning.

I saw beside it a light spray of water showering from outlets along a pipe that ran above logs and planks piled neatly in tiered pyramids. They stood on a raised brick platform, the wastewater leaching down into a wide drain, its grill lid visible at the base of its foundations.

'This is our little miracle,' Cain told us. 'She's our water pumping windmill—the beating heart of the process here. We're in trouble she ever breaks down.' He tapped Axel's head with the knuckle of his forefinger. 'Touch wood she won't and we don't run out of wind.'

Beyond the mill lay a spectacular wetland surrounded by reeds and willows. We stood and admired the lake as Cain explained that it was the sedimentation pond, purifying the run-off water drained from the sprinklers, as well as brackish water pumped from the ponds, which the pumping mill then recycled.

'We run the sprinklers to avoid the timber drying out. You'll find out why once you start work.' He pointed at the pyramids of wet logs. 'Logs piled high like this can be dangerous, especially when they're wet. So remember one thing, boys, above all else. Think safety first! Everything you do here will have an element of danger attached to it. Take your time. Watch how the others approach their work. Do *not* rush in headfirst.'

He reached out and tapped the closest pyramid with his rake handle. 'Let Otello serve as a warning. I'll tell you how he lost his arm. Five years ago, he came down here from the kitchen one morning to take a shower. As you three will, by the way. Every evening before dinner. Anyway, that morning three labourers were building a pyramid, similar to these. They were halfway through the task when the labourer at the top slipped and the logs began to move. Had they fallen, the two below him would have been killed, no doubt about it. Let alone himself.

'As it was, Otello jumped forward without a second thought. His upraised left arm was caught between two rolling logs that wound it in up to his armpit like a wet sheet squeezed through a box mangle. But with the strength of his right arm and the bulk of his neck and shoulder, he stopped the movement in the logs in time for the three labourers to escape and come to his rescue. So did every worker in the yards. He was trapped for almost half an hour while they dismantled the pile. His arm was crushed beyond repair. Sebastiao amputated it right here while he was unconscious. The rope that Abel tied round his stump saved his life. I helped him wind it tight enough to stop the bleeding, using a stick tied through a loop.'

He gazed at us as the story sank in. 'He was in the Gasthuis Hospital for several months. We thought we'd lost him.'

We found the story both horrifying and fascinating, especially when he asked, 'What colour do you think his blood was?'

'Is that a trick question?' Nikolaas asked.

'Do you think it is?'

'No.'

'Then why do you ask?'

'I don't know. Red?'

'You're not sure?'

'Red. It must be red.'

'And what colour is yours? Also red?'

'Of course.'

'If you remember anything from your time here, make sure you remember that.'

'What? That my blood is red?' Nikolaas was incredulous.

Cain did not reply. He was silent as he led us across to a nearby workman debarking a pine log balanced on trestles at either end. When we reached him, Cain turned to us. 'That we all share the same red blood, no matter the colour of our skins or nationalities.'

The Snake Wrangler

1711—Aboard the Zuytdorp on Sao Tomé Island, West Africa.

WHEN THE SENIOR SURGEON visited Sao Tomé hospital during that last week, I accompanied him.

At first, I assisted him as he replenished the dwindling medical supplies in his medicine chest from the apothecary in the infirmary. He was able to procure agave resin unguent for ulcers, and cinnamon and caraway seeds for heartburn and bloating and a handful of shrivelled ipecacuanha roots, along with a single sack of dried Peruvian cinchona bark.

'You crush this up and boil it,' the apothecary said, 'to make a potion the Jesuits claim is effective against tropical fevers.'

'Does it work?'

'We swear by it here,' the apothecary nodded, reaching into the back of his cabinet and retrieving two phials containing small amounts of a pale yellow liquid. 'Would you have any use for one of these? It's Gabon viper venom.'

The senior surgeon held it up to the light. 'Interesting. What do you use it for?'

'We add it to strengthen some potions we use for leprosy and smallpox, though we've had little call for it lately and we are about to discard these. It is used in voodoo medicines on the mainland.'

'I doubt if we'll have a need,' the senior surgeon replied.

I reached across for the phial and turned it this way and that. The liquid seemed to have the consistency of mercury.

'Where do you get it from?' I asked.

'We have a snake pit here. The Angolares who looks after it is an expert.' He looked up at me. 'I can show you if you like.'

I turned to the senior surgeon. 'If we have the time, I'd like that.'

That afternoon we attended when the half-caste Angolares, revered for his sorcery, climbed into the town's snake pit to casually milk one viper directly into a glass phial.

That night I wrote a brief journal entry.

I witnessed today a native who collected the venom of a snake, a remarkable sight he showed to all those gathered there. The snake was the length of my arm, its body of remarkable thickness wound in contortions about the native's forearm. Its scales were patterned in pale brown and purple pentagons, while the belly was pale gold. It had two horns and was thereby recognisable. The native held the monster behind the head, its mouth open against the lip of a phial while teasing the fangs of surprising dimension and thinness and hung with skin webbing from the tissue of its jaw with a bronze rod. The venom slid down the glass, to my mind like yellow mercury. The native wore no shoes and his bare feet were visible beneath cowhide protectors worn from ankle to knee. I saw he wandered among other reptiles of similar size coiled there, as though under the protection of God Almighty—or some other god of his own belief. I found the docility of the snakes and the native's indifference to them beyond belief.

Acknowledgements

T HIS COLLECTION OF STORIES wouldn't have seen the light of day in its current form without the cooperation and advice of others. I owe them my deepest thanks.

Lynne Stringer, my reliable and brilliant editor who has devoted so much time to correcting and tweaking all my work over the years. Lynne's changes are always spot on. They never fail to improve the word choice, plot sequences and storylines. I owe you my heartfelt thanks.

Tireless James Munro of Australian e-book publishing, whose extensive technical skills I have tested many times. Thank you for your creativity in preparing my work for publication to the highest standards and for your persistence and timeliness.

Many thanks also to my pre-publication researchers, readers and advisers whose guidance and interest I value: Mike and Jenny Purchase, Karen, Kaylee and Elly Monaco, Gill Bennett, De Kropach, Bruce and Inka Hutton, Cam and Jae, Jessica Lee, Dayna Norris and Kay Stehn. Without you none of my work would have reached the reading public.

About the Author

Born in Tanzania, from the age of six I was fortunate to grow up in Mombasa on the Kenya coast. One of my goals in life was to research the Arab, Chinese, Portuguese and Dutch explorers who sailed along the East African Swahili coast for centuries.

I migrated to Perth, Western Australia, in 1963. After a 7-year stint as a High School teacher, I transferred to Human Resources and worked on remote mine sites in the Pilbara, Northern Territory and Papua New Guinea. This brought me into close contact with local Indigenous people. I found their culture, deep rooted love of country, resilience and unfailing sense of humour inspirational.

I retired in 2008 and since then have dedicated myself to writing fictional novels based on historical themes. 3 of these comprise the Truth and Reconciliation Trilogy. They draw on 20 years of archival research undertaken in Australia and the Netherlands (Zeeland), and an appreciation of Australia's First Nations people, who have survived the effects of European settlement and colonialism. The trilogy gives you a fresh look at Australia's colonial history and reflects the current dialogue between the Aboriginal First Nation people and the rest of Australia.

I have also written a number of short stories, most of them included in my collection, including some drawn from sections of the trilogy. I trust you enjoy reading the novels and short stories as much as I enjoyed writing them.